Dear Marion —
with appreciation —
of your friendship —
Love sends you on
every visit.

Love,
your Re[...]

FLOWERS & LOCUSTS

FLOWERS & LOCUSTS

MY CHILDHOOD IN ETHIOPIA

MARTHA REID PARADIS

NORTHLOOP
BOOKS

North Loop Books
2301 Lucien Way #415
Maitland, FL 32751
407.339.4217
www.NorthLoopBooks.com

NORTHLOOP
BOOKS

© 2018 by Martha Reid Paradis

Printed in the United States of America

ISBN-13: 978-1-63505-488-0

In loving memory of my parents,
my sister and her husband,
and to the people of Ethiopia

FLOWERS & LOCUSTS
MY CHILDHOOD IN ETHIOPIA

AUTHOR'S PREFACE

The Ethiopia I remember is one filled with the scent of eucalyptus trees, acres and acres of yellow Meskal daisies sprung up after the heavy rains, and the laughter of hyenas at night as they roamed our neighborhood. One reads about a mysterious country called Abyssinia in the Bible, located in the borderlands between the Arabic world and the heartland of Africa. Even as a child I perceived it as a land of stunning contrasts, between arid lowlands and lofty mountain-tops, between the cool altitudes in the north and sweltering humidity of the desert in the east, and between an ancient aristocracy and some of the poorest people on earth. Ethiopia is the soil from which mankind arose in the form of the earliest human ancestor, dubbed Lucy by archeologists. Its geographic remoteness and heroic resistance to Western colonizers gave this country and its proud people an aura of the legendary, while the crystalline air of the capital city Addis Ababa bespoke both a harsh feudal history and hints of the divine in human existence.

My family lived in Ethiopia from 1957 to 1969, a time when Emperor Haile Selassie — who traced his imperial lineage back to King Solomon and the Queen of Sheba — led his country into early modernity, while failing to uproot its feudal foundation. We moved from New York City to Addis Ababa when I was only a toddler, and I think of my childhood and early adolescence as a magical time of adventure, but also a time filled with experiences that confused and sometimes terrified me.

Ethiopia is the country where I came of age; and today, almost fifty years later, memories wash over me and it is as if no time has passed. As I sit in my home in New Jersey and look out my window at the oaks and birches, for a few moments they are transformed into the eucalyptus trees of my childhood.

~ Chapter 1 ~

COUP D'ETAT

As a young girl I used to think of my mind as the wind. At times, my thoughts would wander in gentle gusts as I imagined a friend's birthday party or a lazy horseback ride I had planned with my brother Tim. But then at other times the wind howled as though the very trees in our compound would be uprooted from the earth and even the branches would flee in terror from its ominous force.

The swing I was on had reached its highest arc when a scream pierced the air, rising above the laughter of the other children. There followed a momentary stillness. This was not the last anguished cry I would ever hear, but like a first kiss or the sting of a best friend's sharp words, the memory contains an untainted clarity. Then suddenly, just outside the compound I heard a loud staccato crackling of what I would later find out was a machine gun.

We all ran to the front of the yard where our parents had gathered for our weekly Sunday barbecue. I tripped on a branch and fell onto the gravel driveway. I sat up and looked at my knee that was bleeding a little with small grey pieces of gravel in it. For a second I thought about bursting into tears but then stood up and kept running. And then I saw that two of the children's mothers were sobbing and holding onto each other.

Above the roar of car engines starting up, my father's urgent tone instructed me and my older sister to "get into the back seat as low as possible."

He turned to my mother and said, "We will have to drive through an area where there is fighting, but we have no other way to get to the embassy."

I watched my mother get into the front seat with my younger brother, Tim, her hand over her mouth, her blue eyes wide. I climbed into the car and watched Assefa, our gardener, trying to put a little American flag on the antenna, his hands fumbling as he worked to tie a bracing wire around the thin stick that held the flag. I got into our car, not understanding why, and as instructed by my father lay down in the back seat with my older sister, Nancy, while my mother and brother crouched on the floor in the front. Nancy had pushed her way down so I was on top of her, and I could feel her trembling. She would later tell me that, because she was nine and I was barely six then, she had a better idea of what was going on and knew that if the car was hit it was best to be as low as possible. "You were like my human shield," she would joke.

As the car started up I peered over the back seat and saw my father hunched over the steering wheel. He had recently had a haircut and the back of his neck was neatly shaven. I turned my head and looked straight up out the window and caught a glimpse of the sun through the luxuriant foliage of the eucalyptus trees. On the porch standing stiffly as though at military attention was Mamo, a young man who helped our cook in the kitchen and who still had his white apron on. Next to him stood Astatke, the cook, an older man with silver close-cropped hair who had a habit of whistling when he was cooking. Astatke was tall and thin and his features were delicate, as though the skin was pulled tightly across his cheekbones.

"Why aren't they coming with us?" I wondered as I heard the motor rumble and the car begin to move. I didn't know if I should wave to them or not.

I put my arms around Nancy and held tight.

My father drove very fast up the dirt road that led to the main road to the embassy. The gullies in the road caused the car to bounce and made it hard for me to stay on top of Nancy. The car slowed suddenly and I tried to peek out of the window as we passed low single-storied wooden shops with tin roofs. Usually

2

people were shopping or sitting outside of the coffee shops, but now they were running in all directions. A woman carrying a bundle of sticks hurried across the street, one arm raised holding the load in place. Soldiers seemed to have rounded up another soldier who was blindfolded and stumbled forward, his hands tied behind his back.

I could hear a loud crackling sound in the distance but it suddenly grew closer and louder and in a terrifying instant the side window cracked in the pattern of a spider web. A loud roar enveloped us. My father swore loudly and my mother cried out as the car hit the sidewalk and rocked back and forth. I covered my ears for a minute while trying to cling to my sister. My father regained control of the car and thankfully the cracked window stayed intact and the glass did not hit us. I do not remember much else of the car ride. My legs felt like they were buzzing and I wanted to run — not a calm controlled jog, but as fast as I could until my lungs hurt and I would be gasping for air.

I experienced a similar feeling of helplessness and terror half a century later as Nancy lay dying from brain cancer in a hospice in Florida. It was just a few weeks before her spirit left this world, and we were holding hands in silence. She was wrapped in a beige prayer shawl that a friend of mine had lovingly knitted for her. Soft music wafted from the CD player another friend had lent us. Most of the time her mouth was a straight line, her face without expression, her clear blue eyes staring out into space.

She had slowly turned her head toward me and in a hoarse whisper said, "You know, Martha, if that coup d'etat were today, I would put you underneath me to protect you."

After three surgeries and radiation and a persistent bacterial infection, the top of her skull was rotting away and caved in. I watched a single tear roll down her face and squeezed her frail hand wishing I could spare her such suffering. There had been many times that Nancy's presence had been a comfort to me, and I prayed that my being there was some kind of solace to her. I simply could not imagine what life would be like without my gutsy big sister in the world.

We pulled up to the huge black wrought-iron gates of the American Embassy. My father rolled down the window and handed something to the blue-uniformed guard at the gate, who cupped his hands around his eyes and peered inside. By then my mother had slowly sat up and I had climbed off Nancy. I moved my body towards the window and looked out, the bright sunshine stinging my eyes. The guard opened each of the documents, looked at the pictures on the front page and examined each of us sternly. He then handed them back to Dad, who gave them to Mom and muttered, "Here, you hold onto our passports."

The guard waved us through, and we passed a low gray building that I recognized as the place we had gone to last year to get five very painful shots. There were flowers blooming in beds on either side of a driveway that led up to the entrance to the ambassador's residence; the soil was wet and the petals glistened as though they had just been watered.

"Everyone out," Dad said as he pulled to a sudden stop. "I'll be back as soon as I park the car."

Mom, Nancy, Tim and I walked slowly up the steps and into a big hallway where we were met by another uniformed man who took us to a large recreation room. I saw sleeping bags lined up against one of the walls and a group of kids my age were working on a big puzzle together. I recognized them as the sons and daughters of some of my parents' American friends.

I know that we stayed in the embassy for a few days while the coup d'etat against Emperor Haile Selassie's government was crushed. About six families were there and all of us kids slept in the sleeping bags I had seen when we first entered the room. I think our parents tried to make it into an adventure for us. I know we made popcorn and roasted marshmallows on the stove in the embassy kitchen. One afternoon we were all taken to an indoor garden somewhere on the embassy grounds and we sang popular children's songs. I chimed in but our singing did not mask the tension in the room that felt like a live electrical wire.

The second or third night there I had been awakened at dawn by a stream of sunlight coming through a gap in the heavy curtains that covered the windows. A fan hung from the high ceiling above me and for a few minutes I watched it going round and round, humming softly. I got up and looked down at my brother Tim, who was a stiff shape under his sleeping bag snoring lightly as though his nose was stuffed up. I thought about waking him but he looked pretty peaceful, so I cautiously stepped over him. I had suddenly felt really thirsty and remembered that the kitchen was only a few rooms away.

The Persian rug that ran the length of a long hallway muffled the sound of my bare feet as I crept down the hall. Men's voices drifted towards me, and seeing that the door to the ambassador's study was slightly ajar, I stood in the shadows and peeked in. All of the men were wearing suits and ties, their shirts pressed as if they were ready to go to work. My father and five other men were talking and I watched him fold his arms across his chest and shake his head vehemently. I tried to make out what they were saying but their voices were low. I cautiously walked past the door hoping that Dad might notice me and come out, but he didn't.

About fifteen minutes later, as I stood by the window in the kitchen, I watched them get into a big official looking car with the embassy flag flying from all four corners and drive out of the embassy compound. My thirst quenched and suddenly feeling scared, I quickly tiptoed back to the room we were sleeping in and climbed into my sleeping bag. Struggling to get comfortable, I pressed my face into the pillow and closed my eyes, but I couldn't fall back to sleep. I was worried about our animals and had asked my mother if anyone was looking after them. I especially wished that Poupee, my scruffy little dog, had come with us. She slept with me at home. I missed the warmth of her body next to me in the sleeping bag on the cold tile floor in the embassy. When we left I had seen her running around in circles on the front porch, shaking like my pony Scout did when a loud noise startled him. "Don't worry," my mother had said, placing her hand gently on my shoulder. "Assefa will be feeding the animals."

Assefa was an older man with sorrowful eyes and salt and pepper hair. As keeper of Mom's extensive flower gardens, he was a reliable nurturer of living things. "He will make sure they are okay," she'd assured me.

I tried to imagine him feeding all the animals by himself, dipping the bucket into the feed bin and spreading it out for the two sheep. He'd pull a big bale of hay for the horses off the shelf in the stables and jumping out of the way at the last moment so it wouldn't hit him. Usually my brother and I helped him.

"I guess he misses us helping him," I said to Tim when I told him what Mom had said.

On our fourth night there, I told Dad that I was tired of being indoors. "It won't be much longer," he had said. He reached out, and gently touched my arm.

But that night he had taken Tim, Nancy and me out onto the front steps of the embassy porch for a breather. The moon was immobile, a great yellow ball suspended in the night sky, the hundreds of stars peering down on us like distant eyes. A light breeze gave the air a chill and I shivered for a few seconds. But I was so grateful to be outside, to smell the night air and look up into the heavens and see if I could find the same stars that I saw from home.

Two days later, what had felt like our jail sentence at the embassy abruptly ended.

"The good guys have won," was all my dad told us. "Come on, let's go home."

I didn't know who the good guys were and was bewildered by what had happened these past four days. I just knew to obey my father. We climbed into the car, but this time instead of being hunched down with Nancy, I sat stiffly in the back seat and looked out the window, relieved to be going home. The roads were pretty deserted and as we drove along I glanced out the window at a field covered in yellow daisies, a cacophony of color. As we got closer to our compound I looked up towards the familiar eucalyptus groves that lay to either side of the road and whose branches were gently swaying back and forth. Every couple of trees it looked like something was hanging from a branch but I couldn't tell what they were. I thought they might be beehives. And then suddenly as the car moved closer I saw that what was hanging from the branches of the trees along the way were the bodies of soldiers clad in tan uniforms. They looked almost like puppets with their heads twisted grotesquely to the side and the flies swarming around their open mouths. I saw my father's hazel eyes watching us in the mirror.

"Kids," he commanded, "look straight ahead." But it was already too late. We drove along in silence.

I was relieved to see Mamo and Assefa come out of the house when we arrived. I saw Mamo go over and speak to my father.

"Astatke has been arrested," I heard my dad say.

I looked at Nancy and asked, "What is arrested?"

"He is in jail," she said.

"But why?" I wondered out loud but no one answered. "Who will fix our lunch?" I thought.

Tim and I started playing a game of marbles on the front porch. Half an hour had passed when Mom came out and said to Tim, Nancy and me, "Dad has to go to the prime minister's office."

She looked at Tim and me. "Mamo and Assefa have left for the day so I can't leave you two here alone. We are going to go get Astatke. And Nancy, I want you to come with me because your Amharic is better than mine."

We got into the car again and I watched Dad give Mom an envelope stuffed with paper money. Mom quickly put it into her orange purse. It was about a fifteen-minute drive to the local police station. I told myself not to look up at the trees along the way. When we got there, we went into the grey concrete building and a coldness seemed to envelop us. I watched Mom pull the envelope out of her purse, and her hand trembled slightly. I reached out and found my brother's hand. Tim's hair was so blond and so short that you could barely see it these days. I liked to tease him that he was bald.

A guard in a tan uniform stopped us, and with Mom giving instructions I heard Nancy say, "You have our cook and his name is Astatke."

The guard was staring at the envelope in Mom's hand, a few bills peeking out.

"Ask him if we can see him," Mom said, and Nancy's lips quivered and she spoke haltingly but the guard must have understood her because he said, "Come."

Mom looked around the small waiting room with an expression of panic on her face. "You can't leave Martha and Tim here alone," Nancy said, "we will all have to go."

"Come," the guard commanded again, this time sounding louder and angrier.

Mom nodded and turned to follow the guard with the three of us behind her. He led us down a dark corridor. I saw grey iron doors to my left and right and behind the doors heard low murmurs and hushed voices. From behind one of the doors I heard what sounded like whimpering and moaning. The guard banged loudly on the door with his club as we walked by and the hallway became eerily silent.

"Stop," the guard commanded loudly, his voice echoing off the concrete walls, rage smoldering in his voice.

We all stood still. I was squeezing Tim's hand and tried to swallow down the painful lump that was beginning to form in my throat. We watched the guard move the bolt aside and open the door. I had no idea what to expect but saw the outline of Astatke sitting on a low metal bunk with his head bowed. The cell was fairly dark, and behind where he was sitting I could make out the blurred images of other people. And then slowly as my eyes adjusted to peering into the cell I began to see heads, faces, and hands, but because of the poor light I couldn't really tell how they all fit together.

The guard said something to Astatke and he stood up. When he saw us he took a few steps towards us, his eyes frightened. The guard grabbed him roughly by his shirt and pulled him forward and, as Astatke quickly turned his head away, I thought I saw tears welling up in his eyes. Speaking rapidly in Amharic, the guard extended his hand toward Mom who quickly gave him the envelope. He looked through the bills for a few seconds, stuffed the envelope under his jacket and quickly ushered us out, Astatke following quickly behind.

We didn't talk about the coup or what we had seen. I think Mom and Dad thought that we were too young to comprehend what had happened, and we were. At age six you are aware of so much, but understand so little. I had heard Dad say that the coup had been instigated by the Royal Body Guard against the Army who had remained loyal to the Emperor. I wasn't quite sure which were the Army and which were the Body Guard soldiers. But that didn't stop me from trying to figure out why the soldiers were hanging from the trees. Usually I saw the uniformed young men on my way to school or near the Army barracks that was not too far from our home. I just knew that something had been terribly wrong and in the ensuing years I would try to piece together much more about what had happened during that first coup.

We left Ethiopia a few weeks later and moved in with my mother's parents in Virginia. My grandparents lived in the small Shenandoah Valley town of Staunton, a sleepy place with one main downtown street where farmers and tradespeople ambled about.

The town was built on a series of hills, and there was a lovely big park with a circular drive around it called Gypsy Hill Park, at one end of which was a pond with geese and ducks. There were big wooden picnic tables here and there, and you'd sometimes see groups of people chatting around a barbeque grill. It wasn't home, but my brother and I squeezed some entertainment from things like going to the five-and-dime or watching cartoons on television. The TV programs started at dawn, and we would creep from our upstairs bedroom down the wooden stairs of my grandparents' century-old home — sometimes sliding down the curvy banister — and plop ourselves right in front of the big, boxy television set. The first show each morning was about agriculture, with some man talking on and on in front of a paper screen with numbers. We didn't understand anything he was talking about, but Tim and I didn't care. Then came our favorite show featuring a guy called Captain Kangaroo. He was kind of pudgy, with a friendly grin, and he'd parade animals around and tell stories. When it came time for breakfast and our mom or grandparents called us to the table we'd protest, refusing for a few minutes to budge until the warnings got more serious.

"But Mom," I remember Tim saying once, "we don't even have TV in Ethiopia, and the lights go off so much that we'd be sitting in the dark half the time." Mom smiled, and said to come on and we'd get some extra pancakes. Dad had gone back to Ethiopia and I didn't understand why we weren't all together.

Sure there were some fun things about being in America, but most of the time I was miserable. I missed everything about Ethiopia — our pets, the people who worked for us, the view from my bedroom window of the Entoto mountain range. I just wanted to go home. My grandparents' house was across the street from a cemetery and the window of the upstairs room I was sleeping in looked out over the gravestones. It felt creepy. I tried to keep the curtains drawn, even in the daytime. And my grandparents were strict southern Methodists who read the Bible at every meal, and I soon developed a healthy fear of their stern and unforgiving God, who bore little resemblance to the gentle Jesus we sang about in Sunday school, a savior who, according to my grandmother, loved me. Hell and the wrath of God always overshadowed the love of the Shepherd, and this image was reinforced by some of the sermons and meetings by visiting preachers that my sister, brother and I were hauled off to.

My grandfather was proud of his three grandchildren who were already speaking three languages, and he would order us to sing in Amharic or German. We hated it and Nancy taught Tim and me all the curse words she had picked up in Ethiopia and we would string them together when we sang, smiling secretly. I adored Nancy, even though I wasn't sure she knew it because it seemed like most of the time I annoyed her. I would do anything she suggested even if a part of me suspected we'd be in trouble if the adults found out.

My grandparents did not drink alcohol; in fact they assured us it was a one-way ticket to hell. Which explains my reaction when, one evening after dinner, Nancy took Tim and me to an upstairs bedroom and had us sit on one of the beds. The bedspread was soft and pale blue. Nancy liked explaining things to us — she was after all the wiser, older sister.

"I guess we'd just better accept it," she said solemnly. "Dad is going straight to hell. He likes to have a beer when he plays poker and drinks wine at dinner."

Tim and I just looked at her. I was shocked. I didn't want my father to be in a place filled with fire and brimstone.

Since we were there in September, my parents thought it would be a good idea for me to be in kindergarten. I don't remember much about it, except that there was something about a bomb. A bell would ring three times and we would march out of the classroom and then sit in a hallway with our hands over our heads in total silence. I asked Nancy about the bomb and she said that they were worried about something called a nuclear attack that would be like a fireball that would vaporize us all and blow my grandparents' house to smithereens. I'd asked Nancy what the word vaporize meant and she told me that it would melt us all. That sounded as bad as being in a place with fire and brimstone.

After five months with my grandparents we flew back to Ethiopia. The journey was long and tiring, seeming to last forever, and I remember isolated moments along the way. At Staunton's deserted little rail station, the train conductor called out in a sing-songy way, "All aboard," as we climbed onto the train. It was not even dawn but we needed to travel to a city — New York or Boston or somewhere like that — to get on a plane flying to Athens. The last part of the trip back to Addis Ababa, the capital city, was on a propeller plane. I remember it had a big yellow lion with its paws in the air painted on the green tail section. The hum of the propellers was constant, and the plane would get buffeted about. It scared me.

"I think we are going to fall out of the sky," I said to Mom.

"No we aren't," she answered, but I saw that her hands were gripping the armrests on either side of her, and her mouth looked tight and grim. But then she put her arm around me and smiled at me and I felt myself relax.

My brother and I played games with little plastic trinkets that were handed out in zippered bags by the tall, thin Ethiopian stewardesses when we got on the plane. After what seemed like forever, we finally crossed into Ethiopia from the endlessly flat and barren deserts of Egypt we'd been flying over.

"Take a look out the window," Mom said, gently jostling us awake.

Tim pulled up the shade and I stretched myself over his body so I could look out of the window too. We saw beneath us a gigantic jigsaw puzzle of colors — yellows, oranges, browns, and greens — cut into different shapes.

"What are those?" Tim asked Mom.

"Those are Ethiopia's farms planted with beans and *teff*, and where families graze their cattle on little strips of grassy land," she answered.

The Addis Ababa airport was not much more than a big cement hut until a new modern airport was built a few years later. But crowds of people came out to watch the one or two planes that flew in to land each day. Women stood silently with umbrellas to shade themselves from the midday sun, and men draped their arms over their wooden walking sticks. I remember driving down the last stretch of road leading to our home, willing my father to drive faster even though there were deep gullies in the road left over from the rainy season. I could feel my heart pounding with excitement that in a few minutes I would be able to run down to the stable and see the horses; the dogs would be barking and jumping all over us; and Mamo's smiling face would once again appear at my door in the mornings with a laughing "Time to get up, Martha, it is time to get up."

The years that followed, from when I was about six to nine, passed with a comforting rhythm. The combination of familiar voices, daily routines and childhood adventures quieted for a time the terror I had felt during the first coup against the Emperor.

My father took us to school each morning in our family's dark blue Opel. The school day started at seven thirty in the morning, and Dad would drive us from our compound on roads along which we passed the occasional beaten up car. Women in brilliant white *shamas*, the traditional finely woven shawls, skirted the side of the ragged pavement on their way to pick up a pail of water or bundle of firewood.

We'd be dropped off by Dad at the school entrance and I would wave forlornly as he sped off toward the Prime Minister's head-quarters where he had his office. I always felt a moment of panic when either Mom or Dad disappeared from my direct vision and my heart would beat faster and I would feel a little sick to my stomach. I would linger for as long as I could to watch the car grow smaller and smaller. It was then a short distance from the metal school gate to the broad steps of the main school building that led to an entryway bordered by rectangular windows. From there a series of hallways led to the classrooms where the kindergarten and grade school classes were held. Because the school was small, many of the grades mixed together and friendships and rivalries developed.

We went to the German School, where all the subjects were taught by very strict German instructors. By the time I was in fifth grade I had noticed that an older boy named Asfa-Wossen, who was probably around Nancy's age, had an uncanny way of appearing whenever I was about to get into an argument with an older student. There was something about his presence that ensured that I would be left alone. Many aristocratic Ethiopians claimed to be related to the Emperor, but when I asked Dad about Asfa, he said that while some of those claims might be dubious, Asfa definitely was, both on his father's side and his mother's. I was never sure whether the fact that he was closely related to the Emperor was the reason for the unspoken power that he seemed to have, but I am sure that his protective presence helped me during the rough and tumble years of later elementary school.

We went to school six days a week — Monday through Saturday — and the school day ended at one. Mom would pick us up, and Nancy, Tim and I would smush into our family's other car, a little Fiat that looked like a curvy cut-off section of an egg carton. Our afternoons were our own, and sometimes we'd be driven to the home of a school friend who lived nearby, and as we got older we would ride our horses into the countryside accompanied by our groom, Worku Eyasu and then later on our own. Worku had been employed by an Ethiopian family for ten years before he came to us and was highly recommended as one of the best grooms in Addis. He was tall and athletic looking with long legs and arms. He wore his curly salt and pepper hair cropped close to his head and his eyes were a deep dark brown that looked moist and teary even when he was laughing. I sometimes wondered if tears would start running out of his eyes because he did like to laugh at Tim and me a lot.

But a lot of the time, my brother and I just played endless games of marbles, or stacked up bottle caps that we'd knock over with a pebble from longer and longer distances. Every once in a while we'd be dropped off at one of the downtown movie theaters for a triple feature, crammed into the packed old buildings with hundreds of Ethiopians to watch movies from India, or France, or America. These movies were sometimes dubbed into Arabic, or had Arabic script running at the bottom of the screen. We'd leave the theater from these marathon five- or six-hour sessions with glazed eyes, but happy as only kids can be who never got to watch television except on our summer trips every few years back to Mom's home town.

And then, one ordinary summer night, when I had just turned ten, fear and confusion once again entered my childhood world — not with a terrifying ride through the streets of Addis Ababa in the midst of a coup d'etat, but in the cold back bathroom of our home.

~ Chapter 2 ~

CHILDBIRTH

Almost as soon as I learned to walk I was running. I loved to run. Down the back stairs and at the second to last step I would grab the steel railing and swing my body up and to the side and land like the gymnast I had seen in a book about the Olympics. Then the quarter mile to the stable, the aroma of the eucalyptus trees in our back yard filling my lungs as I breathed in. Then from the stable to the tree house where I would touch the second rung of the ladder twice for good luck. And finally around the side yard, squeezing my way sideways because the distance between the high stone wall and the house was at points so narrow.

"Whoa, slow down," Dad would command when he heard me scampering down the hall from the kitchen and dining room into the hallway that led to my bedroom.

I would slow down for a minute, but as soon as I was out of his earshot I would start running again.

On one of my runs I wound up in the kitchen trying to catch my breath, and found myself the butt of some typical ribbing from our amused household staff.

"Where do you think she is running to?" Beheilu, (pronounced *bah-LOO*) our replacement cook, asked Mamo.

"Maybe she thinks the hyenas are chasing her," Mamo said.

"Or maybe she is practicing for the day the boys will be chasing her," Beheilu added. "She's almost ten years old so it won't be long," and he wiped his hands on his apron and turned around to wink at Mamo who just couldn't stop laughing.

I had a few minutes to spare so I climbed up on the kitchen counter and watched Beheilu and Mamo prepare the evening meal. Pretending that I was not even in the room, they kept up the banter. And somehow I loved it, maybe because I felt like I was the center of attention, and because I loved them and liked seeing them happy.

Beheilu's last name was Gebremariam and Mamo's was Abebe. Mom had explained to me that it was important to know the last names of the people who worked in our home because to know someone's last name gave them dignity. So I quickly learned that our nanny Belaynesh's last name was Bayu. And I made sure that I knew the last names of the people who worked in the garden and the stables.

Beheilu was a slightly overweight man of around thirty-five whom I had never seen without a white apron on. He had a round face with the beginnings of what would probably become a double chin. His almond shaped eyes were deep-set and colored a rich chocolate brown. A wide forehead and widow's peak were set under his black closely cropped hair. Tim and I liked to sneak up behind him and then quickly run past and poke his belly and say, "Shakes like jelly, just like Santa Claus," and Beheilu would laugh at us and stick his belly out even farther.

Astatke, our former cook, had shown up to work drunk one morning when I was about seven and Dad had fired him on the spot. In an instant he was gone without a trace. I wished that I could have said goodbye. For a long time I missed him terribly. He was always joking with me and had a warm smile and I wondered where he was, and I prayed that he was okay. Sometimes I would have an image of him when we had gone to rescue him from the police station all those years ago and a hard lump would form in my throat. It was years before I had the courage to ask Dad why Astatke had been arrested.

Mamo had come to the capital city to find employment eight years prior and had been hired by my father to help our cook with his duties. He had been with us since I was three. Even though I knew that he did not have a lot of money or material possessions, he seemed to possess an innate sense of joy, something that

I sensed in a lot of Ethiopians. When he would take vacation time to go back home to visit his family, I missed his good-natured laugh that greeted me as I got off the school bus and rushed into the kitchen hoping that Beheilu had made my favorite, french fries sprinkled with *berbere*, the fiery Ethiopian spice.

Now they kept up their bantering until, my wind restored, I hopped off the kitchen counter and out the back door to run some more.

"There she goes!" they both called after me as I vanished around the side of the house.

As close as I was to Tim, I wasn't sure even he understood how much the running calmed me. Often when Tim and I were playing a board game or lying on our beds reading I'd suddenly feel the urge to run, like a low level of electricity had begun to buzz in my legs and I needed something to help me take in a deep breath.

On one such occasion I sat up and, swinging my legs over the side of the bed, said to Tim, "Give me ten minutes, I have to go out and run."

"Sure," he answered, and he let out a loud yawn and looked up at me. "I will just be lying here resting."

He rolled his eyes at me and I barely escaped the room before the *Superman* comic book he was reading sailed past my head, hitting the door.

I loved the sound my feet made when I ran. On the gravel driveway a 'crunch-crunch' as compared to the hard 'thud' they made on the packed dirt of the side yard. Sometimes I would turn my run into a gallop, imitating the sound of the horses' hooves as I ran through the house on the wooden floors. I liked to run when it was hot but not unbearable. And if there was a breeze in the air I asked Worku to go with me and we jogged the mile to the Kebena River, down the soft dirt trail that gave my legs a welcome relief from the pounding on the hard dirt in the side yard. But whatever the sound, that left-right staccato rhythm, it was always somehow comforting.

Sometimes if we were not in a great hurry we would sit by the river. I remember the first time Worku had taught Tim and me how to skip stones, how careful he had been in choosing the right stone, flat but with an edge so you could spin it off your finger at just the right angle.

"Watch this one, Martha," he'd said, his face lighting up as the stone bounced in the air and then glanced off the water.

"Why are you always running, Martha?" Belaynesh asked me once when I came into my room huffing and puffing. She was putting away the laundry. "You will miss out on so much of life it you do not slow down."

"What do you mean?" I asked, moving from one foot to the other to keep my legs from cramping up. A cool breeze through an open window blew my hair over my eyes and I brushed it away.

"When you are still, you see so much more of life," she said. "You have time to let pictures come into your mind."

For a long time I thought my father's job was "Jack of All Trades," since that was how he described his official position as legal adviser to the Imperial Ethiopian government. He had his office right next to the Prime Minister. He told us that on any day he might work for any ministry or department in the entire government, and he met with Emperor Haile Selassie when the Emperor called for him. He wrote laws and many of the Emperor's speeches. For some reason that I never understood at the time, he told us that when he spoke to the Emperor it was always in French.

There were times, when he came home after a long day, that I could tell he was totally frustrated. I once heard him say to my mother, "It's so hard to get things done in this country." I wondered if that had something to do with an expression that Ethiopians seemed to use all the time, which was "*Ishi Nega*," meaning "Yes … Tomorrow."

I knew that Ethiopians were very hard working, but the traditional way of doing things was so rooted that they often seemed to be standing in place.

One night, when I was about six or seven, I was awakened by the moon shining through my window and made my way to the kitchen to get a drink of water. I saw that the light was on in my father's study, and the door was slightly ajar. I knocked softly and then went in. He looked up and moved his reading glasses to the top of his head.

"Why are you working so late?" I asked. The light came over his shoulder from the tall standing lamp and into my eyes. I moved into a shadow.

He leaned back, stretched, and told me that the Emperor and other leaders were trying to find a way to work together to help their people. He said it was somewhat like when I played soccer at school — one fares a lot better acting as a team member than when each player is running around trying to score a goal on their own. The group they were putting together was called the Organization for African Unity and would be located right in Addis Ababa.

I sat down and asked Dad if, when he was a kid, he thought he would be doing this kind of thing.

Dad paused for a moment, smiled at me and told me that it seemed he had come a long way from the small mill town that he'd grown up in. He added that he wished his mother could know what had become of her son.

Dad told me that he had grown up during a time called the Depression. He said that he didn't have much so they did what Depression kids did. He picked blueberries and dug for clams and sold them both door-to-door, along with something called *Octagon* soap and *Liberty* magazine.

"I babysat for five cents an hour," he said. "My mother and I would sit on our back porch pulling threads from lace, spun by one of the few mills that remained open. She made me promise never to tell my proud father what we were doing, and I never did. We earned four cents for every yard of lace we pulled. But I didn't know any different, so it seemed normal to me."

During the following year, my brother and I got glimpses of the impressive round building called Africa Hall, as we rode along with Mom or Dad on shopping trips or other excursions around Addis. Dad had said to us that "Addis Ababa is now the official diplomatic capital of Africa."

Once, a few months after it was completed, Tim and I snuck into Africa Hall when Dad had to drop off some documents and had left us sitting in our car. The towering interior was fairly dark when we entered, casting us into a dim twilight. We moved forward slowly and suddenly found ourselves staring up at a huge stained glass window that covered an entire wall in the foyer. And as the sun must have come out from behind a cloud and streamed through the windows, the hall was suddenly filled with light and the red and yellow and orange colors glowed like the flames of a fire. I felt the presence of someone behind me and slowly turned around and saw Dad watching us intently. Dad spoke quietly as he told us that the images symbolized African nations uniting to tackle poverty and disease. The three of us then stood together in silence for a few minutes and then walked back to the car past rows and rows of colorful flags of all the African nations.

But what Dad's job also meant was that my parents led a very busy social life and were out most nights to affairs at the many different embassies, or at times at the Palace when there were visits by foreign heads of state or other dignitaries. These were usually black tie events, and my mother owned a number of long evening gowns and cocktail dresses that she would wear depending on the formality of the occasion. I loved watching her get ready, putting on her makeup, and I would ask if I could do the clasp at the back of her necklaces. She owned one in particular that I loved, made of turquoise and gold that my father had given her as an anniversary gift. I trace my love of the color turquoise back to that necklace.

At that moment, Dad's voice interrupted my thoughts, as he said, "Your Mom and I are leaving for a reception at the British Embassy. Belaynesh will be with you and Tim tonight. Don't stay up too late."

I pressed the side of my face up against Belaynesh's hard belly. I felt the warmth of her hand on my forehead. She was wearing a new *shama*, the border of which she had only finished embroidering the night before. I watched her handiwork for weeks, fascinated by the way the colorful threads were transformed into a pattern.

"I don't hear anything," I said, looking up at her soft face and moist dark brown eyes. Belaynesh had been with our family since I was three years old.

"Maybe the baby is sleeping," Belaynesh had looked down at me and smiled. "You must tell your mother you need a haircut, you are almost ten years old now, Martha, you need to start caring about how you look," she said, and then gently brushed my blond hair off my forehead.

I felt the warmth of her hand on my forehead. I looked up at her dark, big eyes and sensual mouth that gave her face an exotic look. I hadn't known that she was pregnant until about her seventh month. I had been noticing that she walked more slowly and would often stop in the middle of her chores to rub her back. I just thought that she was getting fat.

"Is Belaynesh sick?" I asked Beheilu.

He must have heard the concern in my voice because he had turned away from the stove and come over to where I was sitting on the stone counter, my favorite perch for watching him prepare dinner.

"No, Martha," he said. "She is not sick. She is going to have a baby."

"A baby? "I gasped. "When?"

"In about two months," he replied.

From that moment on I watched Belaynesh like a hawk, fascinated that a baby was growing in her belly. I watched the changes in her form as her whole body seemed to ripen with the life that was growing in her.

Three or four times over the next month she came to work with a dark bruise under an eye or on the side of her face. Her eyes were red and bloodshot. I asked Beheilu why the baby was making her face hurt, as he had become my primary source of information regarding this pregnancy.

"That is not the baby," Beheilu said. "Her husband hits her sometimes because she is moving so slowly."

Our kitchen was painted a cheery yellow with white curtains covering the small windows that looked out over the back yard. I just stared at Beheilu for about thirty seconds feeling like a dark cloud had just swept over the room, and then I ran out the door, down the back steps, and back and forth on the hard dirt of the side yard. I kept trying to concentrate on the sound my feet made and block out the awful reality of what he had just told me. That night as Tim and I sat on the front porch engaged in our favorite pastime of watching the moon traverse the skyline, I told him what I had learned. I told him I'd gone back and asked Beheilu what we could do, like call the police or something.

"What did he tell you?" he asked. Tim was holding a flashlight and shined it toward the tree house as he spoke. Its narrow beam traveled from tree trunk to tree trunk illuminating the ground beneath.

I saw something silvery streak through the light as I thought back to what Beheilu had said and relayed it to Tim word for word: "There is nothing we can do. A husband may do what he wishes. In Ethiopia a woman has no voice."

"We will figure something out," Tim said, and reached out and touched my arm.

When I was younger I loved pretending that Tim and I were twins. Sometimes I would imagine that we had rocked next to one another in our mother's belly with our hands occasionally touching. I did not have a single early memory that did not include him. And now, just knowing that he also knew the truth about Belaynesh and would be thinking about it, somehow helped me.

My brother was fourteen months younger than I but was already the same height and was my closest friend, and I always felt safer if he was around. Tim and I shared a bedroom when we were younger; he was in the top bunk and I slept in the bottom. We were creative in making up our own games, like jumping off the roof of our stable onto a huge pile of hay and mud, or collecting as many different colored rocks as we could find from the neighborhood and river and then polishing them till they shone in the sunlight.

With a lot of pets in our house the constant infestation of fleas was awful, and despite the DDT that was liberally sprinkled into our beds, they seemed to particularly love my blood type. I had wakened once and seen where they had feasted, my legs covered in welts, and bright red blood on the sheets where I had scratched them during the night. My brother and I counted forty-two bites on my legs and arms and back. Mamo had taken my mattress outside the next day and Tim and I helped him beat it with eucalyptus branches. I gave Tim my favorite rocks in trade for scratching the bites I couldn't reach, and he must have taken the job very seriously because I wound up with blood poisoning from the ones that got so infected.

And at night, after the metal shutters had been pulled down, as Tim and I would be lying in bed, I would sometimes hear the hyenas roaming around our house looking for trash.

"What's that?" I'd whisper up toward Tim. "Did you hear that?"

"It's nothing," he'd say, "go to sleep."

Holding my pillow over my head for protection, I would scoot down further under the covers, and wait for the next howl from outside. But having my brother in the bunk above made it all just that little bit less scary. When I turned eight, and then a few months later he turned seven, he moved out of the room we shared, down the hall into another bedroom. Even though the distance between us at night was now a few dozen yards or so, it felt like an ocean or desert separated us.

A few days later, when Tim and I were walking home from the school bus with Assefa, whose last name was Azir, we passed the small group of mud and tin huts, called *tukuls*, where Belaynesh lived. A few men were outside sitting together smoking and chewing on *khat*, a local leaf that made you high. I decided to take my chance and asked Assefa, who seemed in a hurry because he wanted to get to the weeds in the flower bed, which one was Belaynesh's husband.

Assefa looked at me with a quizzical expression, before pointing and saying, "That one, the one in the blue shirt."

I wanted to run at him, to tear his eyes out, to make him hurt the way he was hurting Belaynesh. But instead I just kept walking, concentrating on putting one foot in front of the other.

I told Tim that now that we knew what he looked like that was a start.

A few days later, I said very nonchalantly to Assefa, "Where does Belaynesh's husband work?"

He didn't answer immediately and I held my breath.

"Why do you want to know?" Assefa asked. His voice dropped into a deeper tone. I didn't answer.

"Oh, you know Martha," Tim jumped in and I shot him a grateful look. "She just likes to know all kinds of weird stuff. The other day I heard her asking Beheilu how many children his brother has. She is nosy isn't she, always wanting to know everything, whether it's her business or not."

Assefa hesitated for a moment but then said, "I am pretty sure he works in Aware Kebena. It is about a twenty-five minute walk from here. Sometimes I see him on the road when I am on my way to work."

Later that afternoon Tim and I were sitting up in the tree house. I looked down through the eucalyptus leaves and suddenly saw a stretch of road that seemed to wind its way directly under us. I grabbed my brother's sleeve.

"Look," I said, "we can hit him with our slingshots from here and we will be hidden in the trees."

I often thought that the eucalyptus trees had a spirit, and that this helped me do my best thinking when I was perched on one of the branches or leaning up against a sturdy trunk. I would call to mind the big storm when the wind blew so hard that the branches were forced over and I felt like they were struggling to stay upright and not snap in two. It looked like lightning was embroidering the sky with each loud clap of thunder. But I knew that the trees' roots were strong and deep and held the earth together and was not surprised the next morning to see the trees standing proud and tall. Sometimes if I was lying on the ground and looked up it felt like the trees were so tall that they held up the sky.

When we were in the trees I loved feeling so close to the birds and watching the sunlight play with the shadows through each branch and leaf. From its highest branches I could survey the yard below me. If we were in the trees during the early morning hours, my nose would perk up as the smell of the coffee Beheilu was brewing wafted out of the kitchen window. A while back Assefa had made us slingshots using a branch, a piece of rubber, and a leather strip. Tim and I practiced almost daily shooting a can off a tree stump, keeping score on a pad of paper we kept in a can.

Tim looked down, then turned to me and grinned. "Great plan," he said. "Sunday morning we don't have school, but he should still be going to work. I heard Belaynesh say once that his day off is Monday."

We spent the weekend finding the perfect size pebbles. "Try to make sure they are sharp," my brother said.

When we had about fifty of them we practiced shooting the can off the box, wanting to be confident that our aim was as accurate as possible. We woke up early the following morning. It had been an uneasy sleep for me during the night. I would awaken with the thought that we were about to do something very wrong. But then the image of Belaynesh and the bruises on her face would come into focus, and a sudden rush of protective anger and wanting to hurt her husband would flood my body.

Tim and I had crept out of the house at six in the morning. My head ached. It was not hot yet, but once we had climbed up into the tree house I could feel the sweat collecting on my temples and running down my neck. I found a good seat and leaned back feeling myself relax a little as the familiar and comforting branch against my back gave me support. I knew it might be a long wait.

As the sun rose, the flies began buzzing all around us, landing on my head and forehead. Tim and I looked down through the branches and we could make out people who were walking or riding old bikes underneath us. A farmer pulled a pig by a rope down the dusty road and the pig squealed as if being slaughtered. An old woman shuffled along slowly, clinging to the arm of a teenage girl who might have been her granddaughter. The minutes crept by, and my brother and I began taking turns leaning off the platform to try to see as far down the road as we could. I began to hum a little to myself, hoping that might help the minutes go by faster.

I was holding onto Tim's shirt as he leaned far off the platform, my legs pushed hard up against a sturdy branch to give me additional strength, when he said "I think I see him," and I pulled him back. "He is about three minutes away, I would guess."

Neither of us spoke as we each placed a sharp rock into our slingshots.

"Don't aim for his head or face," I whispered to Tim, "and don't shoot while he is right under us. We don't want him to look up."

"Okay," Tim mouthed back at me.

I closed my mouth and forced a deep breath in through my nose the way I would at the start of a race at school. My chest was tight though, and the air seemed to get stuck somewhere in my throat. I placed a sharp rock in the leather pad and pulled back on the elastic thongs. Suddenly Belaynesh's husband was right under us. We waited, poised on the platform until he was about ten feet past us and then, as I met Tim's clear blue eyes and nodded my head, we both aimed and fired.

One of the rocks must have hit the bare skin of Belaynesh's husband's arm, because he let out a sound and clutched his arm right above the elbow. The other shot must have hit his foot, but with shoes on he may not have felt it. Within seconds we had reloaded and since he was now standing still, I took my time, counted up to five and aimed straight at his back right between the shoulder blades. He jerked as the rock hit him and then his right arm grabbed his thigh, the target Tim had chosen. He was looking around, trying to gauge where the attack was coming from and suddenly turned looking straight up into the trees in our direction.

Tim and I both froze. He cursed loudly, shook his fist in our direction and then set off down the road.

"How about a last shot?" my brother whispered.

I shook my head no. We stayed up in the tree house for another half hour or so, neither of us talking much. I don't know what I had imagined I would feel the rest of the day. But basically I felt sick to my stomach and anxious. I had never before consciously sought someone out with the intent to harm them.

The rest of the weekend seemed to drag by. The next morning when we left for school Belaynesh had not yet arrived. When we got home, I immediately noticed that one of the baskets filled with dirty sheets was still sitting outside of the wash room.

Beheilu caught me looking at it and said, "She did not come to work today." There was something tough and hard-edged about the way he said it, his tone different from his usual one.

And she did not come to work the following day either. I was too afraid to ask anyone where she was. And I wondered if she was ever going to come back. Three days later she returned and the relief washed over me.

Dad almost always came home a little bit before dusk and I had begun to associate the darkened sky with his arrival. How the evening would go was usually determined by his mood and I would try to gauge that mood by the sound the Jeep made as it came into the compound. If his mood was good, he would get out, close the door quickly, and immediately stop to pet Rafe and Jambo, our bigger dogs, who would come bounding up to the vehicle. But if it had been a very rough day and he had a lot on his mind, the Jeep door would slam and he ignored the dogs and marched up the front steps and into the house. My mother's voice would change at those times. It would lose the Southern lilt of her background that I loved and she would speak to us in a hushed whisper.

If Dad's mood was good, he would play the piano and we would gather around and sing. He taught us three-part harmony and at the end of a song often said, "Well, we aren't quite the von Trapp singers, but that wasn't bad."

I think I fell in love with music around that piano. I don't really know if our voices were any good, but music allowed me to sing words I could not voice in real life. And music became my companion when Tim was not around. I would hum to myself or repeat the words to a favorite song over and over in my mind.

Dad was a handsome man, about six-two with dark brown hair, a chiseled face, and piercing dark eyes with a steely gaze that embodied authority. His rules were clear and when his voice lowered and he turned his head the slightest bit to the side, I think each of us kids feared him. When he came into a room his presence filled the space with a keen charisma. Women liked him and he could be flirtatious and charming. And men wanted to be his poker buddy and hunting companion. He played the piano in a jazz band and some of my favorite days were the Sundays when we went to hear him play. There were many nights, when I was tossing and turning in bed, that the faint sounds of a piece he was practicing would gradually lull me to sleep.

My mother was a beauty, possessing one of those faces that was simply lovely from every angle. Her light brown hair was cut short and her eyes deep pools of blue liquid. She wore beautiful silk or cotton suits in bright colors like lemon yellow and ruby red. But I have never seen a photograph of her that truly captured what she looked like, at least not what she looked like to me. It was almost like she was suddenly shy in front of the camera as though she might reveal too much. She was soft-spoken, gentle and kind but hard for me to read at moments. I'd never seen her outright angry, but I'd watch her withdraw into herself and I spent many hours studying her and wondering what she was thinking about.

But when I hugged her before she went out the door for the evening, I would be wrapped in her scent, a mixture of Ivory soap and Joy perfume. I had a small stash of spices, grasses, crushed flower petals and leaves, and her scent was one that I would try to recreate. I would fill a bottle with a sudsy tablespoon of water and Ivory soap and then add the oils that I extracted from my own ingredients. I'd shake it gently and watch all the ingredients mix together. I was told that I most resembled my father's mother, the Paradis side of the family, but when I dabbed a droplet of my mother's scent onto my wrist, I imagined for a moment that I looked like her. But I think it was Tim who held a special place in my mother's heart. I watched her soften when he would come into the room. Maybe it was because he was the only son, or perhaps because he would always be her baby, her youngest.

While my father seemed to thrive on my athletic accomplishments, my mother seemed to fear the speed with which I would race one of the horses out of the compound for a two or three hour gallop through the countryside. And I had begun to notice that in the show jumping competitions at one of the embassies or at the Jan Hoy Meda Imperial Racing Grounds, while my father would stand up urging me on as I glanced into the sea of spectators, my mother would sit stiffly by his side, and once or twice I caught her with her hand over her eyes. The past few times that we had been in the center of Addis shopping for groceries I had begun to notice that wherever we went men looked at her out of the corner of their eye. Once or twice a man had stared at her in a way that made me uneasy, like there were dangers prowling just around the corner.

We were all in the house awaiting my Dad's arrival. I heard the Jeep door slam and then his footsteps up onto the front porch.

"Martha, Tim — in here now," he shouted, his voice echoing off the walls down the hallway.

I had been lying on my bed looking at the ceiling, and kicked off the light sheet I had pulled over me; the air coming in through the window had been chilly. Tim and I got to the living room at about the same moment. Dad was standing by the mantle and his big frame seemed to loom over us. He turned towards us, his jaw clenched. I dug my nails into my palms.

"Goddamn it, you two, what were you thinking?"

I could hear a trace of fury in his voice. He took a handkerchief out of his pocket and wiped his forehead.

"You know we cannot interfere with how things are in this neighborhood. This is a different country, a different culture, the rules and laws are different."

When Dad was like this I felt a trembling begin inside of me, and I wanted to become invisible. But then the bruises on Belaynesh came into my mind, and because deep down I knew that Dad did not like seeing innocent people hurt, the words "But he is hurting her!" burst out of me.

"You always tell us to stand up for what is right," Tim added, straightening his shoulders.

Dad paused. "Sit down," he said. "Look you two, I know you love Belaynesh like a second mother, but you can't go shooting rocks at people."

"Then what can we do?" I asked and kept my eyes as steady as I could. Willing myself not to blink, I met his gaze.

"I am not sure," he said, his voice a little softer. "Let me give it some thought, but for right now the two of you are in your rooms right after you get home from school for the next couple of days."

I don't know exactly what Dad did, but he left the house about twenty minutes later and I heard the Jeep's door slam and then it leaving the driveway. He was gone for an hour or so. When

Belaynesh returned to work the next day, there were no new bruises that I could see.

"We saw your father in Belaynesh's village," Assefa told us a few days later.

"Oh," I answered innocently, and quickly changed the topic.

"Yes," he said looking at me intently, "and now her husband has a new ten-speed bicycle. Imagine how quickly he can get to work."

"Oh," I said again. I didn't want Assefa to know what we had done, but I think he probably knew already.

That night when I said my prayers I asked God to take care of my family as I always did. But I also told God what a wonderful thing Dad had done and that I loved him for it. I think that was the first time I realized that there were things you could do if you had the means, and that being able to give someone something they coveted gave you a certain kind of power.

It was raining the night that my parents were going to a party at the British embassy in honor of Queen Elizabeth II, who had arrived for a state visit a few days earlier.

It was unusual for it to be raining in February, one of the many months where Addis Ababa's glorious highland weather had earned it a reputation for having endless stretches of sunshine. Addis lies on a 7,000- to 10,000-foot central plateau which extends out like a huge rock citadel, a sort of inner altar within the empire. As I listened to the gentle patter of raindrops on our home's tin roof, I thought with some anticipation about the upcoming rainy season which I loved. For a few months during the Little Rainy Season, every afternoon, almost like clockwork, the skies would open with a gentle rainfall that made a hypnotic puttering sound on our roof. Then, during the later Big Rainy Season, a storm of tropical fury would occur each day, pounding our roof and soaking the ground so that deep puddles formed in our yard that my brother and I would splash around in. Sometimes we'd sit outside and wait and watch the clouds threatening a storm finally relent, and the skies would open up releasing a torrent of water. We'd look up into the grey heavens and laugh and get drenched. Beheilu and Mamo scolded us but we didn't care because it was just so much fun. At night when I couldn't fall asleep I would listen to the sleet tapping at the windowpanes and imagine hundreds of tiny fists beating on the shutters.

Earlier in the day, Tim and I had gone with Assefa to stand along the route of the procession to catch a glimpse of the Queen and Haile Selassie in the royal carriage. The streets were lined with vendors selling roasted chickpeas and water. Some people were dressed in the traditional *shama*, others in pants and shirts, but many were wearing shabby, threadbare t-shirts and grimy shoes or sandals. As was often the case when Tim and I were out, some people stared at us and our blond hair. I walked quickly along the dusty sidewalk looking straight ahead, keeping my eyes fixed on some distant point. I noticed that for the first time I could ever remember, we were not surrounded by beggars.

"Where are the poor people we usually see when we are in this part of the city?" I asked Assefa, tugging at his sleeve.

"They were rounded up in buses and taken away to somewhere in the countryside while the Queen is visiting," he answered. "The government would not want her to see how poor and sick some people are."

We had cheered as the long line of dignitaries and soldiers marched past. We were holding little Ethiopian and British flags and waving them. As the Emperor and Queen Elizabeth rode past in an ornate carriage, the vast crowd, as if one being, prostrated itself on the ground with frenzied cheers.

The next day we had gone to Jan Hoy Meda to see a stunning gathering of thousands of fierce Oromo warriors. They carried their decorative shields of animal skin covered in brass buttons and were wearing the traditional lion's mane headdress. They had come in from the countryside on horseback and reenacted for the royal visitor the way in which they had fought off the Italian invaders armed only with spears. Small groups would face off against each other, and at an unspoken signal charge at break-neck speed unleashing their spears when they were only yards away from their opponents. Dad told us that the Emperor had spent five years in exile in Britain while his country was occupied under Mussolini during World War II and that that had drawn the Emperor even closer in his friendship with Britain.

"It will be a very late night out," Dad said to us as he finished tying the bow tie that he wore with his tuxedo.

"Dad looks like a duck," my brother whispered to me gesturing toward the tails of the jacket.

We stood on the front porch with Belaynesh as the Jeep pulled out of the driveway. Nancy was away at boarding school in Switzerland, and on my list of things to do on the yellow legal pad Dad had given me I had written, "Write Nancy a letter and tell her about Belaynesh."

Belaynesh was now in her ninth month and her belly stuck out so far and was so hard I was sure she could not see her feet. Her ankles were swollen and Tim and I started doing most of her chores for her so she could rest.

We ate dinner and then Tim and I decided to continue the game of Monopoly we had started a few days earlier. It was already close to ten o'clock, but knowing Mom and Dad would be out late we were in no hurry to get to bed. We could hear Belaynesh in the kitchen straightening up, and I heard her go into the bathroom down the hall near the door to the veranda and shut the door. Tim rolled double sixes and then a four and a two and let out a whoop as he moved his piece along. He asked me to give him Boardwalk and handed over the money.

I was half listening to him because I was waiting to hear the bathroom door open and Belaynesh come out.

"What is taking her so long?" I said out loud.

I returned to the game for a few minutes, but couldn't really concentrate.

"Let me go see where Belaynesh is," I said to Tim and got up and tiptoed quickly down the hall.

I stood outside the bathroom door and listened intently. For a few seconds I wondered if some wild unidentified animal had crawled beneath the house and was whining. I slowly opened the door and peered into the dimly lit room. I saw a figure curled up on the floor, and I cried out.

"Belaynesh, what is the matter?"

The floor was wet in spots and I almost slipped as I moved over toward her.

"The baby, Martha, the baby is coming," she whispered, and it sounded like her teeth were clenched and she was breathing rapidly.

"I don't know what to do," I said, not knowing what else to say, and I was afraid to move too close to her. It took a brief moment for my eyes to adjust to the darkness. I almost wanted to keep them tightly shut.

"You must get my mother," she said quietly but with a sense of urgency in her voice. "Please get my mother."

I ran out of the room and back down the hall to Tim, who was still sitting in front of the Monopoly board.

"The baby is coming and we have to get her mother" — the words burst out of me before Tim had a chance to respond to the look that must have been on my face.

I liked to think that I had perfect control of my face and Tim and I sometimes played a game where he would tell me something very funny or very sad or horrible and I wouldn't move a muscle on my face. But the look on it now must have been anything but impassive because he immediately stood up.

I told Tim that I was going to get the night guard and run to the village. I was just beginning to move when my brother grabbed me by the arm.

"Hey wait," he said. "I know you are the faster runner, but one of us has to stay with her and it can't be me." He did not let go of my arm.

"Why not? I asked, but I already knew the answer before Tim let go of my arm.

"Because Belaynesh is a girl and you are a girl and you know where babies come out." He gestured down towards his privates. I nodded slowly and told him to please go as quickly as he could.

I went back into the bathroom where Belaynesh lay moaning on the floor.

"Tim is going to get your mother," I said, and I sat down next to her praying that somehow I would know what to do or how to comfort her. She was sweating so hard that the cloth of her *shama* seemed to be made of gauze and I could see the outline of her swollen breasts pressing against the fabric.

A small fan hung from the ceiling and I could hear it moving. There were no pictures or mirrors on the whitewashed walls and the tile floor did not have a rug or bathmat on it. This was a back bathroom and not used a great deal.

"Does it hurt real bad?" I asked her.

"Yes," she said, and let out another moan that grew louder and more urgent and suddenly the words, "my back, my back," burst out of her.

I leaned over and awkwardly tried to rub her back not understanding why it hurt her there and not her stomach. Most of me wanted to bolt out of the room but we sat in silence for a few minutes. I thought about my father's mother, the grandmother I had never met, who had died giving birth to Dad's younger brother. I wondered how far the British embassy was. I rode over there frequently and since it took twenty minutes at a gallop, it was no doubt at least three miles away. I didn't have a number for the embassy and Ethiopia had no directory assistance and this was long before the invention of the cellphone. I wished that I was the one running over to the village. I knew Tim would do his best, but the night guard who was with him was not a young man and I wondered how fast he could go.

"Can I get you something?" I asked Belaynesh and brought my head down toward her face to wait for her answer.

Her lips were dry and cracked.

"A glass of water," she said weakly, "that would be good. And a washcloth."

Grateful to have a reason to leave the room and a task to take care of, I stood up and walked out toward the living room, through the dining room and into the kitchen. We had to boil all of our drinking water at 100 degrees centigrade to get rid of bacteria and all of our fruits and vegetables were washed in Clorox. The boiled drinking water was then stored in big jugs in the refrigerator. I remembered when we had last visited my grandparents in Virginia, I drank water straight out of the tap and we had gone with my grandfather to a peach orchard and had eaten the fruit we'd picked straight off the branch. I poured a tall glass and started back toward the bathroom, but then went back into the kitchen and began looking through the drawers trying to find where the straws were kept.

I was delaying going back into the room with her and I paced ten steps in one direction and then ten steps back hoping it would calm me. And I felt guilty. But I also knew that I had to go back, that no matter how afraid I was, leaving her there alone for more than five minutes was simply not an option. I made a detour on the way back though, and went to the linen closet and got a pillow, the washcloth she'd asked for and a flashlight, and then made my way back to the bathroom. When I came in, Belaynesh's eyes were closed but she opened them as I sat down next to her again and first lifted her head onto the pillow and then brought the glass with the straw in it up to her mouth. She took a long drink.

"That tastes good," she said simply as she turned her legs first to the left and then the right as though she could ease the pain.

I handed her the washcloth and she bunched it up and put it between her teeth and bit down hard.

"Let me turn out this bright light," I said, and with light now coming in only from the hallway, semi-darkness filled the room.

It had begun to rain, loudly pounding on the tin roof of our house. I shuddered with each clap of thunder. Things seemed to remain quiet for about ten minutes and then I watched her pull her legs up again and moan loudly. The room was warm, but I felt very cold, like my feet and arms were in a bucket of ice.

"Where is Tim?" I wondered. I concentrated hard trying to get an image of where he was. Recently I had begun to wonder if emotions had a smell or a taste that we could transmit unknowingly by vibrations in the air. Maybe he would sense how scared and worried I was and he would walk faster. I focused intently on sending him the thought, "Hurry, Tim, hurry."

For a minute or two I counted up to sixty and then started over. I couldn't really tell how much time had gone by. I saw that the washcloth was no longer in her mouth but lay next to her head. Belaynesh moaned quietly, sometimes it sounded like a whimper, but then suddenly she would cry out, the sound rising up into a scream. I looked out through a tiny window and caught sight of the moon, a shimmering white disc with an outline of vapor around it. My gaze became fixed on the small square patch of sky that I could see through the window and, as the sound of her screams became eerily distant, I felt myself float away and I was suddenly looking down at the scene in the bathroom. My mind began to drift to running — down the back steps, and then on the hard dirt of the side yard, "thud, thud, thud," the sound like an echo inside my own head. I began to click the flashlight on and off on the wall that Belaynesh's back faced, and with every click, for a split second, the outline of her curled up body glowed in the light.

My brother told me later on that he had gotten to Belaynesh's village quickly, but that it had taken a long time to get back because Belaynesh's mother was old and walked so slowly, and it had started to rain which slowed them even more. I did remember hearing them at the front door and I got up when Belaynesh's mother came into the bathroom. Her face was creased with wrinkles and she had tied a scarf tightly around her head, no doubt after she had been awakened from sleep by Tim. She was holding a knife and a little pot with some kind of oil or butter in it. My brother and I hung around outside the bathroom for a little while as Belaynesh continued to moan and scream and then we each went to our respective bedrooms.

I had started keeping diaries a year earlier when I was nine and I wrote all the time, especially when I couldn't fall asleep. I left a wide margin next to what I wrote and would jot down little details that I saw. Tim had asked me why I wrote so much and I told him that it somehow made moments that went by quickly more permanent. I started a new journal entry and titled it, "Belaynesh is having a baby." I didn't know yet if the baby was going to be a boy or a girl and then with a shudder I thought, "The baby might be dead."

Shortly after midnight Dad and Mom got home and I heard them talking to Belaynesh's mother in the hallway and then I stood outside my bedroom door and watched Dad carry Belaynesh out and put her gently into the back seat of the Jeep. Her mother went around to the front of the Jeep and got in.

"Dad is taking her to the hospital," Mom said. "See if you can get some sleep now."

She gave me a hug and for a moment stroked my head softly and I leaned into her wanting to stay that way forever.

I went into my room and put on my nightgown and then looked at myself in the mirror. A different person from a few hours earlier looked back at me. For a split second I thought it was my ghost, barely transparent, staring at me — it was one of those moments where the world I knew had ceased to exist. Suddenly I started to sob, tears running down my cheeks. I wasn't even sure why I was crying, but the tears just kept coming. I felt my heart pounding fiercely in my chest. For a few seconds an unknown terror washed over me and I lay down on my bed and pulled the light comforter up over me.

A light breeze drifted in from the hallway and the chill crept slowly under the covers. My legs were suddenly cold and as I lay there I felt the cold move up, settling in my chest. My heart continued to pound and I couldn't get in a deep breath as though someone were pressing on my chest. A flickering shadow from the light through the slats in the metal shutters washed over the room. And then gradually, the pounding grew quieter and was replaced by numbness as though a steel trap had been erected inside my chest. And as the weariness and exhaustion moved through me, my breath became slower and deeper and I gradually fell asleep.

The next morning Tim and I were sitting at the breakfast table eating when Dad came in, dressed and ready to go to work. He told us that she had had the baby, a little girl, and that they had named her Rebecca.

"I am really proud of you two," he said, and then he looked directly at me. "Sounds like you got quite an education last night, Martha."

And that was the last time that night was ever spoken of for many years. My mother stood there wordlessly, a silence that I would experience many times at those awkward moments when a child had been exposed to difficult facts of life that a child couldn't make sense of.

A few days later my brother and I walked over to Belaynesh's mud hut with Assefa. I was a little worried that her husband might be there and was relieved when I did not see his bike leaning up against the fence. When we entered the *tukul*, Belaynesh was lying on a straw mat with little Rebecca swaddled in a light tan cloth next to her. Belaynesh had four or five other children who were playing on the mud floor, and the oldest one was stirring something in a pot. One of the little ones toddled over and started banging on a pot with a stick.

"Do you want to hold her, Martha?" Belaynesh's mother asked me. I nodded and she picked up Rebecca and gently placed her in my arms. I couldn't believe how tiny she was. Her eyes were closed, the curve of her light brown eyelids so delicate and her fists were balled up tightly. She seemed to be in a deep sleep. I wanted to tell her that she was beautiful but the words stuck in my throat. Slowly she stretched like a cat waking up and she opened her eyes and looked up at me, unblinking. It was at that moment that I first had the thought, one that I would try to hold onto frequently over the next years, that even on the most difficult days there is the possibility for joy.

~ Chapter 3 ~

FRIENDSHIP

O ur home had a high stone wall around the perimeter of the property and a wrought iron gate at the front topped with iron spikes. A small guardhouse stood right next to the gate and a night watchman was in it at all times after dark. But this didn't seem to completely deter the thieves who could still find their way over the wall at least once every couple of months. At night I could hear them outside the window of my bedroom on the veranda.

Every night heavy metal shutters were lowered over the windows but a number of times I had awoken from a sound sleep to a loud clanging, as someone who had gotten into the compound was no doubt hoping that one of the shutters had been left unlocked. And I could hear our dogs Jambo and Rafe — the doberman pinscher who had bitten just about everybody in the household but Dad — barking loudly from different parts of the yard. Some nights Dad would take his revolver and go out onto the front steps and fire off a round.

"Just want to make sure everyone knows we are armed," he said to Tim and me who would be standing in the doorway watching him.

I couldn't understand what was happening to me at moments. There were days when I was just fine. But there were increasing periods of time where I would feel like I was in something of a daze. I'd be going about my day, but it felt like another part of me was watching me go about my day. And I was beginning to worry more when my family was not at home in the compound. At night when my parents were out, I would wake up at least every hour to go to the living room and look out of the metal shutters, holding my breath and slowly separating them. I would peek out and feel either a rush of relief that they were home or a flood of anxiety.

"I feel worried when you and Mom are out at night," I said to Dad one night as they were getting ready to go to a diplomatic reception at the Italian Embassy.

"That is probably Nancy's fault," he answered, and he began to look through some papers on his desk, then stopped. He folded his hands beneath his chin and looked at me. I felt immobilized under his intense gaze.

"You probably don't remember this but when Nancy was around seven or eight, and you and Tim around four and three, when your mother and I would be going out, as we'd be heading out the door, she would get the two of you up." Dad paused and I waited. "And as we were leaving," he continued," she'd have you all on the porch and she'd be wailing 'promise us you'll come back, promise us you'll come back.'"

And even though Dad reassured me that they would always come back, I felt like I was never totally sure and always wondered what would happen to me if the day ever came when they didn't. But guardian angels, who helped me feel we might be okay, did sometimes appear in the most timely fashion.

We met one such angel, who was destined to become a regular fixture of our childhood, soon after I began the fifth grade.

There was an American School in Addis, out by the airport and the U.S. military commissary. Our parents sent us to the German School instead because Dad said he didn't want us surrounded by "Bozos from Texas." Every subject was taught in German from kindergarten on, and Amharic, English, French and Latin were added as you grew older. Looking back, I'm surprised I didn't start mixing up languages, and I know that I dreamt in at least three of them. Sometimes when I first woke up, if I could remember enough of the dream, I'd lie in bed and try to translate it into another language.

The German School was located about halfway between Arat Kilo and Sidist Kilo, the main traffic roundabouts where many roads came together and that marked each end of the broad avenue running from central Addis up towards the American Embassy and Entoto mountain.

The school day ended at one in the afternoon. That always seemed like long enough to be away from our animals and Mom and Dad and the people who worked for us, but the German School didn't think so because we went to classes on Saturdays as well. When we first started in kindergarten, the number of kids was growing fast, as many of the foreign families in Addis sought out the strict discipline of the school. About half the students were Ethiopians, ranging from those with aristocratic backgrounds to the humblest scholarship students wearing the same pair of shorts day after day. Everyone seemed to mix on the playground during recess, roughhousing and running about, at least during our earliest years.

By the time my brother and I got to grade school, the old hotel where the school was first located had been pulled down, replaced by a couple of two-story cement and steel buildings, painted all white, that were set at perpendicular angles to each other. The new buildings took years to complete, so we always seemed to be going to school on a construction site. But for Tim and me and our friends, this meant that we had more materials like scraps of metal and plaster for our endless games during free moments at school.

The buildings were really bare; they reminded me of the barracks that I saw when we drove by the Army headquarters. The walls on the inside were painted a stark white and there were hardly any paintings or posters on the walls. And it was in those buildings that we were taught not only history and math, but discipline and how to endure pain and humiliation. Corporal punishment was permitted and shaming and ostracism were common. Nancy, Tim and I were among the few Americans and we sensed among some of the teachers a visceral anti-Americanism that was expressed in extra discipline or dirty looks. Tim told me once on the bus ride home that no matter who started the chatter, he always got the blame.

"Paradis, shut up. You aren't that stupid, Paradis, so why do you pretend to be?"

He mimicked the voice of Herr Buber, a short, stout man who taught us geography and seemed to be in a constant state of annoyance and frustration.

"One of my friends told me he says it even when I am not there," Tim continued with an exasperated sigh.

We had heard some rumors floating around the older students that two of our teachers had been with the S.S. during World War II, and like many former Nazis had fled to Africa after the war.

Since the teachers were permitted to hit us I spent a good deal of time figuring out the best ways to avoid their wrath. The fact that I was a diligent student and athletic helped me except the time that I forgot my crochet at home and was rewarded with fifteen hard blows to my knuckles with a pair of knitting needles by a middle-aged female teacher. She had her hair pulled back in a severe bun and her face was so red it looked like she had fallen asleep in the midday sun. I didn't mind the pain so much as I did the embarrassment, of having to take my punishment up in front of the whole class. I avoided making eye contact with any of my friends during recess that day and stayed by myself near the swing set. No one really tried to speak to me and I was grateful to have a day to recoup.

During the early years we were driven to school in the morning and picked up in the afternoon. But when I entered fifth grade, and my brother the fourth, we started taking the school bus. The bus dropped us off at the top of a hill. From there it was about a ten-minute walk to our home, down a dusty road with no sidewalk. Right next to where the bus dropped us off was a small grove of eucalyptus trees. I loved the smell of eucalyptus, and the leaves were used in all sorts of ways.

Once a year, armies of red ants marched through the compound heading straight towards the front of the house, while trying to make their way from the fields in the front to the Kebena River which lay behind the house. Assefa, sweat running down his face, showed my brother and me how to spread the leaves out on the gravel walkway that led up to our front door. The eucalyptus leaves acted as a natural insecticide, steering the ants away from the front of our home. Tim and I once spent an entire afternoon moving the leaves slightly to the left and then to the right, and watching the columns of ants change their direction with military precision.

One afternoon as the bus had just pulled away Tim noticed a group of boys almost hidden in the grove.

"Martha, let's get moving," he said, and reached out and tugged at my sleeve.

My brother's voice was lower than usual and I glanced over to where he seemed to be looking. A group of six boys began to walk towards us. Tim and I looked at each other, both uncertain now whether to stay standing where we were or begin to hurry down the road to our home. Tim shifted uneasily next to me.

"What should we do?" he whispered.

"I don't know yet," I answered quietly. I looked past Tim to a group of small shacks hoping I might see an adult.

Suddenly the backpack I was carrying felt as though it was filled with bricks, although a moment earlier I had barely noticed it was on my back. The boys were now about six feet from us and a boy who looked to be the oldest, around twelve, stepped forward.

"Hey *Ferenje*" he demanded, "give us your *genzeb*," which I knew to mean money.

I felt my chest tighten.

"We don't have any," I said, thrusting my shoulders back the way Dad had instructed me to if I wanted my words to be taken seriously.

As though he had not heard me he repeated, "give us *genzeb*," and he took a step forward with the other boys right on his heels.

I glanced over at my brother who was standing very still. I cleared my throat and as Tim looked over I mouthed in German — grateful that Dad had insisted on our learning another language at a young age — "run, on three."

Tim nodded and I yelled "*eins, zwei, drei*" and turned and bolted up the little rise before hitting the stretch of road towards our home.

I could hear my brother right behind me and when we had gotten no more than twenty yards away I suddenly felt the sting of small pebbles and rocks hit my backpack and the back of my legs.

I yelled over in Tim's direction that he should cover his head and at the same time I put both my arms up and crisscrossed them over the back of my head.

The sharp sting of the rocks decreased as we neared the gate to the front of our compound. Assefa pulled open the gate to let us in.

As we walked up the back stairs and into the kitchen and hung our bags on the hooks by the door I asked Tim what he thought we should do. He shrugged and said he didn't know but that we were not going to tell Dad. I nodded. Dad would get so angry he would storm over to the village and find whoever the head guy in the village was and "those boys will be in a heap of trouble." Dad's wrath could be intimidating both in its swiftness and ferocity.

"And then we will never be allowed to leave the compound alone again," Tim said.

We had only this year been permitted to leave the compound on our own and walk to and from the bus stop, a privilege that we had been looking forward to for as long as we could remember. For years we would climb one of the big trees a few feet from the stone wall that surrounded our property and look out toward the mountains beyond. If there was no wind, in the month or two after the rainy season we could almost hear the roar of the Kebena River, the deep water now buffeting the trunks on the river bed.

Tim always asked me, as he looked out toward the horizon, when I thought we'd be able to be out on our own.

"Maybe next year," I had answered for the past couple of years. And then finally, at the start of my fifth grade, when we would start taking the school bus back and forth, the long awaited time had come. "But if you get into any trouble, you will be right back to having Assefa accompany you to and from the school bus," Dad told us, looking down at us sternly.

We also didn't have any money to give the boys. Dad and Mom made us do chores for sure, but did not believe in paying us for them.

"Helping out is just a part of what it means to be in this family," Dad said the one time we had told him that some of the kids we knew got something called an allowance.

And because this newfound freedom of being dropped off at the top of the hill was so important to us, we did not say a word to anyone but decided to take our chances. We became experts at getting off the bus, already at a run, and had taken to wearing two sweatshirts to lessen the sting of the pebbles. One afternoon as the bus pulled up, right before we started our run down the hill, I noticed a slightly older boy standing by himself on the opposite side of the road from the grove of trees. He seemed intent on watching our courageous sprint off the bus; he was neither frowning nor smiling but just stood very silently. When he caught me looking at him, he ducked behind a tree.

"There is someone over there watching us," I said to Tim.

"Where?" he asked looking around.

"Over there by the trees," I said, and gestured in that direction.

"I don't see anyone," he responded. "You must be imagining things."

"No, someone was there." I looked over in the direction of the trees again and wondered if I had only imagined it.

Our desperate, daily flight off the bus lasted for about three weeks. It seemed to have become a game for the group of boys who would be gathered close to the bus stop anticipating our arrival. Tim and I would look out the window, and as soon as we saw them begin to make our preparations.

"Tie your sneakers tighter," I would tell my brother, "and you set off before me."

I had been blessed with the gift of speed. But speed alone was not enough for what happened the beginning of the third week. This time when we got off the bus, the boys had formed a line about twenty feet wide, and as soon as the roar of the bus signaled that it had pulled away, they began moving slowly towards us. Suddenly, as though it had been planned well in advance, the boys had surrounded us. I felt my heart begin to race and a prickling sensation raced up my spine. Tim and I both stood totally still, waiting, not knowing if we should speak or not. I stiffened as we waited. The ringleader moved out of the circle and came and stood right in front of us. There was a swaggering cockiness to his walk and a slight smirk on his face. He half smiled and I could see that his two front teeth were chipped and yellowed.

"Give us *genzeb*, or fight us," he said loudly, his tone suddenly cold; and the smirk was replaced by a glare as he took two steps toward us.

"We don't have any *genzeb*," I started to say, but before I had finished getting the words out, the ringleader took a swing at Tim who stumbled backwards almost losing his balance.

That seemed to be the cue for them to attack us. Hands were pulling at my sweatshirt and two boys grabbed at me and tried to pin my arms, but as they pulled me down I reached out and scooped up a handful of hard dirt and threw it into one boy's face. Sputtering, he let go of my arm long enough for me to wiggle out of the second boy's grasp and crawl back on my hands and knees and quickly get up again. My backpack had slipped all the way down my one arm and now, using it as a weapon, I swung it as hard as I could at the other boy while the first boy was wiping his eyes trying to get the dirt out. The backpack flew open and my books and pens and pencils came tumbling out.

Glancing to my left I saw that Tim was on the ground but kicking hard and fast with both his feet as two of the other boys tried to grab his legs. I felt a sharp pain in the middle of my spine and fell forward, and then the hard thump of a heel against my back that brutally knocked me down. My face hit the ground hard and I could not see or focus. But the combination of fear and a surge of adrenalin must have forced me back up onto my feet because I was standing with the world spinning when I suddenly heard what sounded like a sharp crack followed by a howl.

I looked quickly to my right and saw the tall boy from the bus stop holding the ringleader by the shoulder and with a swiftness born of experience he slapped him hard across the face for what must have been the second time. He let out a stream of curses in Amharic, and letting go of the ringleader, he advanced on two of the other boys with his fists raised. The bigger boy took a step towards him and the tall boy delivered a punch that seemed driven by God himself and the boy's nose exploded with blood and I watched it run down his chin. The tall boy's fist then caught the second boy in the left temple and sent him spinning wildly backwards. He continued yelling as the two boys he had hit scrambled to their feet and the rest of the group scattered. It had all happened so fast and my heart was pounding wildly. The tall boy leaned over and extended his arm to Tim who grabbed it and was hoisted back to his feet. I began to wipe the dirt off my face and I moved over to stand next to my brother and for about a minute we just stood looking at each other. His dark eyes seemed to be taking us in.

"Thank you," I finally said, not sure if I should smile or not.

He did not answer immediately, but then slightly bowed his head and said, "My name is Sileshi Teferra." When he looked up I saw a flash of something melancholy in his eyes as though he was a sentimental soul with the heart of a poet. He was tall and lean with the long fluid-shaped muscles of a swimmer.

He extended his hand towards me and I took it and felt the rough callouses on his palm.

I told him that my name was Martha and gestured toward Tim, "and that is my brother Tim."

"Yes, I know," Sileshi said, letting go of my hand and extending his to Tim.

"You live down the road and your father drives a green Jeep, right?" he said in a soft, earnest tone.

I saw Tim nod, his head bobbing up and down.

All three of us began to pick up my books and pens and pencils and put them back into my backpack.

"I must go, I am late," Sileshi said. "You will be okay now. They will not bother you."

And he turned and walked back toward the grove of trees he had emerged from. Tim and I stood there watching him go.

The next morning was a Sunday and after a quick breakfast my brother and I went down to the stables behind our house. We liked climbing to the top of the roof above the horses in our tall rubber boots and then jumping down into a huge pile of hay and dirt and mud, seeing who could make it the farthest. Sometimes we would just sit on the roof and try to listen to the roar of the Kebena River, but today we had decided to practice our jumps.

We were on about our third round of this pastime when Tim suddenly tugged on my sleeve and said, "Look over there."

I turned and standing in the middle of a field on the other side of the wall about twenty feet away was Sileshi. He was simply looking up towards us squinting into the sun, and the fine, angular cheekbones of his face looked even more prominent.

"What is that?" Tim asked me, gesturing toward what looked like a long whip in his hand.

"Let's ask him," I said, and we moved to the furthest side of the roof and Tim said at the top of his lungs, "What is that in your hand?"

"This is my bullwhip," Sileshi answered loudly. "Do you want to hear me crack it?"

"Oh yeah," Tim answered, and we watched Sileshi draw his arm back and then with a quick jerking motion bring it up and forward and a loud "crack" broke the stillness, startling a few goats that were grazing nearby.

Tim yelled over to him, asking if he'd let him crack it.

"Yes," Sileshi said, "but either you have to come down here or I have to come in there."

"What do you think?" Tim looked at me with an expression on his face that seemed a combination of hesitancy and excitement.

"I think it would be alright," I answered.

"Okay," Tim said looking back at Sileshi, "come to the small gate at the back, right behind the stable."

We jumped off the roof and ran around to the back and got there just as Sileshi's face appeared at the gate. I quickly looked for the hook where the key was hung, found it, put it into the heavy padlock, turned it, slid back the hard metal bar and then pushed open the gate. Slowly, as though still somewhat unsure, Sileshi stepped forward and came into the compound.

We spent the next couple of hours learning how to crack the whip. We showed Sileshi the tree house we had built, propped at the fork of the largest branches. It had three walls and a thick wooden floor. Sileshi laughed when a breeze came through and the bamboo wind chimes that Dad had brought back from one of his trips, and that we had hung from a nearby branch, made their hollow haunting sound. Sileshi told us that we could add some rope swings and then we would be able to swing off the platform and grab onto one of the branches of a skinny eucalyptus tree and shinny down the trunk.

He said that that way we'd have two escape routes if the neighborhood boys ever found their way to the tree house. I wasn't sure if he was serious or not, even though he was smiling.

The addition of the rope swings became our first project with Sileshi. Materials were easy to come by since there was always a lot of extra rope around the stables, and we got a hammer and huge nails from Dad's workbench in the basement. Sileshi would show up in the field behind our house after school and as soon as we came out to the back porch would crack the bullwhip to get our attention. We ran down to the stables to let him in at the back gate. This was always after our homework was done, usually by mid-afternoon, but we soon noticed that even if we were in the middle of something he would leave shortly before 5 o'clock, the time that Dad would get home.

One afternoon we were up in the tree house just about to practice swinging from the rope when we unexpectedly heard Dad's voice under us: "Martha, Tim. Who is that with you up there?"

"Why don't you all come on down," he said, his voice more of a command then a question.

I turned and glanced at Sileshi, who looked like he had just heard a ghost and his fingers were anxiously tapping on his knee. There was a look of terror in his dark brown eyes and they sparkled as though holding back unshed tears. His thin lips were pulled tightly together as though he was about to whistle.

He didn't seem able to move, so I whispered to him telling him that it was my dad and that he had to come down with us. I reached out and tugged on his sleeve. We slowly climbed down the ladder and went over to where Dad was standing. Sileshi was walking very slowly and I got to Dad ahead of him. Dad didn't say anything to me but seemed intent on watching Sileshi's slow walk toward us. When Sileshi got to us he had his head bowed and he was looking at the ground.

My dad suddenly smiled and said warmly, "I hear you helped out my kids."

I glanced over at Tim who shook his head. I couldn't imagine how my father had found out, but somehow he always seemed sooner or later to get wind of anything Tim, Nancy or I had gotten ourselves into. Dad extended his hand toward Sileshi, who still had his head bowed and very slowly Sileshi looked up and took Dad's hand. Dad placed his other hand over Sileshi's other hand and thanked him and assured him that he was now always welcome in our home.

We climbed back onto the platform and I asked Sileshi why he had been so scared. He told us that they called Dad "*Jibo*" in the neighborhood, a name given to someone who was considered fierce and aggressive.

"Look at how he drives his Jeep, always creating a great dust storm and with the gravel flying under the tires. And at night he fires off his gun. We can hear it in my village."

I thought about what Sileshi had told me, that they called my dad *Jibo* in the village. And I could see why. He could be so intimidating and take-charge in his approach to life. But there was this whole other side to him that I saw and felt. There was this gentleness in his touch when he would hug me goodnight before going off to some evening function. And whenever I would come to him to plead the case of one of the people who worked for us — that they be given a special day off or be permitted to come to work late — he always said, "Yes, of course. What goes on in their life is important too."

I had noticed a while back that no one who worked for us ever asked Dad anything directly but would call me over and say, "Martha, can you ask your father if I can have the Monday after Easter off?" And I would wait and try to gauge when Dad didn't seem to have too much else on his mind. I never told my father that I had been asked, but would say something that suggested that I had heard Mamo say that if he had Easter Monday off he could go visit his children and then innocently propose that maybe we could give him the day off. Only a couple of rare times had Dad said no, and I felt that I had somehow failed when I had to go back to relay the answer.

Tim and I never did find out how Dad learned of our experiences at the bus stop and Sileshi's intervention, but with the entrance of Sileshi into our lives, the world outside our compound opened up for us. Well, initially at least, the world immediately outside the compound, which included the villages where Sileshi and Belaynesh lived. But as we began to venture farther and farther away from the compound, Ethiopia emerged like an echo of a period in history that was frozen in time. And the little that I knew of the world outside Ethiopia, from our few visits to Staunton and trips that we took in the summer, made that world seem pale and devoid of life in comparison.

~ Chapter 4 ~

FLOWERS & LOCUSTS

I have never been able to see a floral display without remembering the gorgeous palette of Ethiopia's wildflowers.

My mother loved flowers and recreated Ethiopia's natural splendor in our home. There were always fresh flowers in the center of the dining room table, their scent mixing in with the herbs and spices that Beheilu used in preparing a meal. The midday meal was the one we ate together as a family since Mom and Dad were out almost every night. After having my first lunch with my parents and Tim, I would run down to the back of the stables and have a second lunch, sitting on the ground with Assefa and Worku around a basket of *injera* and *wot*. A lot of the time it felt to me like I had two families.

Mom spent hours with Assefa planning the flower beds, especially the one in the center of the circular driveway in front of the house. I could see it from the living room, looking out of the front window by the armchair I liked to sit in sometimes when I was reading. I watched him trim the leaves off the rose bush. Mom told me a long time ago when I had tried to pick one of the roses and a thorn had pierced the skin on my forefinger, that the only rose native to the African continent was the cream colored Ethiopian rose, also referred to as the Abyssinian rose. Sometimes when I watched Assefa in the garden I would see his lips move and I was sure he was talking to the flowers. Some flowers were invaders who would overrun the garden if Assefa did not prune them back. And at times it seemed like the flowers played a frustrating game with Assefa. The buds would look ready to bloom and he'd water them furiously and the next morning if they were still closed he'd shake his head and frown, muttering under his breath.

It was mid-afternoon and I put my book down and watched Assefa clip the hydrangea bushes, plants that produce fragrant white, green, orange or purple flowers. His heavy shoulders and thick arms moved back and forth under his thin cotton tunic, and I wondered whether he might have been a boxer in his younger days. His small brown eyes were hardly visible because of the way he screwed them up in a perpetual squint after years and years in the sun. His face looked like that of someone who had lived deeply and perhaps suffered a lot. But there was not a bug or butterfly that drifted into our lives that Assefa couldn't identify. In my mother's garden he showed my brother and me where the turtles hid their eggs beneath the thick brush on the edge of the garden. And he taught us how to dig up earthworms when we wanted to go fishing at the river, and how to identify the ground that would yield the most crawling little bodies. I didn't like to admit it when friends of ours talked about having gotten a television set, but secretly I was glad we didn't have one. I felt like nature was a much better teacher than staring at a screen.

As I watched, Assefa squatted down to weed the flower bed, and suddenly he swayed and tipped over and was on the ground. I dropped my book and raced out of the house, tripping on the front steps and almost falling over myself, and then I was by his side and knelt down. His eyes were closed and his face was moist with a light veil of perspiration. I wanted to reach out and trace the lines on his forehead. He looked older than he usually did. I had not noticed until this moment the grey at his temples and now tears seemed to rim his eyes. Maybe all the years of working in the garden in the hot sun had left its mark on him. Worku, who must have been at the stables, suddenly appeared behind me and knelt down next to Assefa.

"Is he dead?" I whispered quietly.

"No," Worku said.

He had taken Assefa's hand in his own and was feeling his pulse.

"He has fainted. It is Ramadan and he is fasting."

"What is Ramadan?" I asked, hoping that I was pronouncing the word correctly.

"Ramadan is a month of fasting. He does not eat or drink from dawn to sunset."

"But it gets so hot in the middle of the day," I said. "That seems mean."

"His religion is Islam," Worku said. "Ask your father to explain."

I looked at Assefa's parched lips.

"Can't we give him a little sip of water?"

Assefa's eyes were open now and he shook his head, "No."

"He is not permitted to eat or drink. Not even the tiniest drop of water. Let's get him into the shade," Worku whispered as he drew his face closer to mine putting a thin finger over his lips "Martha, help me. Take his other arm."

I put Assefa's limp arm over my shoulder and together Worku and I gently moved him to a spot where it was shady and cool under one of the tall eucalyptus trees.

"I have to water the flower beds," Assefa said, his voice hoarse. "I cannot let the flowers die in the heat."

He tried to stand up.

"No," Worku said, and gently touched his shoulder, "you rest — Martha and I will do it."

I followed Worku to the hose and for the next hour while he sprayed the flowers in the circular driveway and by the side of the house, and the large vegetable garden in the back, I ran back and forth with buckets of water, tipping the water slowly onto any dry patches he had missed.

As we were walking back up to where we had left Assefa I asked Worku, "Do you fast?"

"Yes," he said, "I fast every Wednesday and Friday. It is part of the Coptic Church's regulation. It means I only eat one meal on those days soon after sundown."

"Last year before Easter Tim and I gave up eating dessert for a week," I said.

Worku looked at me and smiled.

"That is good, Martha. It shows discipline. During Lent I fast fifty-six days, during Advent forty days, and leading up to *Kweskwam* forty days."

"What is *Kweskwam*?" I asked, trying to remember if I had heard the word before.

Worku told me that *Kweskwam* was the feast having to do with the flight from Egypt and that he could not eat dairy or meat.

"No ice cream?" I said, thinking about the homemade ice cream Beheilu made and my favorite flavors.

"No ice cream," Worku said, a smile appearing on his usually solemn face.

When we reached the eucalyptus tree Assefa was still leaning against, his eyes were closed and he was snoring lightly. Worku gently woke him up. I went back into the house and a few minutes later watched from the kitchen window as Assefa slowly laid out a prayer rug facing east, then crouched down on it and began to recite his prayers silently.

"I guess when he is done he will be able to eat and drink," I said to Poupee, my little dog who followed me around like my shadow.

Then I thought about an incident from a few years back, that began when my brother and I were in the house playing an interminable card game and we got bored.

"Let's go outside and find something more interesting to do," I said to Tim.

We walked past Mom and Dad's bedroom and I caught a glimpse of my mother standing by their bed, wearing a pale blue robe and methodically brushing her hair.

"Come on," I whispered to Tim, "let's go spy on Assefa when he does his afternoon prayers."

On the way to the back yard, we stopped by the linen closet and carefully pulled two small towels from the neatly folded pile. We then crept down the back stairs close to where Assefa would lay out his prayer mat. Hiding behind the cellar door we peeked out every few minutes and watched the sun make its slow descent. It was dark and humid in the cellar and the smell of stale incense permeated the air. At last Assefa came in and we watched him wash his hands carefully, scrubbing the dirt from under his nails.

Then he picked up the colorfully woven straw mat that was rolled up in the corner, stepped out onto the lawn and laid out the mat facing east. I watched him kneel and then bow down, letting his head touch the ground three times.

Cautiously Tim and I moved forward with our towels and spread them out about ten feet behind him. We knelt down and began to copy his movements.

Suddenly I felt someone yank the back of my shirt hard and hiss, "Come back inside." Beheilu's dark eyes bore into me.

I touched Tim's shoulder and we backed away and then turned and went back into the house. I wasn't sure what we had done wrong but sensed that we were in trouble.

"Don't do that," Beheilu said. "You are not Muslim and Assefa will think you are mocking his beliefs."

I felt confused because if anything I liked Assefa and that is what drove us to mimic — not mock — his prayers. And so, years later, on the day that Assefa fainted, I had learned to satisfy my childish curiosity with a more direct approach. When I got the chance, I simply asked Dad:

"What is a Muslim?"

Mom and Dad were getting ready to go out to an affair at the palace. Some head of state or dignitary was visiting. It always took Mom longer to get ready than Dad who was sitting behind his desk doing some paperwork.

"You know the way we follow the teachings of Jesus, and we are called Christians?" he said.

I nodded and Dad then told me that Muslims follow the teachings first told by a prophet named Mohammed. He said their bible was called the Qur'an and their religion was called Islam.

"But I thought Ethiopians were Christian?" I said, thinking about all of the churches that I saw when we drove around Addis.

"Most are, mainly the Amharas," Dad said, "but there are many Muslims in the south and then some Jews in the north near Gondar."

"Do they believe in the same God we do?" I asked.

"Yes," Dad answered.

Recently I had overheard Dad tell Nancy that he was an agnostic, that he wasn't sure about the existence of God. But I knew Mom was sure. Nancy had recently started telling everyone that she might be an atheist. Dad told Nancy she'd better not tell Mom that.

They'd glared at each other for a moment, and to defuse the situation I had said, "Nancy, can you help me with the essay I am writing?" Nancy was one of those teenagers who seemed to always make people, especially grownups, go slack-jawed. She just said what she thought in a very matter-of-fact way.

But more recently it felt like I was always diverting my father and sister from an argument. And my mother's face was always anxious whenever she witnessed the chilly interplay between Nancy and Dad. In some ways they seemed so much alike to me. On the outside, so tough, like nothing scared them. But then this other part of them was deeply emotional. And they cared so much about the people and things that were important to them. I hated it when they would argue and they both had such a stubborn streak, as though actually agreeing with the other person's point of view meant losing some kind of battle.

"They call their god Allah," Dad said.

"Do they pray to that Mohammed person or to Allah?" I asked.

For some reason it seemed important to have it right, to know what was happening when Assefa knelt on his prayer rug.

"They pray to Allah," he said as he stood up and went into the living room. But Mom still wasn't there, so he sat down on the sofa to wait for her. I followed him into the room.

"Didn't you used to be a Catholic?" I said to my father.

Dad then told me that growing up he was a devout Catholic, that he attended a Catholic school and became an altar boy, walking the mile and a half to church every morning to serve at the seven o'clock mass. He said that he was often called out of class to serve at weddings and funerals.

"What was that like?" I asked, thinking that I'd love to be called out of class.

"I much preferred weddings," Dad said, "funerals were pretty sad and dreary affairs. The mourners were so worried about how to pay for the casket and the headstone and flowers that they never thought about the altar boy."

I asked him if the weddings were any better.

"A wedding was a happy and joyful event and I could count on at least a quarter, or perhaps even fifty cents," Dad answered, looking down at his watch.

"Dad, why aren't you Catholic anymore? "I asked.

"Well, I knew enough about the birds and the bees and the facts of life to wonder how the Catholic Church to which I was so devoted could oppose birth control when the price I had to pay was the death of my mother," he answered. "Remember, Martha, I told you my parents had been advised not to have another child?"

I wasn't quite sure how that all worked. I had heard something about birth control from listening to Nancy and her friends. I decided I'd wait and ask Nancy more about it. I didn't want Dad to have to keep talking about his mother who had died. And I wondered if faith was patient and if the Catholic Church would wait for my father to return one day.

My mother finally came into the room and Dad stood up and whistled softly. "You look beautiful," he said. My mother blushed and took Dad's arm.

"There will be fireworks from the palace tonight at around ten," Dad said to me. "It is a clear night so you should be able to see them from the front porch." Dad gave me a quick kiss on the cheek and gave Tim's shoulder a squeeze. Mom kissed us both on the cheek and I caught a whiff of her perfume.

Later that night Tim and I stood on the front porch and watched the fireworks. Dad had given us a guide to types of fireworks so we could try to identify them as they shot up into the sky.

"That's a chrysanthemum," Tim said looking at the book, as a circle of colored stars that left a visible trail of sparks shot up high above the eucalyptus trees.

"It's sort of funny how fireworks are named after flowers," I said, my eyes looking up into the night sky.

"And that's a waterfall," he continued, pointing to a group of heavy long burning tailed stars that traveled a short distance from the shell and then burst, leaving a "waterfall" of glittering points.

I half listened to Tim and continued to look up into the heavens. I somehow found it comforting to imagine that God was scattering little dots of colored lights over us to bless us. I was glad that the stars were so far away that predators, human or animal, could not reach them.

I had once asked Mamo what he thought stars were, and he said without even stopping to think about it, "Messages from God."

"What do you mean?" I asked.

"Every time a star blinks, a baby has been born," he answered.

The day after Assefa's collapse I woke up early, pulled up the shutters, opened the window and looked out. The day seemed to unfold to a different rhythm as the dark grey light snuck across the horizon. I sometimes wondered what it would be like to see the earth millions of years ago. I knew Ethiopia was one of the oldest civilizations on earth. Had it been like this? Is this what it was like in the beginning — dark, peaceful and motionless?

I shifted my gaze to the eucalyptus trees and saw the very faint outline of the tree house. When far away each tree looked the same, maybe one a little taller than another but basically the same. But once you were up close each of the trees was unique. The bark could be light grey or almost dark brown, the leaves every possible shade of silver. I loved listening to the sounds of morning, especially when the eucalyptus branches would brush up against the metal shutters, as though welcoming a new day. Far off in the distance I heard a sound. I couldn't even tell if it was a bird or a person calling. The sun had just begun to peek over the horizon and my eyes took in the rest of the compound. Dad's Jeep was gleaming from the wash the night before. Somewhere over where the grass gave way to the thin dirt path that circled the house, I heard a scuffling noise as though a small animal was making its way out of the brush.

A few days earlier Tim and I had been up in the tree house when Dad came out and told us that Granddaddy Reid, Mom's father, had had a heart attack and was very sick.

"Where is Mom?" I asked.

Dad told us that she was lying down and would be flying to the States in the morning.

We didn't see Mom the whole rest of the day. She wasn't at dinner and I watched quietly as Beheilu prepared some soup and crackers. I followed him down the hallway and when he opened the door I peered into the semi-darkness hoping to catch a glimpse of her. That night, Tim and I sat in my room and talked about our memories of Granddaddy Reid from the three times we had visited Staunton.

"Remember how he would take us to the Reid Grocery stores and let us get anything off the shelves and we didn't have to pay for it?" I reminded my brother. Granddaddy Reid and his brothers had started a small grocery store when they were in their twenties and it had grown into a chain of seven stores. Once I got four boxes of Oreo cookies and Tim and I had eaten them all as we sat in front of what Dad called "the idiot box."

"Let's watch as much TV as we can now," I would say to Tim each of the three times we visited Staunton, "before Dad gets here." Dad would be joining us in a few days. Dad was always stressing the importance of reading and saw television as a meaningless activity that would no doubt rot our brains and turn them into mush. "One of the reasons I moved you to Ethiopia," he said frequently, "is because they don't have television yet."

One of the things that I had noticed about Mom on our last two trips back to Staunton, though, was that she seemed to become a different person when she was in her home town. She seemed in command of herself and the world around her in a way I did not see in Ethiopia where the depths of foreignness seemed to bring a kind of anxiety to her that she handled by keeping the household in perfect order. But both in Staunton and in Addis she accepted everyone as an equal regardless of their race or class. That quality was true for both my parents and something that united them in spirit. My father seemed proud of my mother's graciousness as a hostess, referring to it as her "Southern charm," and I noticed that she always was able to put anyone who came into our home at ease.

So now Mom was off to Staunton once again, on a sad mission. She had left on the first flight out that morning and I wasn't sure how long she would be gone. I wished she had said goodbye to me but I guessed she didn't want to wake me that early. After a quick breakfast prepared by Beheilu, my brother and I decided to go down to the river.

"Give me a boost up," Tim said, and put his foot into my tightly clasped hands.

"On three," and he grabbed the top of the wall and pulled himself up.

"Okay, now give me your hand and I will pull you up." I scrambled up the wall.

Once on top of the wall we dropped down and rolled, and then stood up and started jogging down towards the Kebena River. We didn't really know if we were permitted to go out of the compound on foot on our own, but now that we were allowed to leave with Sileshi, we took it as tacit permission. But we didn't leave by the back gate because that would have meant leaving the key in the lock, where someone might spot it, so instead we climbed over the wall.

Unlike the crisp weather that was typical at this time of year, the air was hot and heavy. Before the rains came, the trees and scorched fields took on a desperate, haunted look and I worried what would happen if the rains did not come.

As we ran in the direction of the river I noticed that the cattle were not grazing but all lying down. As we jogged past, a few of them struggled up and began twitching their ears and twisting their heads.

"It almost seems like they are listening for something," I thought to myself.

On some of the really hot days when we got to the river we'd wade in waist deep and pretend to be crocodiles, diving into the rushing water at the spot where it was deep enough that we didn't hit our heads. Sometimes the river was so cold it felt like my legs were on fire when we'd first wade in. Closer to the banks of the river there were areas of rippling, tangled black weeds. At moments I imagined that I saw something large and ominous moving by the shore, but when I moved closer I would realize it was only a log or clump of wet leaves from a fallen branch. I thought about Mom and what she had told me about herself when she was my age. She said her parents were so conservative that her mother had sewn sleeves into her bathing suit and that she hadn't been allowed to go on a school camping trip because they were having root beer and the word "beer" was in the name of the popular soda pop. She said that she had to be home right after school every day and that her weekends were filled with church related activities.

I loved all the freedom Tim and I had, just to be able to run down to the river and spend hours there without anyone checking on us. I decided I would have hated growing up in Staunton, Virginia.

My brother and I didn't look for danger but we did like challenging ourselves. A few weeks earlier Tim had found a long branch that had fallen across a narrow part of the river. The wood was no thicker than my thigh and Tim and I spent hours crossing it. We had to turn sideways, arching the sole of a foot over it one step at a time, as we had inched along. I could hear the river rushing underneath me. Once or twice I had stumbled and almost toppled over but using my arms for balance somehow caught myself. At other times we liked to race upstream, the cold water rushing against our legs. But today we decided that we wanted to add to our rock and pebble collection, so as soon as we got to the river we took off our socks and sneakers and waded into the water. I loved trying to find the special ones with my toes.

I stopped when I had the sense that something worthwhile might be under my big toe and reached down with my eyes closed, retrieved it and then said to Tim, "Okay, should I open my eyes or throw it back?"

Tim had looked at the rock and most times said, "Throw it back," which meant that it was just a gray rock.

But every so often he told me to open my eyes and there in my wet hand lay a spectacular rock. There was one time when after a half hour of wading in the water I was rewarded with a white-washed pebble as pure a white as a piece of typing paper. Another time the compensation for my patience and instinct was a smooth rock that seemed to have a rainbow of colors embedded in it. Tim and I also had three pink rocks which we were convinced were either marble or granite and a dark black stone that we were sure was onyx. Dad told us that the river's waters carried the rocks and pebbles along the bottom of the river bed.

"The sharper or more angular the rock is, the shorter the period of time it has been moving. Pebbles that are really even and flat have been moving for a very, very long time," he said.

Sometimes after a day at the river collecting rocks, if at night I was having trouble falling asleep I imagined the journey that one of our rocks had been on. Where had it come from and what had it witnessed along the banks of the river? Had it traveled the length of the country and met waters that fed the Blue Nile, that eventually reached Egypt? Had it been picked up by other human hands, perhaps by some women washing their family's clothes in the river's cool waters? Was a rock's life as random as a human's life seemed to be?

We had been in the river for about half an hour when I glanced to the east and said to Tim, "It looks like a thunderstorm is coming. Maybe we should get going."

"Just a little while longer," he said without lifting his head, his eyes focused on the water rushing over his feet. "I know there are still some good ones down there."

I resumed feeling around the stones and pebbles with my toes, taking a step forward and then stopping, closing my eyes and trying to sense a good one. About ten minutes passed and I looked out toward the east again. The heat was building up and I wiped the sweat off my brow with the back of my hand. I watched the cloud, which was now a dark purple bruise against the blue sky, advance toward us. The river suddenly turned muddy with the advancing rain and began to rise and would soon spill over the banks.

"Let's get moving," I said to Tim and got out of the water, sat down on a patch of grass and began waving my feet in the air to dry them before putting on my socks and sneakers.

Tim flopped down next to me.

"We got a couple good rocks to polish up," I said standing up and reaching out my hand to give Tim a tug up.

The half-mile walk back to the compound was mostly uphill and while we had run down to the river, our pace was always much slower on the way back. A light breeze came up and rolled the dust up along the sides of the path where the earth was bare. My eyes began to water and sting and as I wiped them I heard a faint noise, like the purr of an electrical wire or faint rumble of a faraway Jeep, behind me. I turned around and saw a churning black cloud moving over the river toward us. I stared at it for a second without recognition and then grabbed Tim's arm.

"Locusts, there are locusts. Run, Tim, run!"

My brother spun around and then we both began scrambling up the path, behind us the sound of the locusts' beating wings increasing in pitch until it resembled the steady rumbling of an ancient army marching into battle. Within minutes the thick ravenous swarm was upon us. I thought I was being pelted by a million tiny stones thrown from unseen hands as the insects smashed into my back and shoulders. For a few seconds I closed my eyes and looked down, but when I opened them it looked like the brown dirt was moving until I realized it was a seething mass of insects crawling forward.

Suddenly it got darker and felt like nightfall as the insects blocked the sun like a thick, dark cloud. I glanced around quickly, unable to fully grasp that a whole area which a few seconds ago had been covered in grass and daisies now appeared as if it had been burned dry and brown. I started frantically swatting at my arms and legs but the locusts caught onto my shirt and shorts with their hooked legs. Wave after wave of the insects kept swarming through the air and covering the ground like a thick mat until the thudding of our feet on the hard ground was replaced by a crunching and crackling as we stepped on them in our desperate attempt to get away from this living, breathing, winged nightmare.

I was a few feet behind Tim and saw him raise both his arms and run his hands over his blond crew cut and then shake them vigorously, and for a few seconds I watched brown winged bodies fall to the ground. Almost without thinking I did the same, but when my hands moved over my head I screamed as I felt crawling bodies that were now tangled in my hair.

"Tim, Tim, help me," I cried out.

He turned around and looked at me and then, realizing why I seemed rooted on the spot with my hands in my hair, he moved toward me holding his own hands in front of his face in a vain attempt to protect his eyes and mouth from the locusts.

"Help me, help me, please."

I kept screaming and Tim grabbed my hair at the roots and pulled his hands downwards trying to dislodge some of the bugs.

"It's no good," he said, "I can't get them, they are too tangled in your hair."

I tried to move, but couldn't and I felt Tim take my hand and pull me forward. I did not look at him, but returned the pressure and began to take in short quick gasps of breath so the locusts wouldn't fly into my mouth and I tried to steady myself.

"It will be okay, it will be okay," he said over and over, his voice a deep hoarse whisper as he kept pulling me forward. "We just have to get back to the house."

I don't know what would have happened or how I would have ever gotten back to the compound without Tim. Maybe I would have just stayed rooted on the spot for eternity while the locusts set up house and laid their eggs in my hair. But instead for twenty minutes my brother encouraged me and prodded me along.

I tried to focus on his words of reassurance — "We are going to make it, just keep moving, keep moving, Martha, we are almost there!" — and the feel of his sweaty hand in mine as he tugged me along.

I tried not to think about what was happening in my hair. When we reached the compound we climbed over the wall and ran through the back yard up the back steps and then into the kitchen. Mom was gone and Dad was still at the office but Beheilu and Mamo were in the kitchen when Tim and I entered. Mamo stared at me and then seemed to almost shrink away. But without a word, Beheilu opened one of the kitchen drawers and pulled out a pair of scissors. He motioned for me to sit down on one of the stools and for the next fifteen minutes I watched long strands of my hair and cut up locusts fall to the ground around me. My heart was pounding against my ribs as though hoping to escape my body.

"I'm so sorry, Martha," Beheilu said gently, "I wish there was another way, but this is the only way we can get them out."

"I don't care, I really don't care," I said, twisting my hands and then sitting on them to stop myself from reaching up and tearing at my hair. "Just do it."

Mamo found a broom and swept up my hair and the locusts and when he was done, Tim held up a mirror to me but I barely looked into it. I didn't even think about what it would feel like going to school the following day with my close cropped uneven haircut. I just desperately wanted to get into the shower and I scrubbed my scalp over and over. I let the spray flow fiercely over my eyes and face hoping that I could wash away the images of the locusts.

Later in the afternoon my brother and I went outside. All over the ground were the corpses of the wounded and the dead, the ones that had blindly smashed into a tree or the walls of the house. We made our way toward the stables where we found Assefa alone in one of the small rooms in the back. He was kneeling upright on his prayer mat with his back to us. When he heard us he slowly turned around away from the blank wall that he seemed to be staring at.

"How bad is it?" he asked, his voice gravelly.

"Bad, it is very bad," I said quietly.

Assefa stood up slowly and we all went outside and together we looked at the devastation without any of us saying a single word. I was glad that Mom wasn't there to see it. The locusts had eaten every leaf off every tree. Every blade of grass was gone leaving behind the brown dirt, and the flowers had simply vanished. What had once been a kaleidoscope of color in the circular flower bed and the beds running along the side of the house was now barren and desolate. Very slowly Assefa walked over to the rosebush and tore off one of the bare stems and held it gently in his hand.

"It is the will of Allah," he said in a quiet voice, but when he turned back to us I watched the tears run down his face.

The next day I asked Beheilu if he believed everything that happened was God's will.

"It is and it isn't," he said. "God may give us a road to follow. But how we follow that road is up to us."

I wondered if Assefa thought that God had sent him on a bad road by having the locusts destroy his garden and all his hard work. My answer came the next morning when I awoke to the sound of a shovel digging into the hard earth and looked outside to see Assefa digging a new flower bed. I stopped off to watch him for a few minutes on my way to the school bus.

"Now flowers will be blooming by the time your hair is long again," he said to me and stopped shoveling and leaned up against the tool catching his breath.

"Aren't you just still so sad that you have to start over," I asked.

"Even when your garden is full of weeds, Martha, if you look hard enough you will see the remains of what were once flowers," he said and went back to digging.

At night Belaynesh began to brush my hair a hundred strokes, carefully pulling it backward away from my scalp.

"It will grow faster if we brush it every night," she said when I asked her why we had to do it.

"Your hair is very beautiful," she told me softly. "In the sun it shines like gold."

~ Chapter 5 ~

EMPEROR

In our childhood travels around Addis Ababa we constantly saw the most grim and heartbreaking poverty, which made the Imperial Palace seem even more imposing and opulent than it probably ever was.

On the route to the palace, the first sign of the imperial compound was the crowds of people pressing up against the wrought iron gates hoping for an audience with the Emperor. My father explained that this was the only opportunity for justice that the vast majority of Ethiopians could expect.

The gates were surmounted, on either side, by sculptured representations of the regal lions forever associated with the Emperor.

This Ethiopia of my childhood seemed frozen in time. It was a country with stark contrasts between wealth and poverty, but these were softened at times in my child's mind by the rituals of religion and culture that brought color and joy to countless festival days. At times, for the briefest moment I wanted to flee this land, to exist instead in the perpetual clear skies I had grown to know during summer trips to Greece where we had spent the past four rainy seasons. But that thought would evaporate in an instant when I thought of our caretakers who were like a second family to me, and the meskal daisies, and the smell of eucalyptus in our back yard.

Addis Ababa itself, where we lived for my entire childhood, was such a strange city to me. There were these huge imposing ultra-modern buildings in the central parts with a few sleek cars idling in front. And then ten minutes away mud huts, with scrawny children playing outside while their mothers pounded handfuls of *teff* in big stone mortars. I had to accept that this was just the reality of Ethiopia, the only home I had ever known.

By the time I was five or six I'd been picking up many of the basic words and numbers in Amharic, the ancient language spoken by Ethiopia's highland lords and their peasant farmers whose fields we'd seen from the air. Sometimes when my brother and I went on walks outside our compound with Assefa, we'd hear the rhythmic chants of the neighborhood school kids as they learned to count. The high-pitched sound would drift through the air from the rickety wooden schoolhouse with its slanted tin roof — *and, hulet, sost, arat, amist, sidist, sabat, simint, setegn, aser* — and on up to one hundred they would count. I took note the roads entering the busy downtown roundabouts one day to confirm that *Arat* and *Sidist Kilo* matched their names numerically.

At other times we'd hear the Ethiopian kids reciting the Amharic alphabet, which sounded like an endless song with only a couple different notes — *ha, hu, he, ha, he, hi, ho / le, lu, li, la, le, li, lo* — until they reached the total of two hundred sixty letters, Assefa once told us. Because kids absorb language like a sponge, without even really realizing it Tim and I were just naturally speaking more and more Amharic.

"Martha, Tim," my dad called, "your mom and I need to talk to you."

We both appeared at my father's study the same time to find Mom and Dad sitting together in the armchairs in front of his desk. I saw a white card with black calligraphy in Mom's lap and immediately recognized it as the invitation to the Emperor's Christmas party held at the Jubilee Palace. We were invited each year, ever since I was four, along with the children from all the foreign embassies. I remember one year at the palace Santa Claus arrived on an elephant, and once he flew in on a helicopter. Santa handed out gifts and we played games and there was a lot of food piled up on silver platers on tables covered in white linen. The part I hated though was having to wear a frilly dress. I didn't feel like "me" in dresses. I felt like me when I was in jeans or jodhpurs, but when I sort of suggested to Mom that maybe I didn't have to wear a dress, she didn't even answer, which was an answer in itself.

Mom told us that the party would be in two weeks and that we shouldn't make other plans.

Mom got up and left the room and my brother did as well. I sat down in the armchair across from Dad. Sometimes I felt like I was drawn to that armchair by something outside my control.

"What's up, Martha?" he said.

He laid the dog-eared copy of the book he'd been reading onto the desk and smiled because I think he suspected that I was about to ask him a lot of questions. He always told us that asking questions was how you learned things, and that you should never feel stupid if you didn't know something but "just ask the question." I relaxed back in the chair and started talking, remembering what I had seen. My father leaned forward listening attentively.

I told Dad that the other day when we were out riding on the way to Jan Hoy Meda all of a sudden three big black cars drove by with the Ethiopian flag on them. First there were motorcycles out front. Before I even saw the cars, I heard all this cheering and as they went by everyone knelt to the ground and Worku had gotten off his horse and done the same.

Dad said that that was the Emperor on the way either to or from the palace, the same palace where the Christmas party would be held. I asked Dad if he liked working for him, and he said that most times he did but that sometimes it was frustrating because Ethiopia was a very complex society, and getting things done could seem to take an eternity.

"My official title as 'Legal Advisor to the Imperial Ethiopian Government' would seem to suggest that I should be told of what's going on at all times," he said, "but that's far from the case."

"When you were a kid did you even know Ethiopia existed?" I asked.

Dad looked out the window for a few seconds before answering.

He told me that he had first learned of a country called Abyssinia back in 1935 when he'd seen a photo in the newspaper of barefoot warriors, clad in their traditional costumes. A few were armed with rifles but many with spears and swords and rhinoceros-hide shields, some on gaily-decorated horses, preparing to launch themselves against Mussolini's machine guns and tanks and poison gas.

He then told me that he had only been a few years older than I was now when he had seen pictures of Emperor Haile Selassie as he addressed the League of Nations and warned of what would happen if Mussolini, the Italian dictator, wasn't stopped after invading Ethiopia. The Emperor gave an impassioned speech asking for the assistance that had been promised to Ethiopia eight months earlier after the Italian army had invaded Ethiopia. Haile Selassie's eloquent speech moved all who heard it that day at the League of Nations and made him *Time* magazine's "Man of the Year," Dad said. But the League did nothing. As the Emperor left the chambers, he was heard to mutter with a sigh, "It is us today; it will be you tomorrow."

"What did that mean?" I asked.

"Hitler followed," Dad said, and while I didn't know much about history, I did know that Hitler had been a very evil man.

Dad seemed in a talkative mood so I decided to press on.

"People seem to worship the Emperor like he is a really good ruler, but there are so many poor people in Ethiopia and the rich people are so rich," I said.

Dad tilted his head to the side as though considering his words carefully before he spoke.

He stopped speaking for a moment as though trying to decide how to answer a difficult question in a way that I could understand.

And then he told me that it was complicated because the Emperor, although he seemed all powerful, was something of a prisoner of the system that had existed for centuries, that there were dukes and princes who were the powerful landowners in Ethiopia's many provinces. Some of them were set against progress. Not all of them, but Ethiopia was an ancient society that the Emperor was trying to modernize, but it couldn't be done overnight. He said that in many ways the Emperor was a hostage to the aristocratic landowners who felt threatened by the modern world, but whose support he needed to hold the country together.

"But things were slowly changing," he said. "For example," he continued, "the schools used to be totally based on the teachings of the Ethiopian Orthodox Church, and the Church is very old-fashioned. That is no longer true, and Ethiopia even has a first class modern university now."

I told Dad that Sileshi's mother wanted him to go to school there, and that some of the older kids at our school would be going there too, unless they went overseas for their university education. I already knew that some of their brothers and sisters were studying in Germany, or France, or the U.S.

"I want to stay here and go to Addis Ababa University," I beamed.

I wasn't sure if Dad heard what I'd said, but if so he ignored my comment and continued talking, explaining that the government led by Haile Selassie had also built a lot of roads which brought trade and business to otherwise totally isolated parts of the country

"Remember that first coup in 1960?" he asked.

I nodded.

"It was awful, but it also has given us an opportunity to leapfrog into the modern world, because it shook people up and made clear that things can't stay the way they are forever. There have been some major changes but there are still ethnic and tribal rivalries that make everything much more difficult."

My father seemed to be on a roll, so I just kept listening as he said that people should remember that it took Europe centuries to change from their traditional system, and it's unfair to expect Ethiopia to achieve that overnight. He asked me if I remembered when we had visited Staunton that first time and were so shocked to see separate waiting rooms at the train station for white and black people. I did remember that and how it had upset me.

Dad said that while slavery in the United States had been ended almost exactly one hundred years before, the system of keeping people apart was still pretty much in place.

He glanced at his watch, and I hoped he would keep on talking. My facial expression must have communicated that because he explained that Ethiopia's diversity made things harder.

He said that he found the Ethiopians such captivating people, self-controlled and well-mannered toward outsiders but with a strong sense of their own moral superiority, and that often they were very secretive. He added that Ethiopia was both traditional and modern — fast moving cities not far from rural areas set in a time warp, part African and part Middle Eastern, really like no other place in the world.

Dad wiped his forehead and looked at his watch again and I knew this conversation would be coming to an end soon, but he was still sitting and leaning back in his chair so I kept talking. There was a question I'd had for a while now, so thinking this might be a good time I asked if he had considered staying in the States after the first coup.

"I thought about it," Dad said, "but your mother and I talked about it and I really felt like I could do something useful and of value here in Ethiopia."

"I am glad you did," I said. "I love Ethiopia. I don't think I would have liked growing up in Staunton."

Dad smiled and said he doubted we would have grown up in Staunton.

"I would have earned a lot more money if I had stayed working on Wall Street," he said, "but it just wasn't for me."

But without really realizing it at the time, I had initiated a ritual with Dad. If I saw that he didn't seem particularly busy at his desk and was just looking out the window, I would plop myself into the armchair in front of it and begin to ask questions.

A few weeks earlier we had visited the ancient city of Axum and looked at giant granite columns.

"They are believed to be the remains of what was a great Empire that stretched over much of East Africa and Western Arabia," Dad told me, and he explained that Ethiopians believe the Empire was ruled by the Queen of Sheba.

"The legend is that she visited Jerusalem and became pregnant with the child of King Solomon," he added, "and Emperor Haile Selassie is claimed to be one of the descendants of that union."

"Do you think it is true?" I asked.

Dad said that in Ethiopia, truth and myth are often indistinguishable, and what people believe matters more in the country than what is literally true.

"But do you think it's true?" I pressed on.

He responded that if those massive pillars in Axum, some taller than the tallest obelisks of Egypt, are not the remains of an Empire, then what are they, and how did they get there? And he said that the Christian Coptic Church in Ethiopia was very powerful and fully believed that Emperor Haile Selassie — King of Kings, Elect of God, Conquering Lion of the Tribe of Judah — was in fact Ethiopia's 225th Emperor in the dynasty of Solomon and Sheba. If you believed otherwise it was blasphemy.

We had learned what the Emperor's full title was in school but I had no clue what blasphemy meant and asked Dad.

"Blasphemy means showing great disrespect for something holy," he said with a little shake of his head.

I thought about how much Dad knew, and how he liked answering questions about historical or factual things, but that somehow I didn't frequently ask him questions about many of the things that I saw or was confused about, that somehow I just knew that I wasn't supposed to.

A few days before the Emperor's Christmas party Dad called us into his study.

"You two are old enough now that you will greet the Emperor formally. But you have to know something about it."

Tim and I both sat down and listened attentively.

"There is a time during each of the Emperor's working days that he hears the pleas of his subjects," Dad said. "He sits on his throne and they approach him, bent low, and after he has heard their request and made his decision they bend low again and shuffle backwards out of the room."

"Why do they do that?" Tim asked, a confused expression on his face.

Dad explained that no one is allowed to turn his or her back on the Emperor, so after you greet him just walk backwards till you get back to the group.

Tim and I spent the rest of the afternoon practicing our backwards walk, sometimes falling over and rolling on the floor laughing. But it was clear to us that on the actual day this would be no laughing matter. The night before the party, Mom put curlers in my hair. I glanced up at her. She was standing by the window, illuminated in the moonlight that cast a silvery glow over her.

"It will hurt to sleep on them," I said to her tentatively.

"It's just for one night" she answered softly," You'll look so pretty."

"Do you ever sleep with curlers in your hair?" I asked.

Mom nodded and somehow the fact that she bore this nuisance made it easier for me. I gazed at my mother, convinced that she was the most beautiful woman in the world. I asked her to tell me the story again of when we had come to Ethiopia.

"Well," she began, a soft smile playing around her mouth, "in the fall of 1957, when you were two, we took the leap into the unknown."

My mother told me that when my father had called her from the law office he worked for and asked if she wanted to move to Ethiopia, her response had been, "Hang on a second, Don, there is something burning on the stove," and she had run for the World Atlas not being certain precisely where Ethiopia was.

She said for her, one of the most painful parts of preparing to leave were all of the vaccinations we three kids had to be given — for smallpox, typhoid fever, yellow fever, and other diseases that had not been seen in the West for decades.

She told me that these were the days of propeller-driven DC-3's and the whole trip to Addis Ababa took well over two days. Her favorite part of the story was that she'd had twenty-two pieces of hand luggage with her. I couldn't imagine how she had managed that and three small kids.

"And when we first arrived I went into a state of shock," she said.

"How come?" I asked, although I already knew the answer.

"Because everything seemed so mysterious and unfamiliar to me — the language, the plants, the food, the fact that we couldn't just turn on the tap and drink the water." It seemed strange to me that all that had seemed mysterious to my mother. For me it just felt normal.

"But," she always concluded the story, "once we got our nice stone house, cozy living room, and patio, I was determined to make it a real home for our family."

That night I had trouble falling asleep. Having spent time with my grandparents in Virginia on three different trips to the States, I felt like I knew a little about Mom and how she'd grown up, since my grandparents' home was the one she'd lived in as a child. I'd visited my grandfather's grocery stores and peach and apple orchards and had sat at their table for what felt like hours as they read the Bible. There were portraits in huge frames of ancestors who had come from Scotland and Wales. I had met some of Mom's childhood friends and her two brothers and one sister and my two cousins. But I didn't really know Dad's father or stepmother and since I was wide awake I began to think about everything I knew about my father, a man I adored and sometimes a man I feared.

From the time that we were little, Dad loved to tell us stories of his upbringing. It was always hard for me to imagine either of my parents as children, but especially Dad. He had an album of pictures that I liked to look at, but even looking at pictures of him as a toddler, I always saw the adult gazing at me.

My father was born in West Warwick, Rhode Island, a tough little manufacturing town. My grandparents, Charles and Elizabeth Paradis, were immigrants from Quebec and Nova Scotia who had moved south in the early 1900's as part of the wave of rural people looking for a better life in the textile towns of New England. Pepe, the French Canadian nickname that everyone called Granddad, had very little formal education, but took correspondence courses, and went to night school to become a qualified power plant engineer.

Dad had said that his father was a fanatic about education and lectured him daily about the value of learning and knowledge. Dad told me once that they were never close, but that he would always be grateful for that lesson. And the lesson must have stuck with Dad. Every day when our family gathered for lunch he would quiz us on the capital city of every country he could think of, and we all competed to gain his nod of approval.

On rainy afternoons, my brother and I would pull out the big Atlas that Dad kept in his office and quiz each other on all the countries and capital cities we thought Dad might bring up next. We thought of different ways to memorize them, and then at lunch if one of us was asked and had forgotten, we'd kick each other under the table and mouth the hint.

For example, Dad would say, "Norway," and Tim would look blank and glance at me.

I'd kick him and mouth, "NO," and suddenly Tim would blurt out "Oslo," the "N.O." being the way Tim and I had worked out to remember that particular combination.

I was never quite sure if Dad caught on to what we were doing, but if he did he kept quiet.

My father's mother died in childbirth when Dad was in fourth grade, just a year younger than I was. My grandparents had been warned before Dad's younger brother was born that another pregnancy would kill her, but somehow that warning had slipped through the stoicism of a good Irish Catholic woman, for whom bearing children was simply a part of the deal. On the day that my grandmother left for the hospital she had kissed Dad on the forehead and said, "Goodbye Donald, I am never going to see you again."

At night, alone in my bed, I would often try to imagine what that had felt like and then try desperately to push away the wave of anxiety before it overwhelmed me with images of one of my parents kissing me on the forehead and saying goodbye forever.

My father once told us that his first words had not been "Mama" or "Papa" but "How do I get out of West Warwick, Rhode Island?"

I thought that seemed like a strange thing for a little kid to be thinking.

But there was one thing I was very sure of. Dad was interested in everything we were learning at school, and at night would have us bring our homework into his study and he would look at it and comment and encourage us to come to him if there was a problem we didn't understand, or if we wanted to explore a topic in greater detail.

"The best learning," he said, "is learning for its own sake — not for a grade which only measures your ability to memorize and spit back, but because there is a big world out there to know so much about."

The morning of the party, my brother and I sat on the front porch waiting to leave for the palace. Tim was wearing a dark suit and bow tie and I had on a cream-colored dress that had a matching sweater. I kept moving around trying to get comfortable even once we were in the car driving toward downtown Addis.

As we got closer I asked my father how long the Emperor had lived in Jubilee Palace.

"Well, the palace was built in 1955 to mark Haile Selassie's Silver Jubilee. He used to live in the Guenete Leul Palace," Dad said. And then he told us that after the coup attempt in 1960 the Emperor decided to make the Jubilee Palace his main residence, because he did not want to remain living where there had been so much bloodshed.

"How do you think Santa is going to arrive this year?" Tim leaned over and whispered.

I shook my head.

"Don't know," I said, still thinking about what Dad had just said. "It's always a surprise though."

I looked over at my mother who looked stunning in a lemon yellow satin suit.

"You look as pretty as Mrs. Kennedy," I said to her.

I had recently seen pictures of President Kennedy and his wife in the newspapers. Dad had brought them back from the state visit on which he had accompanied the Emperor to the United States and Mom and I had read them together, sitting on the sofa in the living room. The Emperor had visited Washington and then New York where he had ridden in an open vehicle down Wall Street. Dad told us that he had been walking behind the vehicle that the Emperor was riding in, the confetti pouring down on them, when all of a sudden he heard voices screaming "Paradis, Paradis, look up!" and looking up he had seen all the girls from the typing pool at Cahill Gordon, the law firm where he had worked before we moved to Ethiopia, leaning out the window and waving.

"That will be the only time your father thought he was a movie star," Mom told us, smiling.

But during one of my afternoon conversations with Dad after that trip to the States, he also told me that while they had visited New York the Emperor had been invited to cruise the Hudson on a private yacht.

"As we sailed past Manhattan," Dad told me, "I stood with the Emperor on the deck and he talked about the future and what he sought and wanted for his people and his nation. He said he wanted all the blessings and advantages of modernity but without the evils which are part of that society. And do you know what he added as we sailed past New York's dazzling skyline?" "No," I asked, "what did he say?"

Dad spoke softly, recalling the Emperor's words: "Alas, I shall not live long enough to see anything like this in Ethiopia in my lifetime."

"Do you like the Emperor?" I asked Dad.

"That's not an easy question," Dad answered." I admire him in many ways. He has suffered the loss of the empress, two sons, two daughters and two beloved grandsons. I think it has made him more withdrawn perhaps. I wish I'd known him when he was a younger man."

The large cream colored palace came into view with the three great pillared porticos on its front that rose to the height of the building. The palace sat behind an elaborate wrought iron gate topped on either side by large carved lions. Guarding the gate were members of the Emperor's Body Guard, wearing red trousers, green jackets with gold epaulettes, black boots that shone in the sunlight, and perched on their heads white pith helmets.

Our car slowed and pulled up to the gate. Dad rolled down the window and handed the guard the invitation. The guard glanced at it and gestured to a second guard and slowly the gates opened and we were directed into the driveway of the palace.

"We'll meet you back at the car when the party is over," Dad said to us.

For the next two hours, my brother and I played in the palatial gardens with their vast manicured lawns and visited the zoo that was kept on the grounds. We saw the lions and cheetahs that were the Emperor's favorite pets, who were led around on leashes by attendants in white suits. We ate pastries and cakes served on silver platters.

"Do you think we can just keep eating?" Tim asked, stuffing a huge piece of cake into his mouth.

I had brought a small white bag with me, and took a handful of cookies and hid them there, planning to share them with Mamo and Belaynesh when I got home.

Suddenly we heard a loud commotion at the front of the gardens, and I grabbed Tim by the hand and ran towards the squeals of delight as Santa Claus rode in on a camel with a loud "ho ho ho."

"I bet he's really sweating in that suit," Tim said.

Once off the camel, Santa started distributing gifts, a bow and arrow set wrapped in blue and white paper for the boys, and we girls received a set of knitting needles and different rolls of colored yarn.

"I'll trade with you," I said to Tim. "No way," he answered emphatically. "This is way too cool." He saw the look on my face and added, "But you can borrow it."

I kept wondering when we'd have to officially meet the Emperor, and began to worry that I might not curtsy correctly or back away properly.

"What will happen if I make a mistake?" I asked my brother. "Will a guard grab me and yell at me?"

At around four o'clock in the afternoon, we heard a bell and I turned around and saw children beginning to line up at the steps to the palace. Slowly, the group moved forward. At the front of the line, a formally dressed attendant asked your name, and then when it was announced you walked forward to meet the Emperor. When I got close enough, and could peer inside, I let out a slight gasp. The entrance hall was so big you could have fit our entire house in it. The ceiling was too high to even make out clearly.

The floor was marble and at some places covered with beautiful Persian carpets. I looked at a wall and a large gold framed picture of a peasant bent over a shovel. It seemed odd to see that particular scene in such an ornate frame.

The line moved forward at a snail's pace.

"What if I trip on my way out?" I whispered to Tim.

"Don't worry, you won't," he mouthed back.

I felt a little dizzy and tried to focus my attention on the paintings that were hung on the walls in front of me that must have been portraits of members of the royal family.

When we were almost at the attendant, I whispered to Tim, "You go first."

"No, ladies first," he responded. "And you're older."

"Okay," I said reluctantly. I shuffled ahead and the attendant asked for my name.

"Martha Paradis," I answered, my voice cracking a little.

I began to walk forward, my black patent leather shoes echoing off the marble floor. I kept my eyes down, but when I looked up saw a large throne, and seated on it the diminutive figure of the Emperor. Two little Papillon dogs lay on either side of the throne. I came to a stop, and the attendant said something quietly to the Emperor, and then gestured that I should approach the throne. I looked up into the darkest eyes I had ever seen and curtsied. He looked at me sternly, and I took in his bearded face, the aquiline nose over full lips. And then he smiled slightly and his face was transformed by such a sad and mysterious expression.

"Welcome."

The word was spoken softly. I glanced at the attendant who nodded, and as my brother and I had practiced for hours began to back away carefully. The last thing I wanted to do was topple over.

During the time that all the children were at the Christmas party, the adults were having cocktails in another part of the palace. On the drive home, Mom and Dad asked us about the party. Tim seemed pretty talkative, but I kept thinking about the Emperor's smile, about how sad it had seemed to me. I thought about what it must be like to live in a palace but not be able to do simple things by yourself, to just leave the palace and go for a walk or drive on your own. And how tough it must be to know that decisions you make will affect so many other people.

I wondered if, even as a kid, the Emperor had just been able to daydream, or think silly thoughts, or had he always had to be serious. And I wondered if my father was ever able to be just plain friendly and chat with the Emperor, or always had to be diplomatic and formal, bowing slightly and backing out when he left the room.

~ Chapter 6 ~

SOFIYA

I was sitting on the floor with my knees pulled up under me listening to the rustling of the trees outside my window when Mom opened the door to my bedroom and stuck her head in. I liked sitting in my room and listening to the noises in the yard, the buzzing of a wasp or tweeting of a beetle just outside or underneath my window. The noises during the daytime were so different than those at nighttime, when the hyenas were laughing as they roamed the neighborhood looking for food, or the drumbeat from the nearby village echoed faintly in the distance. Beheilu in the kitchen must have been chopping or peeling onions or garlic at that moment because the aroma drifted into my room.

I was in the middle of thinking about my upcoming eleventh birthday and making my mental list of invites when Mom walked softly across the floor and sat down on my bed.

"I am starting a new volunteer activity, Martha," she said, "and I thought you might want to come with me."

I got up off the floor and went and sat next to my mother on my bed. I leaned up against her and remember thinking later that her scent at that moment reminded me of the eucalyptus trees after a first rain, sweet, but not heavy. She had on a light lilac cotton sweater, and the fabric felt soft against my cheek as I rested my face up against her arm for a moment.

"Is it another place where you help women learn how to read?" I asked her. My mother spent many hours working for the charities that were dear to her.

"No, it is a place called the Cheshire Home and it is about an hour and a half outside of the city. I thought that if it works out we could maybe stop and have a picnic, but I think this first time we will just drive straight there," she answered. "I will pick you up from school. Tim can take the bus home."

"What are we going to do there?" I asked her.

"I'll explain more on the way," she said, and she quietly left my room.

I got off my bed and sat back down onto the floor to resume my listening. About five minutes later, my brother came into my room. He was wearing glasses these days and he walked over toward my window and looked out. The lenses of his glasses reflected what he saw out the window.

"What do you hear?" he asked.

"Bees, I think," I answered.

He turned around and looked at me, a long appraising look.

"Mom told me I'll be taking the bus home alone on Tuesdays," he said.

"Yes," I nodded, "I am going to start going to a place called the Cheshire Home with her."

"Maybe she is worried you are going to start munching on hay," Tim said. "I heard Mom and Dad talking and they said all you ever want to do these days is ride and spend time with the horses."

I grabbed a pillow from my bed and threw it at Tim who collapsed on my bed laughing. I grabbed Tim's ankles and pulled him off the bed and then sat on his chest with my full weight and dug both my knees into his armpits. He tried to fling his legs up to wrap around my shoulders, but I bent my torso forward so he couldn't reach me. We were both laughing so hard, and convinced he'd think twice before making fun of me again, I stood up and reached out and grasped Tim's outstretched hand and pulled him up.

School let out at the usual time on Tuesday but rather than heading toward the school bus I went to the back gate by the gym where Mom had told me to meet her. She wasn't there yet and I sat down on the bench to wait. About five minutes later I saw her little blue Volkswagen buggy coming down the road. I climbed into the front seat next to her, and when I turned to throw my knapsack into the back saw about six bags filled with pads of paper and boxes of crayons.

We set off down one of the main roads in Addis. The street was alive with market-goers, schoolchildren, beggars, parishioners, cars and vans, bicycles, cows, sheep and their attendants. As we rounded Arat Kilo, the large roundabout surrounded by small shops and coffee houses, the grey government buildings stood out in stark contrast to the sea of color amidst the crowded street. Every time the car came to a halt we were surrounded by children with outstretched hands, their faces covered in flies. I had asked Worku about the child beggars and he told me that sometimes they were assistants to the adult beggars.

"Some of them have a twisted arm or leg," I said.

"Yes," he nodded, "sometimes, when they are young, a parent or relative will break a bone so it will grow to be deformed and arouse greater sympathy."

"Can I have some change?" I said to Mom as we drew up to a stoplight.

She handed me some coins and as the car came to a stop, I rolled down the window and handed the money toward a sea of imploring faces. I quickly rolled the window back up, not to get away from the beggars, but from the dust in the air stirred up by the car. It occurred to me that during the dry season everything in Ethiopia seemed to be covered in dust. The roads were dusty, and the *tukuls* made of mud and straw always seemed to have a thin layer of dust that clung to them. When I would take one of the horses out for a gallop, as soon as the animal began to pull against the reins and paw at the ground, a cloud of dust enveloped me. The equatorial sun could be vicious and, as the earth baked under its glare, was responsible for much of the dust.

As the car pulled away I turned around and looked at the group of thin barefooted children in a haze of dust fighting over the few coins I had given them.

Mom told me that we were picking up a close friend of hers.

I felt disappointed for a moment. I wanted this to be something that just Mom and I did together. But I liked my mother's friend,

87

Mrs. Nolan, and knew that somehow the two of them would feel safer driving out of the city if they were together. Dad had said at one point, in responding to me, that "Colonel Nolan is part of the big American military and security involvement in Ethiopia," so now, that somehow made me feel less worried about a trip away from Addis Ababa.

So I said, "No problem."

My mother looked relieved. We stopped at a gated house and Mom's friend joined us in the car.

As we drove they chatted about the upcoming parties at the various embassies and a big costume party they were planning to throw together. With very few cultural activities available in the city, the big costume parties became major events for our group of about fifteen American and European families who celebrated holidays together and were good friends. Last year our entire home had been transformed into a French bistro with red and white checkered tablecloths on all the tables, and I helped Mom, Beheilu and Mamo cover all the walls of the living room and dining room in French newspaper. Dad dressed up as Quasimodo from *The Hunchback of Notre Dame* and most of the other adults dressed up as various French figures from movies and literature and the party had gone on well into the early hours of the morning.

I loved all the costume parties that we had. The grownups would put on skits and write songs. One of my favorite songs that Dad had written was called "Once You Have Drunk Of the Waters of Ethiopia." It was all about the pull of Ethiopia and how you always wanted to go back. And it ended with the line, "We will be seeing you again."

Now as we drove along I found myself humming that song as I half-listened to Mom and her friend talk about a Safari party they were planning. I glanced out the window as we crossed a river and saw a group of women doing their laundry, their skirts hiked up as they methodically pushed the garments up against the rocks. I slowly ate the sandwich Mom had brought along for me and looked out the window at Mount Entoto, a part of the Entoto mountain range and the highest peak overlooking the city of Addis Ababa. Mount Entoto is considered sacred and is home to many monasteries, and it is also where Emperor Menelik II, who ruled before Haile Selassie, lived and built his palace. I could see the peak of Mount Entoto from my bedroom window and at night would sometimes imagine what the monks in the monasteries were doing or what Menelik's palace had been like. The mountain is densely covered with eucalyptus trees that were imported from Australia during Menelik's reign, but most of the planting took place in the early years of Haile Selassie's rule. I guess because of all the trees, Entoto mountain is sometimes referred to as the "lung" of Addis Ababa.

Whenever we traveled outside the capital city I loved to roll down the window and look at the scenery and breathe in the sweet smelling air. Sometimes we'd have to really slow down when the road turned into an obstacle course as herders guided their cattle across from one field to another, women hurried along with jerry cans filled with water on their backs, and children stopped in the midst of a game of kick-the-can to turn and wave at us. We turned off the main road and drove along a road that was unpaved and ran so close to a ravine that I was afraid to look down. Off to my left was a cattle path that led down toward a stream. And then I saw a small sign: "Cheshire Home."

When we pulled into the driveway, I looked down the dirt road and saw a long, white one-story building. The car slowed to a crawl avoiding some potholes in the road. As we drew closer I saw a group of children by a tire swing, and as we drove past them one of the little girls turned and waved.

"Mom," I said startled, "that little girl doesn't have any hands."

"I know," Mom said. "This is an orphanage for children with physical handicaps. We are going to spend this afternoon doing arts and crafts with them."

She pulled the car into a parking space and when her friend opened the door Mom said, "Give me a moment with Martha."

Mom's friend got out of the car and walked over toward a woman wearing an apron and a nurse's cap who was hurrying toward us. Mom turned around in her seat. She began to speak, then stopped, cleared her throat and started to speak again.

"Most of these children suffer from poliomyelitis, sometimes called polio. It is a crippling disease that affects some of the muscles of the body and makes them totally useless."

I nodded because I didn't know what to say.

"And some of these children, like that little girl you saw, have lost hands or a foot because they stepped on a land mine."

She stopped speaking and then said quietly, "Or tried to pick one up."

I still hadn't said anything.

"Come on, let's get these bags inside."

I took a couple of the bags and followed Mom into what looked like a dining room with long tables set up in a row. Thirty pairs of eyes turned around and looked at me. I slowly walked over to one of the tables and put the bag with the crayons and paper on the table. I noticed that a lot of braces and crutches were lined up against the far wall. Suddenly I heard the screen door open and slam shut and the little girl, who looked like she was seven years old and whom I had seen by the swings, ran up to an empty chair at the table and sat down and looked at me with huge brown eyes.

"My name is Sofiya," she said.

Mom and her friend began unpacking the packages of crayons and colored pencils and put a piece of white drawing paper in front of each child and then began to divide up the coloring materials. I looked around and then sat down next to Sofiya because that was the only free seat.

"Can I have a brown crayon," she said looking up at me.

I reached for one of the boxes of twenty-four crayons and pulled out the brown one.

"Thank you," she said. "Please hold the paper for me."

I pressed down on two of the corners and watched her pick up the crayon with her little stumps and then, using her mouth to guide the crayon, she began to draw the outline of a *tukul*. I kept peeking out of the corner of my eye at the place where her hands should have been. I wanted to stare and I was afraid to look. I looked for a few seconds and quickly averted my gaze. The skin looked like it had been sewn together roughly and unevenly and there were little bumps along the scar line. I looked at her drawing again and saw that she was carefully coloring the roof a light brown, the exact shade of the roofs of the mud huts in Belaynesh's village.

"I need green now," Sofiya said, and again I found the colored crayon for her and watched her trace the outline of a tree.

"Yellow now, please," and a bright blazing sun began to appear above the *tukul*.

I watched her head bob back and forth as she drew the lines of the sun's rays, and then go round and round as she colored in the ball of the sun.

"You are a good artist," I said.

"Thank you," she answered.

"Where is that?" I asked her when the drawing was completed.

"That is where I come from," she said. "That is where my family is."

"Oh," I said, and before I could stop myself, "do they visit you?"

"They will," she said simply.

I heard loud scraping as chairs were pushed back from the tables and I watched as some of the children began to crawl on their hands and knees, pulling themselves along toward the back of the room where all the braces and crutches were lined up. Three or four staff members began helping them don the equipment, an ordeal that took a good fifteen minutes. I remained sitting next to Sofiya who was now busy coloring a scene with a mountain and river in it, interrupting her hard work with a, "Blue please," and, "Now I need green."

When all the children had been strapped into their equipment and were gathering in a circle, she put down the crayon she was using and ran over to join the others. A woman hurried into the middle of the circle with her guitar. I would later learn that her name was Mrs. Stein. She looked to be no more than five feet tall and wore her silver white hair in a tight bun on the top of her head. Mrs. Stein and her husband were the missionaries who had come from a Lutheran church in Minnesota for three years of service running the home.

"Okay," Mrs. Stein said, and as she began strumming, sixteen little voices sang out, "Jesus loves the little children, all the children of the world," a song I recognized from my own Sunday school classes I had attended when I was younger.

When we got home, Mom went into the house and I went down to the stables to feed the horses some carrots. When I got back up to the front of the house, I started to walk up the front stairs but then sat down on a step. I turned and looked up, and watched Dad pull the heavy metal shutter over the living room window halfway down to block out the setting sun. He stood for a minute with his hands on his hips, then checked his watch and reached into his pocket and pulled out a pack of cigarettes. He took one out, lit it, and I watched the smoke curl up towards the ceiling. He had that certain kind of handsomeness that would make aging easier for him than for other men. The only light coming out of the window was the muted reflection of the archway that led from the living room to the dining room.

Suddenly my mother appeared behind him and said some-thing, and I watched her lips move. In a rare gesture of tenderness, I watched my father take her hand and stroke it. I held my breath. I rarely saw my parents affectionate with each other in front of us. My father switched off the light and I watched the window turn a dark shade of charcoal. I stayed there for a while just breathing in the cool evening air thinking about my parents and how they had met and that I loved hearing my mother tell that story over and over and never got tired of the details.

My parents had met in San Francisco where my father was on shore leave while the minesweeper he'd commanded during the war when he was only 19 years old — and which had seen fierce fighting in the Pacific Ocean — was being recommissioned. My mother had come out to San Francisco on a train with her best friend when she graduated from teacher training college. It was the first time my mother had ever been more than a few hours drive from Staunton. I loved the fact that the journey from the sleepy home towns where Mom and Dad had grown up to now living in the remote and mysterious kingdom of Ethiopia was a story full of chance encounters. I had practically memorized the portion of the story about how they had actually met.

"We would never have become a couple were it not for some clever maneuvering on your dad's part," my mother would begin, a quiet smile playing on her lips. "We'd been set up on blind dates with a different young soldier and lady, and we were to go out dancing at one of the packed halls filled with returning soldiers and fresh faced young women. But on a cobblestone street as we walked downtown, your father skillfully crossed behind the group to position himself next to me at the moment that the street took a sharp angled turn. That way he traded the other young woman he was supposed to be with for me."

"Do you know what happened to the other soldier and young lady?" I always asked.

"I only know that they were dance partners that night," Mom said.

"Was Dad really handsome?" I'd press on.

"Yes, he certainly was, especially in that naval uniform."

"And then what happened?" I'd ask, even though I already knew the answer.

Mom always told me that she and Dad married in New York in front of a few friends at a church fondly known as "The Little Church Around the Corner" off Fifth Avenue. The church where they were married is the place where their ashes along with Nancy's are now interred. She would add that their courtship might have broken up over the still bitter divide between Southerners and Yankees, but Granddad and Grandmom in Staunton were impressed by Dad's courtly ways, and that part of Virginia was better known for its peaceful Mennonite communities than as a hotbed of Dixie senti-ment. My parents didn't travel to see Pepe and Dad's stepmother Elizabeth until after they were married.

"We barely had any money, so that's why I got married in a grey suit and your dad was in his naval uniform," Mom would explain.

Mom had a picture of the two of them on that day. My parents kept their personal pictures in a box with brass knobs on it. The sepia photos were wrapped in what looked like cheesecloth and I'd unwrap them carefully and hold them by the edges to avoid leaving fingerprints. Whenever I looked at that wedding photo of my father taken so soon after the war, I would find myself staring into the intense, frozen face of a stranger. So I would search for a trace of the smile I knew or the twinkle in his eyes.

My mother had some photos of her own family and her youth. In one photo when she was about six she is standing in front of a porch in short overalls, her eyes under straight Dutch Boy blond bangs, seemingly focused on some distant point. I always wished that there were some magical way that we could know what kids are thinking because I'd love to know what was on her mind. She had a sister and two brothers, all of whom I knew slightly from our trips back to her home town. There was a family photo of Mom as a teen that I would look at frequently and wonder what her relationships with her siblings had been like growing up. Had she felt as close to them as I felt to Tim and Nancy?

I knew that Dad then went off after they got married to pursue a law degree at Harvard made possible by something called the GI Bill. And that they lived in a place called Boston. He always said he'd made it through law school "by the sweat of his *Frau*."

I would often try to imagine what my parents had been like when they were dating and I wondered what would have happened if Dad had not crossed the cobblestone street so he could dance with Mom. It was so strange to me that that could have meant that I would never have been born, and if either of them had married someone else I wouldn't be Martha but might be living an entirely different life with different siblings and friends. It all seemed very confusing to me. Did God have some kind of grand plan or was it all just totally random? If I thought about it for too long my head would start to hurt and I would start to feel scared.

If Dad happened to come into the room while Mom was telling me the story he'd always hold up his hands and say, "Enough about how I lost my heart in San Francisco." And he'd wink at Mom.

A few days after our first visit to the Cheshire Home, I came into Dad's study where he was reading the newspaper, his head cocked to one side. He reached for the cigarette in the ashtray in front of him, brought it up to his lips and I watched him inhale deeply. He turned the page of the paper and it made a rustling sound. I looked at the stack of books piled on one side of his desk.

Dad devoured great literature, memorizing passages and poems and sometimes reciting them at the dinner table.

Some nights when my parents were out and I couldn't sleep I would sneak into Dad's study and run my hands over the worn covers of books emblazoned with names like Socrates and Shakespeare. I wrote down the names of these books and told myself that one day I would read all of them. I had started my own library in my room and reread my favorite books three and four times. Books opened a door to a vast universe beyond my tiny world. People disappear when they die: their voice, their thoughts, their joys, and sorrows. Soon their bodies rot, just like the animals who had died and who were left in our neighborhood. Soon they are only a memory to the people they left behind. But if they had written a book, we could discover them again, they could comfort us, their writing could make us laugh or cry. In some way they and the world they lived in could come alive again. I hoped that one day someone in my family would write a book.

I coughed quietly to get Dad's attention. He looked up.

"I played with a little girl who doesn't have any hands," I said.

His eyes widened the slightest amount. "And?" he said.

"I held down a piece of paper while she drew a picture with a crayon that she held between the two stumps and she used her mouth to guide it."

I stopped speaking for a few seconds and then continued, "But the most amazing thing is that she seems so happy."

Dad's gaze held me for a second. The smoke from the cigarette in front of him curled up toward the ceiling. He watched it for a second and then resumed speaking,

"Maybe you cannot miss something that you have never had."

He looked back down at his paper, his cue that the conversation was over.

But as I turned to walk out of the room he said, "Mom tells me that you did well."

I felt a flush of pride surge through me. Mom rarely gave compliments. I don't think it was for lack of pride in us, but it was just not her way to be emotionally effusive. Sometimes I wondered about that though.

Once I had overheard Dad say to her, "I don't believe in complimenting children a lot. It can make them conceited. Set the bar really high."

I kept thinking about Sofiya and sleep did not come easily that night. The thought that she had been out playing in a field and picked up a land mine that had exploded and blown off her hands felt unimaginable. I got up and quietly went down to the kitchen to get a glass of water. I wished that we could drink straight out of a tap and that we didn't have to boil our water. The one time a year ago that I had decided to just take a gulp straight from the tap though, I wound up with amoebic dysentery. And I didn't want to repeat that. I lay in bed writhing and shivering, curled up in a fetal position, with high fever and abdominal cramps. For a day Mom and Belaynesh took turns sitting by my bed wiping my forehead with a cool washcloth. There were moments when I seemed to be in some kind of dream or hallucination, floating on a white cloud peering down on the scene in the bedroom with the sound of my heartbeat bellowing in my ears.

After two days Dad had taken me down to the main hospital where a friend, a Danish physician, had prescribed some kind of medication and slowly over the next week I felt better. When I finally got out of bed, I weighed about seven pounds less than I had before and my skin had lost its tan and my eyes seemed vacant the first time I looked in a mirror. I tried to brush my hair which was all matted from sweat. But I would never again drink water that had not been boiled, no matter how thirsty I was.

Dad had said, "Experience is the best teacher."

On my way back to my room I heard the murmur of voices coming from Mom and Dad's room. I pressed my ear up against the door and listened intently. I heard "Martha ..." and realized that they were talking about me. I lowered my eyelids as though they could catch me eavesdropping through the wooden door and pressed my ear even closer, holding my breath.

My mother's voice was too low for me to make out what she was saying but I heard Dad say, "No, I don't think she is too young. We can't protect the kids from life."

I didn't hear my mother's response but I already knew that whatever it was she would comply with Dad's decision. I tiptoed away and got back into bed.

From the living room I could hear the low tones of Dad's favorite jazz records. I had so many questions about Sofiya. How had she gotten to the Cheshire Home? Did someone in her family bring her? How did she feel the first day she spent away from her village?

I suddenly thought about a time Tim and I had been out on our bikes with Sileshi and we had seen a small half-eaten carcass with hawks pecking at the body.

"What do you think that was?" I asked Sileshi as we rode by.

"I know what that was," he answered, and told us that in one of the villages not too far away the people were very poor. He said that they could barely feed themselves and had no food for animals so when a dog had puppies they took the females and left them out for the hyenas because if they kept them, there would just be more and more starving dogs.

My stomach lurched and I felt like I was going to fall off my bike. I just couldn't imagine a hyena eating a poor innocent puppy.

Two weeks later when Tim and I were playing down by the stables, we heard a whimpering by the back gate. When we got there we found four female puppies who looked like they had just been born. I asked Sileshi if he knew how they had gotten there and he had shaken his head "no" although he avoided eye contact with me. Without telling anyone we took them in and made a home for them in one of the empty back rooms and for a few weeks fed them milk from baby bottles. But the day came when they began to whine and bark and I knew we were going to have to tell Mom and Dad.

"What should we do?" we asked Dad, "We can't put them back outside."

Dad told us he had an idea. And that weekend, when my parents were hosting a Caveman costume party, when it came time for the prizes Dad instructed me to go get the puppies. I then watched as the person with the best costume was awarded a puppy, the person with the worst received one, as did the winner of the most original costume, and the lucky winner who didn't wear a costume at all.

Just like that, the puppies were gone. The randomness of life seemed really confusing to me. Would the puppies be happy in their new homes? And would I ever see them again?

The weeks went by and I found that I was looking forward to Tuesday afternoons. I liked being picked up by Mom and the trip out to the Cheshire Home was a change from every other afternoon that I would spend on horseback. As soon as the car turned off the road I'd start to look for Sofiya. Sometimes she'd be waiting by the swings and as soon as she saw the car she started running toward the main house, and as I got out of the car she flung her arms around my waist and then put her stump into my hand and led me to the main building. The first time I held the little stump I felt a shudder run through me and a sudden rush of vertigo, but each time it got easier. Sofiya always wore one of two dresses, a green dress with a white stripe on the hem or a navy blue dress with a little duck on the breast pocket which looked like it had been sewn on crookedly.

"Can you hold down the paper, please," she said, and I would dutifully do as she asked.

But I soon began to notice that no matter what picture she drew the second or third time, her first drawing was always the same. It was always a *tukul*, and a tree under a bright yellow sun. And this routine continued every Tuesday. At times I would find my mind wandering. Once while holding down the paper and waiting for the requested crayon I suddenly thought about the two little ostriches Tim and I had been given as pets a year ago. We named them Salt and Pepper and we liked watching them run around the yard. One afternoon we had seen Pepper under the tree house, but no Salt. This was unusual because they always stuck together, pecking at each other and fighting over the grain that was put out for them. Tim and I started looking for Salt and finally found him under a bush, dead as could be. We pulled his rigid little body out and noticed something purple around his beak. With a little stick we wiped some of the material onto the ground and when I picked it up I looked at my brother.

"Oh no, a purple crayon. We must have left one out after our art show," he said.

My brother and I liked to put on art shows on the front porch, displaying our drawings and insisting that everyone in the household come and look at them and judge which deserved first prize. I might have been the better athlete, but for sure Tim was the better artist and invariably the first place ribbon was placed next to his drawing. We took Salt's little body down to that pet cemetery at the side of the stable. Tim wondered if maybe we should cut him open to be sure he had died from eating a purple crayon, but I glared at him.

"No way," I said.

For the next couple of weeks after burying Salt, we watched Pepper become more and more listless. He no longer ran around the yard and seemed to have lost all interest in food.

"He looks so lonely," Tim said to me after we spent an afternoon observing him.

"Of course he is," I said. "He has lost his best friend."

After mulling over the various options we could think of as to how to remedy the situation, Tim and I emptied the can that we kept our meager savings in, the few dollars from birthday presents that we had saved. We gave it all to Worku and begged him to buy us a chicken the next time he was at the Mercato. A few days later, when we went down to the stable after school we heard a clucking and saw Pepper and his new playmate, an emaciated looking chicken, fighting over the grain on the ground. We named the chicken Cinnamon and he did seem to cheer up Pepper.

About six weeks after I had started going to the Cheshire Home and coloring with Sofiya, as I held down the piece of white paper it seemed like the drawing was taking her longer than usual, and when I looked down I saw that she had drawn a stick figure at the entrance to the *tukul*.

"Who is that?" I asked her, a little startled.

"Oh, that is my mother," she said simply.

I asked Mrs. Stein later when we were having a snack if she thought Sofiya remembered her parents.

"I don't know how she could," she told me. "She was brought here when she was not yet three years old."

For a few weeks the mother stick figure appeared each time she drew the picture, and then one day a second stick figure appeared, this one taller and broader.

"My father," she said to me, not looking up, before I had a chance to ask.

And the routine continued — every week she studiously made the same drawing. I had grown accustomed to the sight of her small stumps and the way she would chap them together when something funny occurred or during the part of the afternoon when the children sang, and I realized that love has nothing to do with who or what you are looking at; it has to do with what you see. I no longer saw Sofiya's little stumps, but only her radiant smile.

That summer, as we had for as long as I could remember during what was the big rainy season in Ethiopia, we went to Kenya, to a resort in Mombasa, a town situated on the east coast right on the Indian Ocean. We spent six weeks at an old fashioned resort called Nyali Beach with Mom, and Dad flew down for the weekends. I had such wonderful memories of miles and miles of white sand, of climbing coconut trees with Tim, and, when Dad was there, of all five of us building elaborate sandcastles. And during the summers Nancy was back from boarding school and everything seemed more exciting when she was around. I told Sofiya that I was going to be away, but that I would write to her and asked Mrs. Stein to give Sofiya my address if she wanted to write back. Three times during those six weeks, I received an envelope from the Cheshire Home and inside was a drawing from Sofiya — a tukul and tree under a bright yellow sun and two stick figures.

When school resumed so did the visits to the Cheshire Home. In the fall, I arrived on Tuesday afternoon and expected to see Sofiya by the swing set or already sitting at her seat at the table waiting for me to hold down the paper. But I didn't see her at the swing set and waited about five minutes at the table before I heard the screen door open and Sofiya come through it. She didn't speak or answer my cheerful, "Hi Sofiya."

She sat down and began the same ritual of drawing the *tukul*, tree, bright sun, and two stick figures. I felt myself relax when she looked down at the paper but then she said, "Black please," startling me because she had never chosen any colors other than the brown, green and yellow.

"Please hold the paper down hard," she said, and I did and watched her vigorously move the crayon back and forth over the paper until the two stick figures disappeared under a black formless shape on the paper.

"I do not want to color today," she said.

Pushing her chair away from the table, she stood up and walked away from me and I heard the screen door slam shut. I didn't know whether I should follow her or remain sitting where I was. Mrs. Stein, who had been at the back of the room, came over and sat down across from me.

"What is the matter with Sofiya?" I asked.

Mrs. Stein reached out and put her hand gently on my knee.

"Once every three months, parents come to visit," she said. "Most of the children who are orphaned have accepted that their parents won't be coming and spend the day playing in a different part of the building. But Sofiya is adamant they are coming and insists she stay with the group whose parents will be visiting and she waits and waits."

She stopped speaking.

"Oh," I said, because I couldn't think of anything else to say.

"She will be okay in a few days," Mrs. Stein said.

When it was time to go I wanted to find Sofiya and say goodbye and tell her that I would see her next week but Mom was in a hurry. As the car moved slowly down the driveway I glanced out the window hoping to see her and as we passed the sandbox I saw her sitting on the edge. She looked up at me and then looked away and a lump began to form in my throat as I felt the deep sadness of a little girl who drew her parents every Tuesday and yearned for these people she did not even remember, a little girl who so wanted to belong to someone, who lived part of her life in a world that did not exist but had such a hold on her.

I kept going to the Cheshire Home for the next few years, watching Sofiya grow, but something in her seemed to have changed with the realization that her parents were not going to be coming to get her. I was realizing more and more that she was going to miss spending all of those moments in childhood with the parents that become a lasting part of who you are.

I felt close to my mother on those trips to the Cheshire Home, and in looking back I realize that she was showing me a life of quiet service.

Family portrait a month before we left for Ethiopia.

My father (on right) with Navy buddies. Pearl Harbor in background.

My parents on their wedding day in New York City.

My mother with me on my first day of kindergarten.

Our home in Addis Ababa.

Belaynesh with Nancy, Tim and me.

Beheilu on our back porch.

Portrait of Mamo.

Assefa by the swing set in our backyard.

Sileshi's school picture around the time
we met him.

Emperor Haile Selassie.

National Palace, also called Jubilee Palace, in Addis Ababa.

My parents at a diplomatic reception at the palace (my
mother far left, my father far right.

My father with Princess Beatrix and Prince Claus at the palace.

Tim and me dressed for the Emperor's Christmas party.

Sofiya at the Cheshire Home.

Nancy, Tim and me in Mombassa, Kenya.

Axum obelisk in northern Ethiopia.

Oromo warrior with decorative shield.

Women in traditional woven shamas.

Priests celebrating traditional festival of Timkat.

~ Chapter 7 ~

EXPLORING

My brother and I owned bikes — we had gotten them for Christmas one year — but so far we had only ridden them up and down the long yard on the side of our house and raced around the circular flower bed in front of our home. Our driveway was not paved but covered in a very fine gravel. Often Assefa, who would be weeding the flower bed, watched us create the greatest dust storm we possibly could, turning the handle bars sharply to the left and then the right so the back wheel skidded and dirt flew up into the air. He would shake his head in amusement or irritation and use this time to take his break and get out of the hot sun for a little while.

A few days after Sileshi had met Dad, a Saturday, while we were at breakfast, Tim and I asked our father if we could take our bikes out onto the road in front of our house.

"Will Sileshi be with you?" he asked us, his forehead wrinkled as he looked up from the newspaper. Beside him the radio played one of his favorite jazz pieces.

"Yes," Tim answered and cleared his throat as I stood there stunned that Dad's answer had not been a firm "No."

"Okay then," Dad said returning his gaze to the paper. "Let him use Nancy's bike."

He turned a page of the newspaper and before he had a chance to change his mind my brother and I raced out of the room.

"Where should we go?" we asked Sileshi as we pushed the bikes out of the front gate.

Before he could answer I said, "I know, I want to see where you live."

Sileshi looked at me for a long moment as though considering the request and then said, "Come, follow me."

I couldn't really believe that we had just left the compound on our own and I was excited and a little nervous at the same time. For years Tim and I had sat in the tree house and imagined what it would be like to be out on our own exploring the world beyond the stone wall and metal gate that was the boundary line to our home.

There was a dirt path off to the left that led to the small collection of mud huts that constituted the village about half a mile away. We rode our bikes for part of the way as the path snaked its way up a hillside covered in thick brush and the route became progressively overgrown. But before long we had to get off our bikes and walk in a single file along a path only about two feet wide. The ground fell away steeply as we emerged into a clearing where there were about ten *tukuls* made of dried mud and straw with a thatched roof on top. This was the village where Belaynesh lived, and as we pushed our bikes along, a group of small kids ran out of their homes to stare at us, and a few mangy looking dogs tied to a tree started barking.

I had been inside a *tukul* a number of times. They were always single room structures where entire families lived, ate, and slept crowded in next to each other. They did not have indoor plumbing, electricity, or running water. I suddenly remembered reading that Abebe Bikila, a great hero in Ethiopia who had won the Marathon race at the Rome Olympics, had begun running as a shepherd boy in the hills around Addis. A few hours before the race, he had decided to run barefoot the way he always did in Ethiopia.

I looked at the kids staring at us, all of them barefoot. Like these kids, Abebe had grown up living in a *tukul*. I was suddenly very aware of the four pairs of shoes that I had lined up in my closet at home. And these kids were so thin. Not thin in a slender and athletic way, but in a malnourished way. It looked like their bones could easily snap. And the clothes they were wearing were all tan in color, but then I realized it was because they were caked in dirt and dust. As we passed one little boy I saw that it looked like some of the skin on his hands and one side of his face had lost its coloring and some of the skin was raised or thickened. I guessed that he was about seven or eight years old and he stood by himself away from all the other kids who were grouped together. As he saw me looking at him he brought his hand up to the side of his face and covered his cheek and eye. I smiled, but he did not smile back.

We continued to push our bikes single file through the smattering of *tukuls* and then, as we crested a hill, we saw a small group of rectangular buildings. They were covered in mud but each had a corrugated tin roof on top. Sileshi led us to one of the structures and when we got to the door said, "Wait here."

He went inside and we could hear his muffled voice and that of a woman. While we were waiting I thought about our home. Compared to Sileshi's house it felt like a palace, although it actually was not nearly as big as my grandparents' home in Virginia, and not grand in the way I remembered the American ambassador's residence where we had stayed during the coup. In fact, our house was rather simple, with small bedrooms off a long hallway. The living room was by far the biggest room and nicely decorated. But what I loved the most was a veranda that looked out over the fields behind the compound. At the end of the rainy season the fields looked like a blanket of yellow daisies had been thrown over them, evidence, I felt sure, that this land was loved by God.

I heard a noise and a moment later Sileshi poked his head out and told us we could come in, that his mother had just finished cooking. We stepped into the room and I looked around. Newspaper on the walls served as some kind of wallpaper, and the floor was made of a mud that seemed to have been pounded so hard it felt like concrete under my shoes. There was a hallway off to my left that must have been where his mother slept because a single bed was pushed up against one of the walls. But what caught my attention was the aroma coming from a pot on a small stove with one burner. Sileshi brought out a basin of water and soap for us to wash our hands with, and his mother gestured that we should sit down on the ground around a *mesob*, a tabletop that is woven from straw and has a lid on it.

Eating *injera* and *wot* was something that I had been doing for as long as I could remember. You ate the whole meal with your hands, ripping off a piece of *injera*, that was like a spongy grey pancake, and dipping it into a fiery stew that usually had chicken or meat, and vegetables, in it. Tim was able to eat the spiciest hot peppers that seemed to make steam come out of his ears. He turned bright red and beads of sweat formed on his forehead.

He would usually say, after swallowing and looking very alarmed, eyebrows raised, "Oh man, what did I do that for?"

But after a few minutes when things had calmed down, he'd say, "Yum, can I have another one?"

I tried to avoid them at all costs.

We were finishing up the meal when Sileshi stripped off a piece of *injera*, rolled it in the *wot*, but instead of popping it into his own mouth he brought it up to my brother's mouth and said, "Here, a *goorsha*, a blessing." And he bowed his head. Tim and I both looked confused but Tim took the offering and then Sileshi repeated the same ritual with me.

"I am giving you a *goorsha*, a blessing" he said.

He told us that a *goorsha* is an act of friendship and the bigger the *goorsha* the stronger the friendship.

I kept glancing out of the tiny window where the interplay of the light and leaves of the eucalyptus trees cast dancing shadows on the opposite wall. I liked the fact that Sileshi saw eucalyptus trees from his small window the way Tim and I did from ours. I thought that maybe our trees were friends too and spoke to each other at night through the howling wind.

His mother ate her meal in a calm, almost meditative way. She told us that she hoped one day Sileshi would go to university, that he would be the first member of their family to do so.

"That's where I want to go too," I said. "Maybe we will be there together. Tim too."

We heard a noise at the door and an old man appeared in the doorway. His light brown skin was crisscrossed by crevices deeper than age could make and he was leaning on a wooden cane. His gait was so feeble that it looked like a puff of wind could knock him over. The *shama* he was wearing may have once been brilliant white, but now was faded and yellowed. Sileshi stood up quickly and his mother rose as well. They both went over to him and kissed him on the cheeks. Sileshi took both his hands in his own and bowed his head and gently helped him over to the bed against the wall. Tim and I had both gotten up and as he passed us I looked into his eyes and couldn't tell if it was the memory of recent pain that put such sadness there. When Sileshi came back he told us that the man was his mother's uncle.

"He is 78 years old," he said. "In Ethiopia that is very, very old. Very few people live that long."

Ethiopian families, I would learn over the years, are very close-knit, with children showing great respect for their elders. When an older person came into a room, everyone younger would stand up and greet them with two kisses on each cheek. Often extended families — including grandparents, aunts and uncles — live under the same roof, and it is a strong tradition that children look after their elders as they age. I was sure my brother, sister and I would look after Mom and Dad when they were old, but I didn't like to think about it.

We ended the meal with a little coffee and then the three of us, after Tim and I had thanked Sileshi's mother over and over, took our bikes and headed down the path back home. Again as we passed through the small clearing with the group of *tukuls*, the kids stopped playing kick the can, although they were using a rock, and just stood silently watching our little procession go by. A few of them sat huddled together and stared at us apprehensively. I saw Tim staring back at them with his blue impenetrable eyes. We pedaled back to our home and Assefa opened the gate and let us in.

"Sileshi," I said, as we were putting the bikes back into the shed, "I noticed that one of those kids had white skin going up his hand and the skin on his cheek looked very thick. What is that?" I closed my eyes and pictured the disfigured skin.

"Leprosy," Sileshi answered. "He will not live in the village much longer."

"Where will he go?" I asked.

"He cannot stay in the village," Sileshi answered, "because he could spread his disease, so he will be sent away to live with other people who also suffer from leprosy."

"Where do they live?" Tim asked.

"I do not know," Sileshi said, as he bit his lip and gave us a wary sideways look. His voice seemed to have grown hoarse and he said, "But they never come back."

It was hard to fall asleep that night. I kept going over the day in my mind, and what it had felt like to be away from the compound. My ability to make sense of the world with some predictability was lost whenever we ventured outside the compound gates. There was an unfathomable strangeness to the conditions of life that so many Ethiopians faced. Even the eucalyptus trees seemed to smell somehow different, and the sky itself took on a surreal dimension at moments.

When I asked Beheilu about the little boy with the disease on his skin, he said, "Sileshi is right. He must be sent away."

I looked away because the thought of it made me so sad.

"But what is remarkable, Martha, is that in the Bible it is a leper who approached Jesus and said, 'Lord, if you are willing, you can make me clean.' Jesus reached out and touched the man and said, 'I am willing. Be clean.'"

I looked up at Beheilu and he added, "Perhaps the little boy will have a miracle too."

And so our explorations outside of the compound continued.

My brother and I always seemed to be a source of curiosity for the kids that we passed, and I often felt nervous remembering what it had been like to have the pebbles thrown at us and how hard Tim and I had fought the bullies the afternoon we'd first met Sileshi. I wondered what might have happened to us if he had not come to our aid, but with Sileshi with us no one bothered us. As we passed a group of boys leaning up against a fence, Sileshi yelled something very rapidly in Amharic to them. Tim and I both spoke Amharic relatively well, but whatever Sileshi yelled to the group of kids included a lot of what must have been slang that I didn't understand.

Once we had passed them, I asked Sileshi what he had said to them and he answered, "I told them that if they bother you I will come down here with your father's gun."

"I don't think he would give it to you," Tim said seriously. "I really don't."

"Yes, I know that, and you know that," Sileshi answered. "But they don't."

And he turned around and grinned at us.

We continued pedaling, but it was tough going because the road was not paved and we had to navigate our way around rocks and holes. Then the dirt road petered out, and we moved onto a very small trail in single file, and after about five minutes we passed another small village, if you could even call it that. There were about six huts, but unlike the *tukuls* that were enclosed and had a certain solidity to their structure — even though they were made of mud and hay and dirt — these huts were just sticks pounded into the ground that extended upwards for about five or six feet, and then on top was a very thin layer of some kind of tin that served as a roof. As we rode past, the people just looked at us, and when I glanced inside one of the structures I saw a cow and a couple of sheep.

Sileshi saw me looking at the huts and said, "They are so poor that the only heat is from the animals." I shivered as though a cold blast of air had just hit me. I saw a man outside one of the huts who had stacked some twigs and branches for a fire. The wood spat out sparks as he waved what looked like a fan, driving the flames from red to orange to yellow. He was gazing at his handiwork as though he could see the struggle and pain of his life in the fire.

"They cannot take the fire inside," Sileshi said as though reading my mind, "because the straw inside could easily catch fire."

When we came to the end of the village, a man was sitting alone leaning up against a tree. As we rode past I saw that his legs were swollen to about five times their normal size, and his pants were cut wide open. He had a can out in front of him and I wished I had something in my pockets that I could give him. I didn't want to stare, but couldn't help it.

When we had gotten about fifty yards away Tim asked Sileshi what was the matter with the man.

"He has the elephant disease," was Sileshi's answer.

That night, as my brother and I would often do, we pulled the *Encyclopedia Britannica* off the shelf in Dad's study and looked up "elephant disease" under "E." I was fascinated by the encyclopedia. It was just so amazing to me how much information was packed into each volume. If my brother and I were bored we'd often pull one of the heavy bound books off the shelf and flick through the pages at random and when one of us said "Stop" we'd read the information on that page.

I told Tim, who was leaning over my shoulder, that I saw something that might be what we're looking for. "Elephantiasis is a disease that involves the enlargement of the arms, legs, and genitals to elephantoid size," I read slowly.

"How do you get it?" Tim asked.

I read quietly for about a minute and then said, "I think from some kind of worm. There are some words here I don't understand," I continued, shutting the book.

"Should we ask Mom and Dad about it?" Tim asked.

"No," I said, "they might not want us out riding with Sileshi if we begin to ask questions about what we see."

I thought about the man with the elephant disease and the little boy with the disease called leprosy a lot over the next few days. I thought about how embarrassing that must be, and how painful to have others shun you because of it. It was hardly the first time that we had seen beggars or disfigured people. Wherever we drove with our parents, whenever the car came to a stop, there were immediately beggars at the window with their hands outstretched, and their faces covered with flies. But there was something very upsetting about being out on our bicycles in the fresh air and riding so closely to someone who was suffering.

A few days earlier on the way to school I had been looking out of the window, watching a man stumble forward with a wagon pulled by an emaciated mule. The man held a whip he used to clip the mule on its hindquarters. Slowly the mule had taken a few steps forward, each step cajoled by more beating, the mule struggling all the while against the weight of the wagon. I couldn't watch and had turned my face away but was suddenly flooded with pictures of pain and suffering, the many times I had witnessed people or animals desperate with disease and hunger. It felt like I had no refuge from it no matter how far I turned my face away. Later that night Tim and I talked about how helpless we felt and that we had to do something. Together we went through our toys and books and games and the next day with Sileshi went back to the group of *tukuls*. When we got there the village seemed pretty deserted.

"It is market day," Sileshi said.

"Can we just leave the things?" I asked.

"I don't see why not," Sileshi answered, so we put the big plastic bag at the entrance to the little village. Two days later Tim and I rode our bikes over to Sileshi's home, hoping that his mother would have some *Kolo*, a roasted barley snack that had become a favorite of ours. As we passed the small village, we saw that the box and board of the board game we had included was now being used to cover up some holes on the side of one of the *tukuls*.

We continued to venture farther and farther from our home, sometimes staying away for four or five hours. One Saturday morning Sileshi told us that he had a special treat in store for us, but that it would mean we would have to cycle quite a distance. On our outings Sileshi would point out details that I hadn't noticed. He would direct our eyes towards unusual flowers or vegetation. He would tell us to listen to the songs of children on their way to school or the muffled conversations of a group of men sitting by a fire.

"I think it will be okay," I said, a quiver of excitement quickening my breathing as I thought about everything we might see.

"Let's go," Tim said, already halfway out of the gate. We rode for about thirty-five minutes until we came to the outskirts of what looked like an open air market.

"This is the Mercato," Sileshi said. We made our way in and suddenly it felt like we were in a sprawling small city. Everywhere we looked merchants were seated on three-legged stools or burlap mats in front of their wares. Children were carrying piles of fruits and vegetables in huge baskets on their heads, each basket looking like a natural extension of the bearer as if a second head had appeared. They set the basket down on the ground and then ran back to get a second load. Men staggered forward with huge burlap sacks filled with grain on their backs. And women balanced fragile pots on their heads, looking straight ahead with each step. It seemed like you could buy anything at the Mercato, from crafts to pottery to food to electronics.

The giant market was a noisy place, but a refrain that I kept hearing above the din was a sing-songy "*Coolie, coolie, coolie, ande birr e semuni.*"

"What are they yelling?" I asked Sileshi.

"They are hoping someone will hire them to carry any heavy items they have bought and they will charge them one dollar and twenty-five cents."

"That seems like a lot of money," Tim said.

"They will not be paid that much because they will bargain until they decide on a price, but they start with those words, because it rhymes."

"It is so busy here," I murmured, the tumult of voices, sounds and smells making me a little dizzy.

"In every part of Ethiopia there are markets like this where people come to trade and meet," Sileshi said. "Probably it would take us two hours to walk through the whole market."

"Let's go," Tim said.

We explored the Mercato with the meticulous care of three reporters or detectives, allowing ourselves to be swept along by the stream of people moving from stall to stall. The fragrances of *berbere*, cinnamon, and other spices permeated the air and Sileshi had us inhale the scent of a particularly pungent *berbere*. Tim started sneezing and my eyes burned and watered. Sileshi couldn't stop laughing behind us. Most of the merchants were very friendly and were happy to answer our questions and show us their wares, but once in a while someone looked at us in a way that caused my heart to race and I just wanted to be back home in the compound.

I knew that Mom came to the Mercato to do some of her shopping. Since Granddaddy Reid owned a chain of grocery stores back in Staunton, I wondered if that was where she had learned to find the best bargains and pick out the freshest produce. Mom had carved out a small space for herself in a corner of the kitchen that held a small desk and bookcase filled with cookbooks. I'd often find her there poring over the books and copying down recipes. Sometimes it just amazed me how she could run our home and organize the many cocktail and dinner parties that my parents hosted. She taught Beheilu how to cook and I loved hearing them discuss menus and ingredients. When Nancy was home she'd join in the conversations and she was already becoming a good cook herself. Not me though. I wanted to be outside in the trees or by the river or roaming the countryside on horseback.

We rode home without talking, the silence broken only by the sound of the bikes' wheels when we accelerated. I thought about everything I had seen in the Mercato and about the people who were so poor that they had to sleep with their livestock. I was sure they did not have a reason or the money to ever go to the Mercato. That night I dreamed that the Mercato was filled with pitiful beggars in rags, skinny and haggard with their huge bellies sticking out. They were standing in front of the stalls filled with fruits and vegetables, rail thin. But the stalls had a barbed wire fence around them and all they could do was look. The morning after the dream, at breakfast, I felt guilty that I did not finish everything on my plate. With each mouthful that I took I could "see" the beggars' pleading eyes watching me. More and more it seemed that when I slept I dreamed about what we had seen, and when I was awake our explorations formed the constant backdrop of my thoughts.

Soon afterwards I began sneaking extra cans of beans or soup out of the pantry next to our kitchen at night, and when I had managed to get ten or so, Tim, Sileshi and I rode to the tin village, as we had begun calling it, and left the box on the ground. We never spoke to anyone in that village. But I think I had somehow decided that I simply would not turn my gaze away from suffering, and I wondered if my life would be harder because of that.

On one of our bike rides to the village we saw a big white tent pitched alongside a house. I watched Sileshi closely as we rode by. He stopped talking and seemed to bow his head.

"What's the tent for?" Tim asked.

"There is a funeral there," he said solemnly. "The burial must take place within one day," he continued, "and if you are wealthy you will have a large tombstone by your grave."

I thought about asking what happened to your body if you were poor but decided maybe I didn't want to know.

In January, Sileshi told us to ask our parents if we could go with him to one of the *Timkat* festivals. At first Mom was reluctant, but Dad seemed to like our adventuresome spirit and seemed to have great faith in Sileshi's ability to look out for us. We waited until very early afternoon and left our compound while it was still chilly, for there was a thin layer of clouds overhead. On our ride to the Trinity Church Sileshi told us that *Timkat* was the most important religious festival of the Ethiopian year.

"It is the Ethiopian Orthodox celebration of the Epiphany — you know, the baptism of Jesus," he said, as Tim and I pedaled on either side of him.

On the approach to the Trinity Church we saw crowds of people, all dressed in white *shamas*, the traditional fine, hand-woven shawl embroidered around the hem with deep saturated solid colors: magenta, purple, bright green, vivid red and sun-kissed yellow. The patterns were simple geometric shapes: diamonds, rectangles and squares. I often saw women sitting together embroidering the *shamas* and always wondered if they were telling each other of their hopes and dreams as they worked together.

As we drew closer I saw one group of women whose *shamas* had no doubt once been white, but now, as the sunlight swept over the sea of people I could see that the cloth was threadbare and the colors of the borders faded. We pulled over and waited with the crowd, and within minutes a group of priests dressed in jewel encrusted velvet and satin robes emerged from the front of the church. They were immediately followed by more priests or monks who, with their bare hands, were playing a steady beat on a double headed cylindrical drum.

Many of the priests carried decorative colorful umbrellas, and as they moved forward, I saw that the two priests in the front were holding something that was rectangular in shape and about the size of an atlas. Covered with an ornamental cloth, it was lifted high above the priests' heads.

"What is that?" I whispered to Sileshi.

"It is a replica of the tablet of the Ark of the Covenant," he whispered back.

As the priests moved forward they began a rollicking, swaying movement back and forth to the beat of the drums, and I was struck by the plaintive sounds of harps and reed flutes that were coming from somewhere to my right. People all around us began ululating and soon joined the swaying movement. I glanced at Sileshi who seemed to have a glazed look on his face as though he had been transported somewhere, and while many questions swam around my mind about what was happening, something told me to keep silent. I watched his mouth move in what must have been a prayer because he crossed himself a number of times, and then bowed his head. The procession moved on and we followed along for a while.

"Where are they going?" Tim asked, and Sileshi stopped his bike and, as we pulled up next to him, said to both of us: "They will eventually go to a river where the priests will say mass and sprinkle holy water. And *Timkat* is a three day celebration all over Ethiopia."

He began to turn his bike back in the direction we had come. "Some people will fight and push to get near to the holy water."

We started pedaling home and I brought my bike up next to Sileshi's.

"What were you praying for?" I asked him as we pedaled along. I pedaled hard to stay next to him.

"I was praying for my family and my friends and for the future of Ethiopia." He let out a long, slow sigh.

"The future of Ethiopia?" I asked.

Sileshi was quiet for a minute and then took one of his hands off the handlebars and pointed off into the distance.

"I feel that there are storm clouds coming in Ethiopia's future," he answered, and averted his eyes.

"You mean the rainy season is on the way?" I asked, unsure of what he meant.

He turned and his eyes seemed troubled, and I thought he was going to say something more.

We pedaled along in silence for a few seconds and then he looked at me, smiled softly and added, "And I pray for rain. There is a drought in some of the provinces."

But the troubled look did not leave his eyes and I seemed to catch it there more frequently in the next months. Or maybe I just thought it was there.

"Will you come back to the festival tonight?" I asked Sileshi.

"Yes," he said, "I will bring my mother and we will spend our night praying, singing, and dancing."

We started cycling home and I thought about asking Sileshi if we could go with him; but I already knew that while my father may have given us permission to go in the daytime, my mother would overrule him when it came to our being out at night. As it was, I often sensed that she felt nervous having us gone with only Sileshi to accompany us. I sometimes wondered why Dad didn't seem worried about us, but I remembered that his mother had died when he was very young and he'd been shuffled from relative to relative and had basically raised himself. Maybe because he had had so little adult supervision and had done okay in life, he just thought that's the way kids should learn how to take care of themselves.

Later that night, after my parents had left for some diplomatic function at the French embassy, my brother and I sat out on the front steps with Belaynesh who still stayed with us sometimes when my parents were out late at night. I couldn't remember a time when she had not been with us. She was so soft spoken and gentle, and I knew she loved me, not that she had ever said the words but I felt it in her touch and the way she brushed my hair.

"It is *Timkat*, we should celebrate," she said simply.

"Yes," I answered, and looked up into her coffee colored eyes. She was wearing an entrancingly beautiful *shama* with a colorful border of red, yellow and green, the colors of the Ethiopian flag. She had told me that she bought the silk threads herself at the Mercato, and had saved for weeks to have enough money. Now Belaynesh went over and spoke to Kadir, the night guard, and he brought a small drum to the porch.

"Would you show us how to dance?" I asked.

"I will teach you the *eskesta*," she answered in a quiet voice, "the traditional Ethiopian dance."

She stood and placed her hands on her hips and as the night guard began to keep a steady beat on the drum, she began a controlled shiver of her shoulders and torso. Tim and I got in line behind her and began imitating the movement, our feet moving to the hypnotic rhythm of the drum beat.

"Keep your waist still," Belaynesh had turned around and was watching us, "only move your shoulders and feet."

And while the night guard continued to hit the drum with a cupped hand, Belaynesh started to sing in the warbling voice common to Ethiopian music. Tim and I danced in a circle around the porch, moving our shoulders up and down.

"Faster," Belaynesh said, "don't think about it. Move the way your heart wants you to move."

She had started clapping and I discovered that the less I thought about what I was doing, the more my body took over. There was a breeze in the night air and the heavens were filled with stars. And Tim and I danced and danced until we fell to the ground and finally crawled into bed exhausted. I knew that Sileshi and his mother were dancing at Jan Hoy Meda and a part of me wished that Tim and I were there with them, but another part of me felt safer at home in the compound.

A few days later my brother and I persuaded Sileshi to take us back to Trinity Church. By this time Assefa would throw open the compound gates as soon as he saw us getting our bikes out of the shed. And we had begun taking a small backpack with us with some water and a snack because we were staying away for longer and longer periods of time. We rode past the roundabout known as Sidist Kilo and I looked at the monument in the center. Dad had explained to us that Sidist Kilo — close to both our school and Ethiopia's only university — was the site of an important memorial where visiting heads of state would always lay a commemorative wreath.

"That's to remember the tens of thousands of people of Addis Ababa killed by the Italian fascist troops," Dad had told us, and he would point this out to us at least a couple of times a week once we began studying Ethiopian history. The idea of so many innocent people being killed seemed to affect him deeply.

One morning Dad had taken us to school on the early side and we stopped by the statue and all got out to take a really good look at it. He had told us that the tall, rounded statue was called an obelisk, a type of memorial known from ancient Egypt. It was made of white stone, and around the middle of the obelisk were carvings of proud soldiers and hundreds of slain bodies, including men, women and children. We had stared at the carvings for a couple of minutes, and when we got back in the car we were all silent.

It took us a good fifty minutes to reach the church. We parked our bikes and snuck in a side door. I looked back to where there were people on their knees praying, their foreheads touching the walls of the church. The smell of incense was overwhelming and we could hear the priests chanting their early morning prayers.

We passed an open prayer hall and I looked up at the ceiling where there were barely visible depictions of Biblical scenes. I suddenly felt that there was something vaguely familiar about being in this church, as though I had known it from another life, another time. But I knew I'd never been here before even though I had driven by it frequently. Maybe it was the stained glass windows depicting Jesus at the Stations of the Cross. I think I may have seen similar scenes years ago at my grandparents' home in one of the religious picture books that were always on their coffee table. But this church was so different from the small Methodist church in Staunton that my grandparents took us to. I remembered a giant wooden cross at the front of that church but otherwise it seemed bare and colorless. This church was mysterious and secretive.

Even in the daytime the paintings were illuminated by a silvery glow of light although there were no windows.

I watched Sileshi kneel at an altar and begin to pray, and at that moment I first had the sense that Ethiopians looked to their faith for spiritual and emotional sustenance, and that they had a connection to God that I did not feel all the time but longed for at moments. I wondered if it was because they saw suffering so often that they developed a true faith in God. Suddenly the sky must have lightened outside because the church floor was covered by a shower of brilliant specks of colored lights that seemed to be dancing on the stone floor right below the stained glass window.

Sileshi stood up and we continued to explore the church for about thirty minutes, hiding behind columns, and spying on a group of older monks with long beards wearing faded robes. Somewhere in the church I could hear the faintest sounds of a *washint*, a hollow reed instrument. We came to a place where there were pews in front of an altar. An older priest was sitting alone in silence, and then words came out of him like an incantation followed again by silence. He raised his hands in a gesture that suggested either prayer or a plea. Sileshi seemed to be listening intently, and then whispered to us, "Come, let's go home."

"What was the priest saying?" I asked Sileshi as we left the sanctuary. I didn't know if it was just my imagination, but his hands seemed to quiver slightly and he looked troubled as he pulled his bike off the wall.

"He is from a church in the province of Tigray," Sileshi said, as Tim and I both hurried after him. "Many people are starving there."

Later that evening, at dinner, Tim and I told our parents about visiting Trinity Church, and Dad explained that Christianity had become the official religion of the Kingdom of Axum, in northern Ethiopia, about three hundred thirty years after the birth of Christ.

"There are many saints' days and festivals," Dad said, reaching for the cigarette on the ashtray at the corner of his desk.

"What's the most important one?" I asked.

"Probably *Fasika*, the Ethiopian Easter," Dad answered, inhaling deeply, "and it is preceded by fifty-six days of fasting and religious services."

I watched the smoke curl up toward the ceiling.

"Boy, you must get hungry," Tim said, staring down at his plate.

"I am sure you do," Dad replied, "but all fasts are broken with huge feasts in which great quantities of meat are consumed, and that prospect is something to keep you going."

"I noticed in the pictures on the stained glass windows in the church that the people all had huge eyes that were turned in either one or the other direction," I said to Dad.

"Yes," he answered, "that is the Byzantine influence, from the time when Ethiopia became a Christian country."

It seemed to me that my father knew so much about everything. And a few months later we took a trip to a rugged mountainous area of northern Ethiopia where eleven medieval monolithic churches are carved out of rock. We had gotten up at four in the morning and driven to the top of a ridge where we parked and waited. By sunrise the mist that hung in the air made everything invisible that was more than a short distance away; but as the mist lifted, the moisture in the air began to evaporate. I saw shapes emerging in the distance and as they moved closer watched a trail of figures dressed in white moving steadily in the direction of the churches. Dad told us that the faithful would walk for days, even weeks, to get to the city Lalibela where the churches had been carved directly into the rocky earth as a symbol of the Holy Land in the twelfth century. He said many of the worshipers crossed the rugged terrain barefoot.

That summer, between my sixth and seventh grade, I fell in love for the first time. His name was Kenn Nielsen and he was the son of a Danish missionary doctor, and I first saw him at a Seventh Day Adventist Summer Bible School program that Mom had signed us up for. Our religious education had always consisted of whatever church happened to have a program for youth that we could be involved in.

I can still vividly remember the moment that I looked across the room that first day and then passed by Kenn in the hallway. He had dark brown hair and smoldering brown eyes with heavy thick eyelashes. His eyes rested deep in their sockets and they followed me unabashedly, as though he was studying me. It didn't take long for Tim and me to become friends with Kenn and his younger brother Jarl. Jarl was a year younger than Kenn and just as good looking but quieter and already seemed like the kind of kid who would be a deep thinker later in life. At least that was what I thought because he'd frequently pause half a minute before answering a question as though he was really considering what the answer revealed. And Kenn was a year older than I was and seemed surer of himself around girls. In some ways Jarl and I were more alike, but I'd seen Kenn first. A few days after we'd met them I saw Kenn and Jarl wave to a little dark-haired boy who was with their mother.

"That is our younger brother, Roy," Jarl told me. "He is nine years younger than I am."

I thought it must be so much fun to have a little brother. Even though Tim was only a year younger than I was, we were so close in age that I never really thought of him as being younger.

After a few days of secretly watching Kenn out of the corner of my eye when I thought he wasn't looking, I found out that Kenn must have liked me too because I got my first kiss the summer I turned twelve in an empty classroom during recess at the Bible School.

The magic and mystery of a first kiss. He ran his hands through my hair and caressed my cheeks and throat. I felt my heart fluttering and my breathing quicken. I was aware of the blood rushing to my ears and the room fell totally silent. Even the air seemed to have stopped moving. His lips brushed mine lightly. I reached up and ran my hand along his arm. There were muscles under his shirt but not bulky the way Dad's were. When we drew apart his face was lit up with a grin and his dark hair had fallen over his eyes. And over the next weeks it felt like some part of me was missing on the days that I didn't see him. I had never had feelings like these before and twice had left the table without eating much of my food.

Mamo caught me sitting out on the porch one afternoon daydreaming about Kenn. He sat down next to me and said, "I want to tell you a story."

"Okay," I said, although I would have much preferred to keep thinking about Kenn.

He told me that there once was a girl who fell in love and stopped eating. His tone was very serious.

"What happened to her?" I asked.

"Well, she simply wasted away and her spirit followed the boy she had fallen in love with and she was jealous of the new girl he was with. But there was nothing she could do, except wave her fist at them and they couldn't even see her."

Mamo stopped speaking and looked at me and the question I was about to ask died in my throat.

I stood up and said, "I think I'm feeling a little hungry."

It felt like things were changing in my life. I was now competing in both track and show jumping at a much more ambitious level, and Kenn had begun to take up more and more of my free time. He loved riding as much as I did so we would spend a lot of our time at the big horse racing arena, Jan Hoy Meda, where I rode for a man named Franco De Santis, an Italian who trained the especially beautiful horses that I competed on. So while my afternoons became more and more consumed with riding and Kenn, my brother's friendship with Sileshi continued to deepen.

Every night after dinner, though, Tim and I would sit out on our front porch and tell each other about our day, and I continued to vicariously take part in his adventures with Sileshi. I thought that perhaps our meeting Sileshi had something to do with fate. Was it somehow part of our destiny that he should have become so important in our lives? And what might have happened to Tim and me if he had not intervened at the bus stop?

Tim told me that they had ridden into Addis and with a throng of people had crowded around a window at one of the hotels and watched a program called *The Saint*, with an actor named Roger Moore, on a small television. They played cops and robbers in the eucalyptus trees behind our home, and Tim said they now carried their pocket knives everywhere they went, and if a group of boys began to bother them they would just pull their knives out of their pockets which seemed to be enough to dissuade the local boys. And we did not abandon our efforts at sneaking food out of our kitchen and pedaling it over to the tin village. And I loved any time that I was able to be out on my bike with Sileshi and Tim.

One day, without asking permission of Mom and Dad, we biked the few miles to the Emperor's Palace. Hard packed dirt roads gave way to tarmac and we were able to pick up speed bent low over the handlebars with the wind rushing through our hair. As we got closer to downtown Addis, where the palace was located, the streets grew ever more crowded with horse drawn buggies known as *garries* and old Italian taxicabs called *Seychentos*.

I began to wonder who'd win in a race between a *garry* against a *Seychento* through the gently undulating streets and alleys of central Addis. I couldn't bear the thought of the emaciated horses being whipped even more than they were on their daily rounds picking up passengers. But the taxi drivers of the beaten up *Seychentos* — I'd heard Dad explain to Tim one day that the word meant "six cylinder" in Italian — used to do something really dumb. Whenever they got to driving on a downhill run, like the few miles between Sidist Kilo on the way to Entoto and Arat Kilo closer to central Addis, they'd switch off the car engine thinking they could save a little gas and a few *birr* over the course of a week.

As the outline of the Palace gates came into view, I imagined that the race might really be won by the *garry*. I'd seen too many times that once a driver turned a *Seychento* off he would struggle to kick it back to life. The vehicle would cough and sputter as it slowly glided to a halt at the bottom of whatever hill the taxi driver and his unhappy passengers were traveling on.

It seemed that Ethiopia truly was caught between the modern world and the ways of the old.

~ Chapter 8 ~

HORSES

My dad first put me on a horse when I was two years old. The horse's name was Scout and I was wearing a white party dress and little black patent leather shoes with ruffled white socks when Dad lifted me up onto the saddle and put the reins into my hands.

"Walk her around slowly," he instructed Worku, who as a young groom had come to work for us and had been with us ever since.

I have no memory of my first ride, but there is a picture of me on Scout in a mahogany frame on Dad's desk. Dad must have taken the photograph. I don't remember Scout; maybe he was old and did not live too long after the photograph was taken. The first horse I remember was a Palomino gelding that we had named Palomine. Everyone said that we looked like we belonged together. His deep yellow coat was only a shade or so darker than my hair and during the summer months when my blond hair turned platinum his white mane and tail matched my hair color perfectly. Tim had been given a horse named Mickey, a grey gelding. By the time that I was seven, I was riding every afternoon for three or four hours and on the weekends even more.

My room was decorated with posters and pictures of horses that I found in magazines, except in the case of the two posters — one of an Arabian stallion and the other of a chestnut thoroughbred — that had appeared Christmas morning under the tree. I had spent hours looking through as many old books and magazines as I could lay my hands on, many borrowed from neighbors, and I'd carefully cut out pictures of horses from Greek myths and illustrated alongside Celtic poems. I remember a shiver of excitement when I had found a book about the western states in the U.S. that had page after page of pictures of horses from the Wild West and Indian legend.

And then one day shortly before Thanksgiving when I was almost eight, my brother and I came home from school and, in the world of a seven-year-old, something truly miraculous had occurred. I first noticed something was different by the way Assefa looked at me when we drove into the compound. As he pulled open the gate, his usually somber face was lit up with a big grin. Dad was home for lunch, and after the customary meal and twenty minutes of questions about our studies and the usual game of "What is the capital of this or that country" he stood up from the table and did not head in the direction of his study.

"Let's take a walk down to the stables," he said.

Beheilu and Mamo both turned away as we made our way through the kitchen and then down the back steps. It almost felt as though they were purposefully avoiding any kind of eye contact with me. We walked across the lawn and I stared ahead to where the stable was and it all looked perfectly normal. I just couldn't imagine what Dad wanted to show us. We entered the dark hallway between the stalls where Palomine, Mickey, and Nancy's horse, Hennessy, were quietly munching on straw. Dad led us to the back stall. It was not well lit but as I squinted into the semi-darkness, I saw three shadowy figures up against the wall. Dad switched on the light and I let out a gasp. A dappled grey mare turned her head to look at us, and beside her were a runt of a colt whose coat was a deep brown color, and a golden chestnut filly. At least that was the initial impression of their colors because all three horses were so caked in mud and grunge that only patches of their true colors came through. I turned and looked at Dad who was smiling broadly.

"What do you think?" he asked. "Here, let's get them outside so you can take a better look."

He turned toward Worku and motioned for him to bring them out.

Worku, who had been standing behind us, slowly went up to the mare and tried to put a halter on her. The mare began pacing the stall, circling it as if caged. She was panting and pawing at the ground and it took Worku a number of tries to grab hold of her mane and slip the halter on. He led her outside and into the fenced-in paddock. The colt and filly came bounding after her and once the three were inside Dad closed the gate. Worku had his hands full trying to keep the mare calm, and while the colt and filly first stayed close to her side they soon began to wander a little farther away.

"They have walked all the way from Asmara, way up north," Dad said. "It took them many, many weeks."

He motioned toward the mare.

"She is not their mother," he continued. "Their mother died three days ago on the trip."

"So," he said, looking around until he saw a bucket near the entrance of the stable, "you two are going to have to feed them until they are old enough to eat grain."

Dad brought the bucket over and inside I saw two baby bottles filled with what looked like watered down milk.

"Here you go," he said, handing one to my brother and the other to me.

Tim and I both slowly climbed through the slats into the paddock. I reached into the pocket of my jeans where I always kept a number of sugar cubes and I handed one to Tim and then slowly approached the filly.

With the sugar cube in the center of my outstretched hand I started speaking to her very softly, "Here you are, girl. Here you are."

I took a step forward and then paused allowing her to grow accustomed to the closer proximity of my body. She pricked her ears forward and flared her nostrils a little. I stopped, stood motionless for a minute and then moved forward again. It was a good five minutes of very slow progress before the filly reached out and I felt her rough tongue tickle my hand as she took the sugar cube. While the filly sucked on the cube I gently brought my one hand up and stroked the side of her neck and quietly brought the baby bottle to her mouth. She latched onto the nipple of the bottle and began to suck.

I looked over my shoulder at Dad who was watching us and he gave me the thumbs up. My brother seemed to have been equally successful with the colt because when I turned and looked to my side, I saw the colt sucking on the bottle while Tim was stroking his mane. They must have been hungry because the bottles were drained quickly. When they had finished the bottles, Tim and I both backed away slowly and went back to where Dad was watching us.

"Good job you two," he said. "For the first thirty-five days of life a foal and a filly need milk. We will be using powdered. You can mix it up".

My brother and I both nodded.

"I figure they are roughly twenty days old so you have fifteen days to feed them from the baby bottles. Then we will supplement their feed with grain. Got that?"

We both nodded again.

"Dad," I said. "What are their names?"

He shrugged his shoulders. "They don't have names yet. You two name them. But first help Worku get them cleaned up. I have to get back to the office."

Tim and I watched Dad walk back up to the house. The crunching sound of his wingtip shoes in the gravel grew fainter and fainter as he moved away from us. For the next hour we helped Worku clean all the mud and dirt off the three horses with buckets of warm sudsy water. It was a tough job, as the horses kept pulling against the ropes we had tied them to the fence with, and by the time they were clean Tim and I were soaking wet.

Naming the new horses became what felt like a full time occupation for us. We quickly decided to name the mare *Tinish Work*, which means "Little Gold" in Amharic. But the colt and filly were a whole different story. We made lists of possible names and at night would go over them. Every afternoon, after we had fed them from the baby bottles, we watched them romp around the paddock and discussed the possible choices.

"Do you think he looks like a 'Bullet'?" Tim asked me. "Or more like a 'Rocket'?"

"You have to decide," I answered.

At night before I fell asleep I went over my own list of names for the little filly, hoping that a final decision would come to me in my dreams. But when the day came that we would begin to introduce them to grain feed, Dad said to us, "Okay, what's the final verdict?"

"Taffy," I said to him, "short for *Taffach*. It means 'sweet.'"

"Good choice," Dad had responded, jotting the name down on his legal-sized yellow pad. He turned to Tim.

"Mac," Tim said. "I want to call him Mac. But his official name will be *Fetan* which means speed."

Dad raised his eyebrow slightly but then wrote down the name. And that was that, they were now officially a part of our larger family.

Tim and I were driven to school at seven in the morning. Classes ran till one, so by one-thirty we were home. After lunch, I would immediately go down to the stables. I didn't want the other horses, especially Palomine, to feel ignored or jealous, so I spent some time with them, fed them carrots and sugar cubes and stroked their long manes. But Taffy, who was in one of the back stalls, would hear me coming and start pawing the floor of her stall. Sometimes she reared up and plunged forward against the wooden enclosure to get my full attention but as soon as she heard my footsteps on the hard floor of the stable coming toward her she calmed down.

Taffy and Mac grew quickly, and when Taffy was six months old I could easily get a halter on her and lead her out into the paddock where the grass was now yellowed during the height of the dry season. The time had come to put a bridle and a saddle on her. For a few days I played with her ears and stroked the front of her face, getting her used to having hands around that part of her head.

"Talk to her the whole time," Worku instructed.

He handed me the bridle and put a sugar cube in my hand and as she opened her lips to take it, I put the bit into her mouth and pulled the bridle up over her head and ears and buckled the strap. She chewed vigorously on the unfamiliar piece of metal in her mouth, foaming at the sides. I walked her around the paddock a couple of times and then went back to Worku.

"For a few days you are just going to put your arms over her back so she can grow accustomed to some weight on her back," he said to me.

On the third day we put the saddle on her back and he gave me a boost up. I did not sit in the saddle though, but lay across her back, lengthwise. Worku took hold of the reins and walked her forward about twenty feet. I slid off, and then hoisted myself back up, and we repeated this again and again as Taffy grew accustomed to the saddle and a body on her back. It was not an easy experience for her. Two or three times she bucked when she felt my weight on her back and I would fall off with a thud onto the hard dirt and quickly roll away from her so she wouldn't trample me. She'd throw her head up and back away with a loud whinny, pulling against the reins that Worku was holding. It took us most of the afternoon of my hopping on and off to get Taffy to walk around the paddock with me on her back. But by the end of a long afternoon I was sitting up on her, holding the reins and making a clucking, kissing sound to urge her forward.

Over the next two weeks Taffy learned how to trot with me moving up and down in the saddle keeping a steady tempo to the rhythm of her stride. Then we introduced the canter, clockwise and then counterclockwise, teaching her to use her left and right leads. Worku told me that in order for a horse not to tire when they galloped, they needed to be able to change leads.

"The lead means which leg comes out first, and especially when going around turns at a gallop it is important to have the right foreleg moving or you will be thrown off balance," Worku said.

He took off his cap and wiped his forehead. Worku always wore a cap and rarely took it off. I had once caught him sitting behind the stables without his cap on and remember thinking it was hard to tell where his brown hair ended and the brown color of his skin started. Worku's manner could be clipped, but with horses he was soothing and totally at ease. He always seemed to be listening hard when he was around them and I was sure he had some kind of mystical communion with them, knowing that a hoof or foreleg was sore or that a bit was irritating a horse's mouth long before there were any signs or symptoms. Grooms like Worku who loved horses collected their knowledge by caring for them through difficult times. When one of the horses was sick, Worku slept next to him on a straw bed. He would watch a horse, learn his language, and then figure out how to speak to him in that language. I noticed that with some horses he spoke as softly as one would to a small child, while with others he gave direct, sharp commands.

"Learn your horse, Martha, learn your horse and then he will do whatever you want," he said to me quietly.

Over the next six weeks we set up cones and Taffy learned how to move through them in a figure eight, responding to the slight change in pressure on the reins or to the slight squeeze of my legs. But she could still get spooked. One afternoon we were working with her when the sky turned dark and the air got heavy. Suddenly the sky overhead was streaked with rain and hail, and the wind whipped up dirt and branches, and a sudden crack of lightning lit up the sky. I was holding on to Taffy, the reins wrapped around my hand. She began to stamp the earth with her front hooves and reared up, her eyes wild and pulling hard. We finally got her back into her stall where she stood trembling against the back wall. I tried to stroke her to calm her down but she shied away from me and reared up again.

"Why was she acting like that, I was only trying to help her?" I asked Worku.

"Horses are always afraid Martha," he said gently. "The only way that they could survive in the wilds if facing a lion or a snake is to run and rear and kick, so that is what they do when they are startled. It is just their nature."

I thought about that and somehow it made me feel better. I loved little Taffy. Sometimes before going down to the stables to work with her, I would stand at the top of the stairs and look down at the field where the horses were grazing and just watch her. Her coat was spectacular when caught in the sunlight, a reddish gold that ran almost to copper, her hindquarters dappled with color.

There was a two-week period when I hadn't been able to see her and it had been really hard. My brother and I had been given twelve white mice neatly separated in cages, one for males and one for the females. We kept them in one of the back rooms behind the stable. One day we took pity on the mice and so we cut a hole between their compartments. In what seemed like just a few weeks' time we suddenly had hundreds of white mice running around the part of the stable where the hay was kept. What we would soon learn is that where there are mice, predators soon follow.

One morning Worku told us that he had seen a huge snake there, and Dad ordered us to stay in the house until it was found and shot. And so we waited and waited until a Saturday morning when Dad was home and together Worku and Assefa coaxed the snake out of the stable.

"I think that may be a cobra," I heard Worku say to my father. "It has the hood that was raised when I got too close."

"What color is it?" Dad asked

"It was yellow brown with crosses on the body," Worku answered.

"Sounds like a cobra," Dad said.

I was sitting in my room when I heard a couple of shots and I ran to the kitchen and looked outside and saw a huge snake lying on the ground with Dad standing there with his pistol. I don't know what happened to the snake's body but I do know Tim and I did not bury it in the pet cemetery.

Worku worked with Mac in the same way I had with Taffy because my brother played soccer every day after school with some of the local older boys. He was determined to make the school soccer team and was convinced that playing with the older boys would bring up his level of skill. Frequently though, in the late afternoon or early part of the evening Tim and I took the young horses for a ride in the fields behind our house and down to the river for a drink. Worku came with us, but often stopped to chat with some friends who lived in one of the cluster of *tukuls* on our way.

It was my favorite time of day. The heat of the day gave way to the chill of the evening breeze. Second only to the nighttime sky I loved this time of day; the light seemed so much clearer than during the heat of midday, the outline of the mountains and trees more distinct. By six-thirty or so, over the crest of the hills in the distance the setting sun cast an orange haze above the horizon. At times the sun looked like a bloodshot fireball, and the sky was lit up ruby red. The clouds were orange, pink and crimson puffs of color. And while Taffy and Mac drank from the river, Tim and I watched the sun sink lower and lower taking with it the warmth of the day. We didn't talk much at those times, perhaps each needing to be alone with our thoughts. And then we'd head home in the chilly twilight, meeting up with Worku on the way back, catching the scent of the fires that burned in front of the *tukuls* but making sure that we were through the gates and back in the compound before dark.

The fall of my eleventh year brought a new challenge into my life. I had been competing in gymkhanas and horse shows since I was eight along with my brother. Most were held at the various embassies and spanned the entire day, with the children's events in the morning and the adults' show jumping competitions in the afternoon. Tim, Worku and I rode Palomine, Mickey and a newer horse, Martini, that Dad had purchased that summer, over to the event site. Taffy would never be a show jumper. She did not have the right build for jumping, but sometimes we would attach a lead to her halter and take her with us just so she could get the exercise and be out with us.

On those rides over I often thought about a time two summers ago when I had visited my grandparents in Virginia.

As a special treat, I had been taken to a place called Shenandoah Farms, one of the most prestigious equestrian stables in the area. We spent the afternoon trotting around an indoor paddock and the highlight seemed to be allowing the horse to canter for a few rounds. I kept waiting for the real riding to begin, that moment when the gate would be flung open and we'd head out at a gallop whooping and hollering and letting the horses run full tilt until they stopped of their own accord fifteen or twenty minutes later, lathered in sweat and panting heavily. That was the way Tim, Worku and I brought the horses to whatever embassy at which the competition was to be held, or to Jan Hoy Meda.

I especially loved going to Jan Hoy Meda where many of the competitions took place. Once there I would give Martini a quick drink of water and a ten-minute rest and then head out to the racetrack for a run. I loved the way Martini moved. Part of it had to do with his size and build — he was lean with longer legs than the other horses. And there was something particularly rhythmic to his stride and the way that he would take hold of the bit. He'd lean into it, grabbing the bit in his mouth and creating a silent intimacy between the taut reins in my outstretched arms and the hard piece of metal in his mouth. At a full out gallop he ran lower to the ground and I leaned forward in the saddle so that the wind rushed over my shoulders. When there were other horses on the track, I could hear their hooves slapping and splashing in the mud when the track was wet. Or a hard thudding behind me if the dirt was dry and packed.

Martini was a particularly spirited horse and if not run enough he would prance rather than walk, and giving him a few laps around the track before the start of the barrel races or pole bending that composed most of the children's events, made it much easier for me to control him. At eight I had begun entering him in the youth show jumping events and was gathering a collection of first place ribbons and trophies. Dad installed a shelf above my desk where they were displayed.

Sometimes when I was doing my homework Dad stopped by my room and looked at the ribbons and asked me questions he already knew the answers to, like, "What color is a first place ribbon again?"

But on this particular afternoon he sat down on my bed and looked at me. I turned my chair around to face him. He cleared his throat.

"Remember last week's horse show at the Italian embassy?" he began.

I nodded. I couldn't imagine where this was going.

"Well, after the show I spoke to Franco De Santis and he has agreed to take you on and train you."

I just stared at Dad. Franco De Santis was well known in the Addis Ababa horse circle as being the top trainer, but he could be very tough.

As though reading my mind Dad said, "I know he can be demanding but he thinks you have a lot of talent and he is looking for a young rider to show some horses."

I still hadn't said a word.

"Why don't you sleep on it and let me know in the morning."

I watched Dad as he walked out of my room. His broad shoulders and the back of his head grew smaller and smaller as he walked down the hallway and turned the corner toward his study. I had difficulty falling asleep that night and my dreams were muddled with scenes that I couldn't quite make out, and after tossing and turning for two hours or so I got up and wrapped my favorite cotton blanket around my shoulders and slowly made my way to the back of the house where my brother's room now was. His door was closed and I knocked on it and waited for a sleepy, "Come in." I sat down on the foot of his bed curling my legs up under me. Tim had propped himself up on his elbow.

"What is it?" he asked.

"Do you think I should do it; do you think I should train with Franco?" I asked him.

Without a moment's hesitation he answered, "Yeah, I do, I really do. You will get to ride his best horses."

"But what if I don't do well, what if I disappoint everyone?" I said, suddenly feeling younger than my eleven years.

"I promise I will watch every round," Tim said firmly. "As soon as my own round is over I will be at the gate that you come out of. Whether you win or lose, when you are approaching the last fence if you glance toward the exit gate, I will be there. Promise."

We both sat in silence for a few minutes and then I got up, and nodding my head said to Tim, "Okay, thanks, I'll do it. I will tell Dad in the morning."

The guard stationed at the entrance to Jan Hoy Meda watched Worku's and my approach with mistrustful eyes. He observed us as though we had some ill-conceived plot in mind, but it was his job to see everyone in those terms. He stood in front of the entrance, a powerful man, dressed in a tan uniform. I had a letter from Dad in my pocket and held it out to him, trying to hold

Martini steady with just one hand on the reins. Martini clearly thought we were here for a race and was stamping his front hoof, then his back one and dancing sideways.

"We are here to see Franco," I said to the guard.

He glanced at the letter, saw it was on formal stationery and while I doubt he read English, handed it back to me and motioned us forward.

"Over there," he said pointing in the direction of the stables in the far corner of the huge field.

We trotted toward the stable and I felt my chest tightening. As we arrived at the entrance Franco stepped out and came forward. Franco looked at me for what felt like an eternity, his dark brown eyes and the expression on his finely chiseled face revealing nothing. I felt as though he was sizing me up and without even a hello he said in English but with an Italian accent:

"Don't be late for practice. We are here to work. I will teach you how to take a horse over the highest jump you can imagine and how to do it in the fastest time possible."

His voice was commanding and I blinked rapidly and felt my face grow warm.

"Come, let's go," he said.

I slid off Martini and handed the reins to Worku and followed Franco into the stable.

Whereas Dad's father never left the mill town he had settled in, Dad wanted to expose us to the world and give us children all the advantages he had had to fight for — education, travel, activities, and hobbies to fuel our passions. But Dad also measured himself and his family by the image he created in the minds of others. And Dad had an almost psychic ability to read others and with his charm and generosity he understood how to appeal to another person's needs, longings, or ego. I knew Dad would ask me how it had gone that first afternoon with Franco, and on the ride home I tried to remember exactly what Franco had said. After dinner Dad took me aside.

"So, how was it?"

I repeated what Franco had said to me almost word for word.

"He is a little scary," I said.

Dad seemed to be thinking something over and then said:

"Do exactly what he tells you to do. Don't question him on anything. Get there fifteen minutes before you are due. If you talk to him, ask him what you can do to get better, nothing about home or school. Trust me, when he knows you are really serious, he will begin to warm up to you."

"Okay," I said, "I will try."

I now trained with Franco three afternoons a week, two during the week and on Saturday.

"When the horse is one stride away, pull the reins back a few centimeters and tighten the pressure with your thighs. Then move forward a split second before he takes off, and move your hands forward a little to loosen the reins. Look straight ahead over the fence."

With time my confidence grew, but lots of things can go wrong when you're taking a horse over a high fence. While it always surprised me a little how much grace and speed a horse could generate at the last second before taking a jump, there were a number of times that Martini refused a jump at the last minute and I sailed off and hit the ground hard. The impact hurt enough but I had to roll quickly curled up in a ball away from as much as fifteen hundred pounds of pure horse bearing down on me. I had already sustained one concussion when Martini had stopped suddenly, planting his front hooves, and I had somersaulted over his head landing hard on the side of my head. The helmet I was wearing cracked upon impact and I lay moaning and incoherent for a few minutes.

Worku must have rushed over to me because I faintly heard Franco yelling, "Do not touch her, she might have hurt her neck."

"No, look," I heard Worku say, "she is moving her legs and arms." I heard the relief in his voice.

They had slowly helped me up. I felt nauseous and foggy and could already feel a headache over the top of my skull.

I must have been very quiet on the ride home because suddenly Worku said, as though he had been reading my mind, "Remember what I told you, Martha. Horses don't stop and think the way people do, they just react."

He reached out and put his hand on my shoulder. "They are not doing it to you personally, Martha. It is their instinct. But think about it, once a horse trusts you he will race into a battle for you."

I nodded. When we got home I went to bed immediately. I had a headache for a few days and Dad told me that I had most likely had a concussion. He had come into my room the next morning to see how I was feeling. I lay watching the steam rise as he worked his coffee with a little stick. I still had a headache.

"Just take it easy for a while," he instructed and stroked the top of my head for a few seconds. "You'll be okay."

Another time Martini had twisted in mid-air over a high three-railing jump and I had tumbled off, but my boot caught in the stirrup and I was dragged about twenty feet as he galloped toward the stable, my body bumping beside his thrashing legs until my boot came off.

"Don't get up," I had heard Franco say, and there was a gentleness to his tone that I had not heard before.

Now Franco's voice sounded like it was coming from far away even though I could see him kneeling directly over me. I slowly nodded and Franco and Worku carried me into the tack room and laid me on one of the long tables where the bridles were kept. Worku found a rag and wiped the mud and dirt off my face and after about fifteen minutes, and with Worku holding me under the arm, I stood up but then quickly sat back down because it felt like the room was spinning. I put my head down between my knees and we waited a few minutes and then I stood up again and began to gingerly move about. Later that night I looked at my thigh and back and ribs, and saw an angry purple bruise beginning to spread over the area. It would probably hurt to take in a deep breath tomorrow. But it occurred to me when I thought back to Franco's voice that he was a little like Dad, on the one hand so tough, but then this gentleness would suddenly appear.

For a few of the lessons, Martini developed a bad habit of running out at the last moment, suddenly swerving to his left or right and avoiding the jump. I hated doing it but for a few weeks

Franco ordered me to use a riding crop and as soon as I felt him begin to veer in either direction, to flick my wrist hard and hit him on his neck. It did work though, and he was soon broken of that particular habit. But what Franco stressed more than anything was that show jumping took teamwork and that the more calmly and confidently I approached the jumps the greater the chances of a clear round.

"A horse has a fine-tuned sense if you are afraid," Franco said. "You are the greatest obstacle to your horse's achievement, Martha. If you are afraid, he will be afraid too. And he senses your fear in your posture and how firmly you handle him."

Later Worku told me that it was not enough to know how to ride a horse, "You must know how to fall."

My brother would sometimes come to Jan Hoy Meda on Mickey with me and hang around while Franco worked with me. I told him what Worku had said.

"Well, you sure are learning how to fall," he said grinning.

The afternoons that Tim was there with me, after leaving Jan Hoy Meda, we would race head to head the last three or so miles back to the compound down the dirt roads that led to our home, slick with sweat when we'd pull up to the gate. There were moments that were scary even though I thought about Franco's words. Once, at a full out gallop, Martini hit a pothole in the road. Like a quarterback smashed on his blind side, Martini staggered and I clung to his mane, grabbing it in both hands as he struggled to regain his balance. I heard his hooves digging into the soft earth, and then, picking up speed, he thrust his neck out and I felt him level out forward.

If Worku had gone on ahead of us to get his late afternoon chores done, and if we had an hour or so to spare, Tim and I would veer off the main roads and take to the back fields. These rides were over hills, along rivers, and across plains where cattle grazed and scattered in all directions as Tim and I galloped past. If a stretch of land was flat, we'd let go of the reins and stand up in the stirrups throwing our arms wide and high above our heads, and just let the horses race side by side. Every twenty minutes or so we stopped to let the horses catch their breath. Then I would gaze out toward an ever-expanding horizon and take in the depth, vastness, and changing light of a land so close to paradise. Dad had told me once that Ethiopia was sometimes referred to as the African Tibet because of the rugged beauty of the landscape.

Frequently Kenn and Jarl would join us on these rides home from a day at Jan Hoy Meda. They lived within the compound of the hospital where their father worked as a physician. Kenn rode a white horse named Comet, and Thunder was the name of Jarl's white gelding. Thunder had been one of the favorite polo horses ridden by the Body Guard. He was fast and a bit skittish. The Nielsens had bought him when he was ready to retire from playing polo. Comet was also white with grey in the roots of his mane and tail, and a dapple around his barrel.

Often, when we'd made a plan to meet up in a field with the Nielsen boys before heading out for a couple of hours to explore the countryside, Tim and I would be waiting and we'd suddenly see two flashes of white on the horizon and then watch Comet and Thunder gallop towards us. Out by the airport there was a stretch of land called Ladies Mile where we liked to race the horses. Like most riders Kenn, Tim and I usually rode with a saddle, but Jarl loved riding bareback, his legs gripping Thunder's sides and a fistful of his mane in his hands along with the reins. The Nielsen boys, both of whom were real daredevils, frequently rode without their helmets strapped on, something I would have loved to do when it was really hot, but my fear of Dad finding out, and memory of the concussion I'd had, deterred me from that particular risky behavior.

One time we were all at the start of Ladies Mile, the flat strip of land an open invitation for the horses and riders to gallop at full tilt. Suddenly Thunder took off, charging way ahead of the rest of us. We followed a few minutes later and saw Thunder standing totally still but without Jarl on his back. We rode up closer, my fear increasing with images of what we might see, images of Jarl injured from a bad fall. We came to a stop at a ravine about six feet deep. Standing in it looking up at us was Jarl, who had been thrown off when Thunder had suddenly decided to come to an abrupt halt. Tim and Kenn both dismounted and threw the reins of their horses over toward me. But before they could each grab one of Jarl's arms to haul him up, he had scrambled out of the ravine on his own.

"You are so lucky you didn't crack your skull or break every bone in your body," I admonished Jarl, who just grinned at me before swinging himself back onto Thunder.

Later that afternoon on the way home we had been trotting through an area where the grass was high. Suddenly a jackrabbit bolted out before us. Why we chose to do so I will never understand, but in an instant, we spontaneously decided it would be fun to chase the little creature. The grass grew shorter and the ground flatter and the little jackrabbit ran as fast as it could, changing directions very sharply, weaving to the left and then right in its desperate attempt to outrun us. We were about twenty-five yards behind it when suddenly from out of nowhere a hawk swooped down and began to repeatedly attack the little rabbit. We started screaming at the hawk who now had its claws in the rabbit's neck. The hawk dropped its prey and we quickly gathered around it, but the rabbit now lay motionless in front of us.

Jarl dismounted and walked over, knelt down and then turned to us. "He's gone," was all he said. We stood around for a few minutes and I felt the tears run down my face. We moved the rabbit under a bush, but with nothing to dig with we couldn't bury him. On the rest of the ride home we barely spoke, and once close to our house Kenn and Jarl veered off toward the hospital compound. That night I thanked God that Jarl had not been seriously hurt, which could easily have been the case. And I begged God to forgive me for the part I had played in the death of one of his innocent creatures.

As the start of the show jumping season approached, the training with Franco intensified. Practice fences were set up in the ring and Franco walked me around the course showing me where quick turns or changes in pace could cut off tenths of a second from the time. He possessed a remarkable ability to judge a horse's pace by sight. Other riders at the stable would often stand around and watch Franco at work as though by osmosis they could take in his keen eye. And then one afternoon when I arrived at Jan Hoy Meda, I saw Franco standing at the entrance to the stables holding the most beautiful dappled grey gelding I had ever seen. He was sleek and tapered and every line on him suggested motion.

"This is Ben Hur," he said to me as I slid off Martini and tied the reins around a post. "He is owned by a friend of mine, but you are going to show him."

The first show I rode Ben Hur in was on the same day as my twelfth birthday. I thought that might be a lucky omen. I almost had a clear round, but he hit a pole on the ninth jump and I came away with four faults. A boy about my age by the name of Mesfin Debebe riding a horse called Awash won that event. Mesfin was distantly related to the Emperor and a member of the Ethiopian aristocracy. He was about my height with the finely chiseled features of the Amharas. As the weekends went by though, a pattern seemed to develop. I would come in first and Mesfin would take second place, frequently after a timed jump off because we had tied. And then the following week Mesfin would take away the first place trophy and I would be in second a few faults or seconds behind him. By the end of the season we were tied. Each one of us had collected six first-place ribbons and six second-place and so the final competition on the last Sunday of the season would determine, in our minds, the overall Junior champion.

The morning of the final competition I awoke to a grey day. I didn't have much appetite for the breakfast that Beheilu fixed knowing that it was my favorite, but I thanked him as I walked through the kitchen. At ten o'clock, Worku and I saddled up Martini and Hennessy, Nancy's horse that Worku sometimes rode, and set off for Jan Hoy Meda. Mom, Dad, and Tim would drive over later before the first event. Since I had started riding Ben Hur, my brother was now competing on Martini and I loved watching them and always cheered the loudest after Tim's rounds. But Tim had taken a bad fall a month prior at the British embassy, one of the other sites where competitions were held, and his arm was in a cast for five months so this season was over for him.

Usually on a ride like this, Worku and I chatted away about what we saw along the route or he would ask me questions about my school or friends and I would ask him about his family. Sometimes he told me a story. The Amhara culture has a wealth of folklore in the form of proverbs, legends, myths, and religious parables and anecdotes. I was particularly interested in his belief in the evil eye or *bouda*. Worku not only believed in the evil eye, but one day I heard him reciting some kind of verse and when I asked him about it he said it was a *kitah* to ward off the ill effects of the *bouda*. He carried some type of talisman in his pocket and I would try to sneak a peek at it when he took it out of his pocket but I hadn't gotten up the courage yet to ask him to show it to me.

Before we left that morning, my brother came down to the stable.

"Do you want me to give Mesfin the evil eye?" he asked with a sly grin. He took off his glasses and placed them on a bale of hay.

"No way," I said vehemently. "Don't you dare, take it back."

I yanked at Tim's sleeve.

"Okay, okay," he said, "don't get so bent out of shape."

What my brother did not know was that I had developed my own thoughts and ways of keeping my family safe. And never giving anyone the evil eye, I bargained with God at night, was one thing on a very long list of superstitions I now had. It was strange that Tim didn't know about it. I usually told him everything.

This morning though, very unlike any other morning, Worku and I rode in total silence while taking a shortcut along the river. I was wearing white jodhpurs, a white button down shirt, black boots — which I had polished to a clear shine the night before — and my black helmet. As we trotted along, I found my mind wandering back to a day that had been filled with both joy and sorrow. Dad had come home from a work trip to Nairobi, Kenya, and when I arrived home from school he was waiting for me with this pair of black knee high boots. I threw my arms around him, convinced that he was the best father anyone could possibly have.

My little dog Poupee had had three puppies about six weeks earlier. We had given away two of them, but kept the third and named him Rascal. He was black with three white paws and a white mark on his face. That afternoon I had been playing with Rascal in the kitchen wearing my new boots to begin to break them in. Rascal circled around me, his tail thumping the tile floor. Rafe, the doberman, came into the kitchen and Rascal bolted to a small space between the fridge and the wall peeking out cautiously at Rafe. I shooed Rafe out of the kitchen and coaxed Rascal out and picked him up. He burrowed in between my neck and shoulder licking and sniffing. It tickled and I kept trying to stroke his ears. Mamo told me that the best way to calm a puppy or dog was by gently stroking and pulling on their ears. Rascal fell asleep in my arms, and I gently put him down on a blanket in the kitchen and went outside.

I remember I was sitting under a tree reading a book wearing my new boots and heard Dad's Jeep start up and then a high pitched yelping followed by silence. I scrambled up and ran into the front yard where I saw Dad standing by the side of his Jeep with Rascal's little lifeless body in his arms.

"He must have gotten out of the house and fallen asleep under the front tire," Dad said, looking at me.

For a moment I didn't understand what he was saying but then it suddenly hit me that when Dad began to back up he had crushed Rascal. I didn't know what to say or do, so I just turned and ran down toward the stable and went to one of the back stalls and climbed behind a huge bale of hay. I knew Dad felt bad about it. I hadn't cried until late that night. I knew that if he saw me crying he would feel even worse.

My brother and I buried Rascal in a shoebox under one of the eucalyptus trees down by the stable and then watched Poupee sniff at the mound of dirt and try to paw at it. We gave Rascal a short eulogy. Tim talked about what a cute little puppy he had been and how his life had been cut short through no fault of his own. We looked around and found a light-colored stone to use as a headstone.

"We should say a prayer," I said to Tim.

"Go ahead, you do it," he said, and I began reciting the 23rd Psalm because it was the only prayer I could think of at that moment.

"Do you think dogs understand anything about death?" I asked Tim, not really expecting an answer. I wondered if Rascal's soul would rise up on the third day the way we had been told Jesus rose from the dead.

That night I kept going over the events of the day, wondering if this was the way life was. Was there some kind of balance sheet where every time something wonderful happened, you were going to pay with something awful happening?

For me, music has always been the language of memory. Every life has a soundtrack. Any time I hear Scott Joplin's jazz piece "Jelly Roll Morton," memories of my father at the piano flood back. The Beatles' debut album, and in particular the song "Do You Want To Know A Secret," has me hiding behind a screen with Tim, watching Nancy slow dance with Gerard, the son of the Dutch ambassador, and hoping they would kiss. On our family trips through Europe and other parts of Africa, belting out the anthems of the four branches of the U.S. military. And of course Dad had to turn it into an educational experience and so we learned that the original lyrics for the "Caisson Song" were written during World War I in the Philippines.

None of us knew what "Hi, hi, hee" meant, but Tim and I would throw up our arms with each word. The Navy's "Anchors Aweigh" was Dad's favorite and I always told him it was mine as well, but in fact the "Marines Hymn" seemed like a real tribute to heroes. I had no clue where the "Halls of Montezuma" were, but I knew the "Shores of Tripoli" were somewhere in North Africa.

On one particular car ride, Nancy sat in stony silence as the rest of us sang the "Marines Hymn."

I nudged her and whispered, "Why aren't you singing?"

"If Dad won't let me hang out with the Marines, I am not going to sing their stupid song," she answered loud enough for Dad to hear.

If Dad heard he chose to ignore her, although as I watched my mother's profile I saw her lips tense slightly; but then taking her cue from Dad she kept singing. Later that night, after I had heard Nancy and Dad arguing, I asked her what it was about.

"It doesn't matter," she said, tears welling up in her clear blue eyes, "but I hate him."

I felt shocked.

"Really, you hate him?"

"Yes," she said, "I hate him, I hate him."

"You can't hate him," the words burst out of me.

"I do" she said, "but at the same time I love him so much it makes me mad. Sometimes I feel like he can't help who he is. His own childhood was so hard and he wants so much for his life and for ours. But it is hard for me to be his daughter, to feel like I have to be perfect."

Small lines radiated out from her eyes like tiny streams. I had only seen her cry once and the tears had run along those streams and then down her face. I didn't know what to say to her and just hoped that my sitting there was some kind of comfort to her. The distance that I was sensing between Dad and Nancy scared me.

Looking back many years later, I realize that most of what I learned about the United States came from those car rides and the songs we learned. "Dixie Land," a tribute to my mother's southern roots in the Shenandoah Valley, to this day I cannot hear it without the scent of her perfume filling the air. And now, off in the distance as we approached the entrance to Jan Hoy Meda, I heard the band playing the Ethiopian national anthem and I would never hear that soaring melody again without thinking about this, my final competition at this place full of memories.

Worku and I came around the corner, and the larger shapes of the stables and the grandstand came into view. We entered the racetrack and as we passed the stables I heard the restless pacing of the horses in their stalls. Slants of light pierced through the stable windows and I knew the grooms were beginning to saddle up the jumpers who would compete in the later events of the day. We broke into a canter towards the schooling ring where the competitors warmed up prior to entry into the show ring. As we arrived I heard the roar of the crowd as someone in the first event must have taken a clear round.

Someone handed me a program and I looked at it relieved to see that I would be competing after Mesfin. I looked over at him already sitting on Awash. He was one of those riders whose grace in the saddle was immediately apparent. Maybe it takes another rider to recognize someone who has that gift of taking a huge animal with lightning fast reflexes over a towering fence. Other than a helmet, we wore no protective gear. The fences were high; a horse jumping over a five- or six-foot fence puts the rider more than ten feet into the air. One wrong move over fences this size could be a catastrophe. I checked the chin strap on my helmet to be sure it was tight and gave Mesfin a half smile. He grinned back at me. Awash's coat glowed from the extra grooming that morning. Awash had everything you want in a show jumper — speed, style, athleticism, and heart.

The jump off was announced and I watched Mesfin enter the ring. Awash pranced around. I closed my eyes allowing the sounds of the crowd to tell me whether or not he had cleared a jump. Ben Hur chomped nervously on his bit and flicked his ears back. In my mind I counted the jumps and was sure he was going to have a clear round and then an "Ohhhh" let me know that he had a refusal because I did not hear a pole hit the ground.

"Three faults," I thought, as I heard the crowd applauding his round.

A refusal gave you three faults, knocking down a pole meant you had four faults.

"Mesfin Debebe on Awash, three faults with a time of 46.2 seconds," the announcer's voice called out over the loudspeaker.

My name was announced and I entered the ring and cantered the courtesy circle. Out of the corner of my eye I saw that the crowd in the bandstand was no longer walking around or eating food from the concession stand. Everyone was crowding the bleachers and I knew that somewhere in the crowd were Dad, Mom and Tim. Franco was not in the bleachers but somewhere along the ring, one foot on the bottom railing. I pointed Ben Hur towards the first jump, a cross rail.

This course was one with tight corners and short approaches so I knew that speed was going to be key to a clear round. Franco and I had walked the course the day before so I could memorize it. Ben Hur felt like he was vibrating like a live wire under my seat. As he took off, I felt him snap his knees up, raising them almost to his neck.

"One down," I thought and I lowered the weight in the stirrups, a signal for him to shorten his stride as we approached the second jump, a high double rail.

His hindquarters gathered underneath him and as I felt him take off I loosened the reins. We landed and he picked up the pace as we raced toward the third jump, two bales of hay stacked on top of each other with a pole a few inches above. I gathered up the reins feeding the leather through my fingers and with a cluck and a quick tap on his sides with my boots, in a perfect orchestration of movement he sailed over the fence.

"Only five more to go," I thought, and I brought him around to the left.

He approached the next jump fast, almost too fast, and snapped his knees tightly, reaching forward with his neck to create a higher arch. For a split second I thought he might come down a fraction of an inch too soon, but he just cleared the second pole.

Next was the wide jump over water where he needed to stretch out, for it is the longest jump on any course. I knew the next three fences were designed to test a horse's balance and courage, for they were verticals — fences that have height but no depth. And they were right in a row which meant Ben Hur would have to keep his legs up tight, and make a short, high arc and then with just two paces between each fence do it again and a third time, but each time the poles would be higher. I could not allow him to get off stride by even one step, in the same way that a gymnast has to calculate the exact point at which to take off so that the routine ends in an exact spot. I took in a deep breath, pulled the reins up tighter, brought him around the last turn, and pointed him straight at the triple.

Franco and I decided a few days earlier not to use a martingale — a leather strap that tethered the horse's head to a strap around his neck, then a strap to the rings of the bit and back to the rider's hands, thus acting almost like a pulley — on him. It would have allowed me a little more control of his neck and suddenly I wished that we had decided to have him wear one because he was pulling at the reins with tremendous force, the raw power coiled within him battling against my arms. I flexed my arms hard to try to keep his stride short. He took the first jump easily and I managed to slow him as he approached the second jump and sailed over it.

"One more," I whispered, and I moved into the jumping position feeling as though everything had suddenly moved into slow motion.

I measured the distance to it with my eyes, then looked over the fence, caught a glimpse of Tim with his arm raised high, and I felt Ben Hur gather up and move into the air and as we came down, a second before we hit the ground, I heard a "crack," and then seconds later a crash as the pole hit the ground.

I cantered slowly out of the ring, barely aware of the applause or the announcer's voice.

"Martha Paradis on Ben Hur, 4 faults, 45.1 seconds."

It didn't matter that my time had been faster, I had more faults. I entered the paddock, dropped the reins and reached up with both hands and covered my ears, and for a few seconds I drowned out the sounds of the crowd and the band and listened to the blood pounding in my head.

I saw Worku up ahead standing stiffly. I slid off Ben Hur. Worku moved next to me and awkwardly put his arm around me. For a second I leaned into him the way I used to when I was six years old and had taken a bad fall off one of the ponies. I wondered if one day a girl my age will lean into me for comfort if her boyfriend had broken up with her or she had had a fight with a best friend.

Tim came over and stood next to me. "It's okay, Martha. It really is," he said quietly.

"Where is he?" I asked. Worku knew I was referring to Franco.

"He is standing over there, by the practice ring." I took in a deep breath.

"Will you come with me," I asked quietly, but I kept staring straight ahead and blinking hard as I felt the tears welling up behind my eyes.

Worku nodded.

"Okay," I said, straightening up, and turned to Tim who had walked over to me.

"I will see you in a little while. I want to get this over with," I said to Tim. "I will meet you back here in about twenty minutes, I hope.

"Let's go," I said to Worku.

I turned around to where Ben Hur was tied up to the railing.

"It wasn't your fault," I said quietly, and I stroked the side of his head for a few seconds.

I lose many things every day. I lose the book I am reading, I lose my favorite pen, I lose the bet I'd made with Tim. But I don't lose when I am riding one of Franco's favorites. This was not supposed to happen this way. I walked slowly toward the ring, Worku a few steps behind me. Even though I knew the sun was shining, a chill had crept into my body and I felt cold and damp. I began to drum my fingers nervously on my leg. When I got to the ring I noticed that the light coming through a tree next to the ring seemed to cast eerie shadows over the field.

I looked at the back of Franco's head. He was leaning over the railing and if he heard me he did not move. I felt Worku's presence behind me like heat drawn from a fire and I wanted to back up closer to him as though needing physical protection.

"I am so sorry," I whispered to Franco's back. I felt my face flush so suddenly and wondered if it might be a crimson hue for the rest of my life. My tongue seemed to have turned to stone as I hunted for words. I couldn't think of anything else to say. It was as though words had lost their shape and clung to the roof of my mouth.

He turned around, his dark eyes revealing nothing as he looked at me. I tried to speak, to say something redemptive, but my vocal cords did not seem to be working and no sound came out.

We just looked at each other and then he turned back to what he was doing.

"I am so sorry," I said to his back.

He nodded and then lifted his hand in dismissal. I thought he was going to tell me that I couldn't show Ben Hur any longer.

"Be here Monday at three."

I felt a rush of gratitude, knowing that that was all he was ever going to say to me about losing the jump off.

I got through the award ceremony in something of a daze and as soon as it was over asked Worku if we could ride home along the river. My brother had gone on ahead with some of our friends. We took a long time, letting the horses stop and graze along the way. Worku didn't speak at all and I was glad for his silence, but when I came through the gates into the yard I felt a lump in my throat as I tried to swallow. I could hear loud music pouring out of the open window from the house. I didn't want to talk to anyone about what I was feeling, not even Tim.

At dinner Dad said, "You gave it your best effort, you really did," and then waited for me to say something but I just put my head down.

Later that evening I filled the tub with steaming hot water. I slid in and let the water cover my shoulders all the way up to my chin. I bobbed up and down weightlessly, my hips floating forward, my shoulders relaxed. I closed my eyes and I told myself that one day, far off in the future, I would not remember this day. I won't remember the ride up to Jan Hoy Meda that morning. I won't remember waiting in the training paddock for my name to be announced to enter the ring, or how tense my stomach felt and then feeling my insides relax as I cantered toward the first jump. But most of all I won't remember the sound of Ben Hur's hooves hitting the pole on the last jump and then the deafening crash as the pole hit the ground.

When we sit around the dinner table years from now and talk about the championship jump off, I will listen politely as someone in my family tells me the story of how Mesfin won by one point. I tell myself I won't remember any of it.

But some things I cannot forget, even though I have longed to expunge them from my very experience of this world.

~ Chapter 9 ~

HUNTING

From the earliest age that my father thought we could bear the physical strain and stand the sound of guns, he took us on his seasonal hunting trips. My brother and I were given the small responsibilities of counting the day's spoils, and whether by foot or on horseback we witnessed the ancient ritual of man pursuing and killing his prey.

The rattle of the grey metal shutters being pulled up woke me from a sound sleep. With the shutters pulled up the early morning light cast a grayish shadow across my bedroom.

"Get up Martha," I heard Mamo's voice as he moved toward the doorway. "They are leaving in twenty minutes."

I glanced out the window where the sun had begun to filter through the branches of the eucalyptus trees, and then squinted toward the sound of Mamo's voice, trying to make out his outline.

"Hurry," Mamo said, "you know your father will not wait. And anyhow, why do you want to go hunting with the men instead of staying home and learning how to sew?" he teased and he smiled and I could see the crinkles around his eyes.

"Okay, okay, I'm hurrying," I said and leaned over the side of the bed trying to find my jeans and the boots that I had thrown on the floor the night before.

Mamo left, closing the door behind him, and I turned on the lamp by my bed and quickly dressed. Some mornings Mamo would ask me to guess what we were having for breakfast by the aroma that would come drifting down the hallway from the kitchen, where I could hear the sounds of breakfast being prepared. But this morning the house was silent.

I grabbed a brush and tugged it through my blond hair. Despite the fact that Dad's nickname for me was 'Ragamuffin', I knew that he would give me that raised eyebrow which signified his disapproval if I showed up looking unkempt. For a moment I stared at my features in the small mirror over my dresser, my green eyes and tanned face and a sprinkle of freckles across my nose. I was almost twelve years old and waiting to have some kind of growth spurt.

"Why do I have green eyes?" I once asked Mamo a few years earlier. "Nancy and Tim both have blue eyes."

"God gave you green eyes to match the eucalyptus trees when you take your horse at the fastest gallop through the trees. Your eyes match the trees," Mamo told me.

"You really think so?" I asked, and he had nodded seriously.

"Martha, you ride in the Jeep with the Colonel and the Ambassador," Dad said as I joined them on the front porch of our home. "Tim and I will go with Kirk."

I reached down quickly and gave Jambo, our golden Lab, a quick pat on the head and then raced over to where the Jeep was parked. This was just the way I wanted it. I loved Jeeps and had been longing to ride in Colonel Nolan's, hoping that after a day's hunting when we were driving back to the city, he would put the top down and open the sides. Dad now had a green Jeep but we didn't need three vehicles for this trip. Colonel Nolan was the air attaché at the American Embassy in Addis Ababa and a good friend of my father's.

Addis Ababa, Dad once said, reminded of him of a human Noah's Ark.

"There seem to be at least two people from every country in the world," he said, "in the clothing of missionaries, diplomats, soldiers, fortune hunters, and spies. But the biggest bunch might be the soldiers and spies," he would add. I wasn't sure what he meant.

I was really happy, at times, that the American bunch seemed pretty big, especially because the military had a commissary out by the old airport. Mom could sometimes go with one of our

American family friends and shop there. We were not allowed to go on our own because Dad did not work for the American government. On those days though, I would beg her to let me tag along, so I could nudge her to buy marshmallows, Tootsie rolls, and other sugary treats that we otherwise never saw.

The Ambassador, on this occasion, was Peter Putman-Cramer of the Netherlands and this was his first time out hunting in the Solulta marshes where we were headed. He made me a bit nervous because he seemed so formal, and even out hunting he wore a starched shirt with a perfectly tied scarf around his neck.

Captain Kirk Hills was standing casually next to his Land Rover. My dad and Captain Hills were inseparable hunting and poker companions, and seemed to drink a lot whenever they were together. A rugged outdoorsman from Montana, he wore a thick mustache and had bushy eyebrows above steely grey eyes. Like my father, he could be stern and intimidating and then just as quickly become jovial and good-humored.

As a senior pilot with Ethiopian Airlines, he would often allow us to join him in the cockpit during takeoffs and landings when we flew to Greece or Kenya for our summer vacations. Once, he scared even my father, when he flew the plane at such a steep angle on leaving Beirut Airport that I was sure the jet was going to flip right over. Dad had flashed him a tight grin, and Captain Hills had just beamed back. It took a while for my heart to stop racing. Over the years, I got to know the Hills family very well, because I would stay with them whenever my parents traveled outside Ethiopia without us kids, but I was often upset because Nancy and Tim would be bunking down with other families. I would have preferred that we be together.

Our small caravan headed out of our compound for the two-hour trip to the Solulta plains. Tim, riding with the captain and my dad, looked back at me with a grin, caressing his new shotgun, a 22/410, which he had just received for his tenth birthday. Dad wanted us skilled in the ways of the outdoors. He had given me a choice on my last birthday between my own gun and a new riding helmet and I'd chosen the helmet. Tim hadn't been given the choice.

The road we were traveling on quickly went from an uneven pavement to a rocky trail and our trip slowed. I stared out the side window mesmerized by the pattern of light and shadow, the shades of green and brown that undulated off the grassy ridges of the Entoto mountains to the west of Addis Ababa as the sun made its slow ascent. This morning the mountain range was devoid of the thin layer of clouds that sometimes lay along its sides. The azure sky promised a perfect day, the dryness in the air characteristic of a plateau set at just under eight thousand feet.

My arm, draped over the back of the seat, warmed as the sun streamed through the side window. I leaned out of the Jeep breathing in the smell of the grass still wet with dew and ahead saw fields of yellow daisies that appeared after the heavy rains of summer. I had left this morning without breakfast and knew it would be hours before we stopped for the lunch that had been packed the night before and now waited in the cooler in the back of the Jeep. I rummaged around in the pocket of my jacket, sure that Mamo had stashed a candy bar in there for me. I felt something a little bulkier than I had expected and when I pulled it out I saw a piece of paper wrapped around a chocolate bar. I unrolled it and slowly made out Mamo's uneven handwriting.

"Be careful," he had written, "your father wants to hunt in a bad area. The people there are not friendly."

I loved Mamo and could imagine him slowly writing out the message on a piece of paper and then deciding how to get it to me. I crumpled the piece of paper and stuffed it back into my jacket. For a moment I wanted to ask Colonel Nolan what Mamo meant, but then thought better of it knowing that if Colonel Nolan mentioned it to my father Mamo would be in trouble. But I shifted uneasily in my seat, feeling my heartbeat quicken with a vague sense of unease. I glanced out the window quickly, but the landscape seemed calm and isolated.

We came around a final bend in the road and up ahead I saw three familiar figures squatting on the ground waiting for us. Makonnen, Aduna, and Haile were the guides who would accompany us on this day of hunting. Sometimes it was guinea fowl that we were after, sometimes wild pigs, but today it was snipe, a migratory bird of the Ethiopian plains, about a foot long with a stocky body and short legs.

Because Ethiopia became almost synonymous with drought over the past few decades, and television images of mass starvation captured the world's attention, it is hard to believe that forty-five years prior rains began in mid-June and usually lasted until mid-September. The roads became impassable, clothes were permanently damp and the smell of mildew permeated the air. But as soon as the rains wound down and the gray skies were interrupted by occasional patches of blue, the message would be carried down from the plains by one of our guides. "They have come, the *foo-fee-ya* have come, they are here."

The Jeep and Land Rover came to a stop at the turn off the main road onto the track that led to the plains. I listened in on the conversation between my father and Makonnen, a tall older man who, while dressed shabbily, still held himself in a distinguished manner.

"This area has been shot over," I heard Dad say to Makonnen. "We have to go further if we want a good day's hunting."

I leaned as far out of the Jeep as I could, trying to make out what Makonnen was saying, but I was too far away and all I could hear was the sound of his low voice, and I watched him shaking his head and then reluctantly nod. I suspected my father had offered to increase his wages and in Ethiopia even a dollar could make a big difference in someone's livelihood. I suddenly wished that Rafe, our doberman pinscher and a ferocious watchdog, had come with us.

We started up again, Makonnen and Aduna on the hood of the Land Rover, Haile on the Jeep, motioning to the right or left so we could avoid the holes and gullies that crisscrossed the many fields. A number of other men loped alongside or behind, hoping that there might be enough work for them to earn a few dollars as well. Looking out the rear window of the Jeep I noticed that as we drove further into this unknown territory all but four of the men stopped, watched us for a few moments, and then turned and headed back toward their own villages.

About twenty-five minutes passed before we came to a stop and Dad motioned for us all to get out. Climbing out of the Jeep I quickly scanned the countryside, relieved that it seemed peaceful and quiet. But I was having a hard time getting in a deep breath and had no appetite for the candy bar Mamo had packed. The sudden craw of a hawk startled me and I jumped.

"Stop it, everything is fine," I said to myself and tried to stifle the uneasy feeling I had by helping to get the rifles out of the Jeep.

Snipe are not easily found, or flushed, or shot. Our guides were the key to finding them. Flushing them was done with a primitive piece of rope, fifty or sixty meters long, hauled through the knee-high grass by two of the men, or sometimes attached to the pommels of a pair of horses which were driven along just ahead of the hunting party. When flushed, snipe literally jump into the air and streak away, never flying in a straight line but jerking in an erratic pattern which makes them hard to hit and adds challenge to the shooting.

We had left our home at sunup, six o'clock. It was now close to eight and Dad told Aduna, who was his main guide, to have some of the men lay out the rope and take their places as draggers and beaters.

"Makonnen, you take five men and go with Captain Hills and Tim. We will meet you back at the vehicles in three hours," Dad instructed.

My brother grinned widely at the prospect of hunting alone with Captain Hills. "We'll bring back twice as many as you," he yelled over to me.

I opened my mouth and started to say that I wanted us to stay together, that I didn't want Tim to be separated from us, but then stopped in mid-sentence. I knew better than to protest a decision my father had made.

Tim was a gentle soul and had recently confided in me that he simply could not shoot a living creature and so he purposely would miss hitting the birds we were hunting.

"I think Dad is getting pretty frustrated with me," he said." He wants to get my eyes checked.

Now as I watched them move off together I suddenly wondered if Dad was sending my brother off with Captain Hills to see if the Captain had any better luck with him.

Slowly our group headed out, Colonel Nolan having moved to just outside the left of the drag line and my father taking the right. Dad asked the Ambassador to walk in the middle, a courtesy, to give him the best shooting. Aduna and I walked slightly behind my dad, waiting for the first snipe to flush as the rope slithered along, bearing down on the feeding birds hidden in the tall grass. I turned around a couple of times and watched the figures of Captain Hills, Tim and their men grow smaller and smaller and then disappear over the top of a hill.

Before us the landscape stretched away, the grass shimmering in the early light. On either side of our route rose gently sloping low hills, dotted here and there with a hut or two, smoke seeping through the thatched roofs and disappearing into the air, the only evidence that there were any other people around. To our rear, perhaps a mile away amid a grove of eucalyptus trees, was a larger group of buildings, their roofs topped with *encorcoro*, or corrugated iron. But except for our small group all was still, the world was motionless, and we could almost have persuaded ourselves that we alone inhabited the earth.

Deliberately we made our way through the tall grass in our high boots, often up to our ankles in mud and water. We had to be sure that we stayed well behind the advancing rope. This was important because the snipe would often fly not directly away but at a diagonal or even parallel to the rope. As we moved forward a bird would suddenly flush and one of the men would take a shot and the bird would drop some ways ahead. One of the beaters would mentally mark the spot and then pick up and bag the bird as we moved over it. If the bird was shot too close up, one was left with little more than a beak, legs, and a mangled body filled with tiny lead pellets.

As we trudged along, concentrating on the unpredictable birds, I suddenly noticed a man who was not part of the hunting party seemingly emerge from nowhere on our right, walking in a line that would bring him in front of the hunters.

"Dad," I said, startled.

He had not seen the man, and only gestured that I should keep quiet. At that moment a snipe jumped up in front of Colonel Nolan and streaked to the right, toward Dad, Aduna and me. Colonel Nolan hesitated just long enough then brought the bird down with a single shot, fifteen or so yards in front of us. The man ran to the bird and picked it up. Dad loped forward, shouting at him to get away from the guns, that he was putting himself in danger, and as they neared one another the man dropped the snipe and lunged for Dad's shotgun. They struggled for a minute and then the man fell to the ground, bleeding from a long gash on his cheekbone where he had been struck by the butt of the gun as my dad had wrenched it from his grasp.

The world started to spin and my heart began to pound. I opened my mouth but no sound would come. Everything took on a dreamlike quality for me as we all stood there dead in our tracks, a motionless tableau.

Slowly the man rose to his feet and Dad backed away. And then suddenly the silence was broken by a piercing high-pitched ululation, the falsetto "la-la-la-la," that strange cry which one encounters in many parts of Africa at certain times, with subtle variations, each conveying a special meaning, and that I had heard at weddings and funerals and other ceremonial occasions. But this time it was a cry for help.

In almost instantaneous response the countryside was transformed. A landscape that had been still, almost devoid of life, came alive, like a termite hill disturbed by an errant hoof or foot, or a suddenly disturbed hornets' nest. From every hut, from every clump of trees, from behind every rise of ground, people appeared, first a few, then a handful, then a hundred. And all moving toward us.

"Haul in the rope," Dad yelled. "Quick, empty the guns, we don't want a bloodbath."

In seconds, the guns were unloaded, the cartridges dropping into the mud and water.

He turned towards me and yelled, "Martha, get near Aduna."

I felt like I was going to topple over, the adrenaline rushed up my legs, but my feet in my boots felt so cold and my boots stuck in the mud like leeches, such that no amount of strength or willpower could move them. I looked over toward Aduna in a panic and he took a few steps towards me, but before he could reach me we were surrounded. There must have been a hundred people around us, many with spears, as we stood grouped together and a man who seemed to be the leader was yelling and suddenly there were about ten men in a circle around me.

I put my head down and squeezed my eyes shut as though I could block out the scene unfolding before me. I heard Makonnen and Aduna talking rapidly in a dialect I did not understand, and then heard them say to my dad, "They want us to go to those buildings." I was suddenly conscious of the bright daylight and the mixed murmurs of the people around us and the one word I kept hearing and understood was *Ferenje*, the Amharic word for foreigner and intruder.

We slowly began walking toward the metal-roofed buildings. My feet kept sinking into the mud and I stumbled forward a couple of times and the water rushed in over the top, soaking my feet and making it even more difficult to walk. We got to the buildings about the same time that I suddenly saw my brother and Captain Hills being escorted down toward us. When they reached us I saw Tim try to make his way through the throng toward Dad, only to be pushed roughly away.

He seemed pale as he looked over at me and mouthed the words, "What is happening?"

All I could do was shake my head. My mouth was dry and parched but I didn't dare ask anyone for water. The men who had been standing around me moved forward to where Dad and the other men moved forward to where Dad and the other hunters were talking to the two men who seemed to be in charge, with Aduna and Makonnen translating.

Tim moved over to stand next to me and in hushed whispers we kept asking one another, "What do you think is going to happen?"

Suddenly, to my horror, I watched them separate Dad from the other men and take him into the building.

Right before the door slammed shut, I heard Dad yell over to Kirk Hills, "Try to find Mamo Tadessa, the Minister of State, and tell him what has happened. And take good care of my kids."

And then the heavy metal door slammed shut and I saw four men plant themselves right in front of the door. Dad was gone.

Captain Hills gestured for Tim and me to come forward and when we reached him he began speaking quietly. I thought I heard a note of panic in his voice. "They won't let your dad leave. Colonel Nolan has offered to stay here with him, but you two and the Ambassador and I are going to go back to the city."

I heard the words, "No, I want to stay with Dad," beginning to form but I had been raised not to question the adults, and Captain Hills wore an expression that told me not even to try to protest.

It took us about fifteen minutes to get back to the Land Rover. It all felt so unreal. Sitting in the Land Rover I suddenly had an image of the lifeless bodies of the rebels who had been hung from the trees along the way swinging back and forth. I shook my head and closed my eyes, as though I could will the image away. I had only been six years old at that time, but had already begun to learn the language of suffering and terror — mine, that of people I loved, and that of total strangers. I knew about the *Shiftas*, bandits, who sometimes attacked convoys on the main roads. Daily I witnessed the cruelty shown by men to their animals and often other men. I knew that there was a deep gap between the rich and the poor and that the peasants resented the government's heavy taxes. And now Dad was sitting in a building that we were moving farther and farther away from.

Tim sat in total silence beside me and neither of us spoke the whole ride back. This was a new kind of terror that I was feeling and I didn't know what to do to keep the image of Dad being led into the hut from playing over and over in my mind. I had to do something to keep myself from imagining what might be hap-pening back where we had left Dad. So during those two hours of silence I tried to remember the words to every song I knew, and if I missed a word I felt I had to start the whole song right from the very beginning.

I was suddenly jolted out of my daze by a heavy thud as the Land Rover reached the part of the road where the dirt and gravel suddenly turned into uneven pavement. We picked up speed and as we neared the city limits I pressed my face up against the window. The city, when we reached it, seemed unreal just because it was so familiar. We passed a bakery, the post office, the grocery store — everything that had been normal yesterday; but it was as if I were looking at it upside down as I rode past people who were shopping or otherwise going about their business like nothing was wrong.

"Nancy," I suddenly thought. "She doesn't know what is happening. I wish she was here right now."

As we passed our school and I saw a couple of teenage girls who were boarders there leaning up against the fence talking to some boys, I felt a deep ache for my older sister.

When Nancy was twelve she had been given the choice to go to boarding school in Switzerland. She said, "Yes, I want to go," and so two big trunks had been packed in late August and we had all driven to the airport where she and Captain Hills' daughter, Connie, were going to take the eight-hour flight to Switzerland on their own. I hugged Nancy really hard when we said goodbye and she had hugged me back, and when we drew apart and I looked at her face I saw that she was blinking really fast and her eyes were all wet.

I remember watching her walk onto the tarmac with Connie. Even though they both were four years older than me, they suddenly looked so young. Nancy's hair was pulled back into a ponytail with a green and red striped ribbon tied around it. She was wearing a skirt and bobby socks and saddle shoes and was walking looking straight ahead. I watched her stiffen her shoulders as she neared the stairs to the plane, a movement I recognized she used when she was trying to be tough.

"Turn around and wave to me, please turn around," I murmured to myself.

But she didn't turn around and the next time I saw her I barely recognized her. The ponytail and bobby socks and saddle shoes were gone, replaced by a miniskirt and boots and a big pink floppy hat and a new way of dismissing me as though I was just far too young and silly to be taken seriously. When her friends were over and talking about boys and experimenting with makeup and hairstyles with the Beatles blaring on the record player, I would hang around the door to Nancy's room pretending that I was looking for something in the big baskets of folded, clean laundry. My hope was that they would ask me to come in and maybe they would put some mascara on my lashes.

"Stop hanging around us," Nancy's friend Diana said to me when she noticed me in the dimly lit hallway.

Then her tone had suddenly changed and she smiled and said, "No — actually, if you go get us some cokes you can come in and we'll show you how to put on lipstick."

I tore into the kitchen and grabbed three cokes from the pantry and raced back down the hall towards Nancy's room coming to a stop right in front of the door. I held out the cokes.

"Thanks," Diana said as she took them from me.

I took a step forward and suddenly felt her push me backwards at the same time that the door slammed shut. Stumbling backwards I heard them all laughing. For a moment I thought about banging on the door. Instead I had gone to look for Mamo.

I asked Mamo why Nancy let Diana do things like that to me and he said that maybe someone older did something similar to her at her boarding school.

Are you going to tell your father?" he asked.

I shook my head, "No."

I had sensed this growing tension between Nancy and Dad and knew he would be hard on her. My father had told me once that his older brother Arthur had run away from home when he was sixteen and they still did not know where he was. One of Dad's ironclad rules was that we three kids stick together and stand up for each other, and telling on each other, unless it was something truly dangerous, was frowned upon.

"She is just going through a phase," I overheard my mother say to my father. "You know she's a teenager."

But Nancy and Dad had a big argument this last time right before she had flown back to school, and now, as the Land Rover sped along through the city streets, I kept thinking about the fact that Nancy would have no idea what was happening back home, and Dad, sitting in a hut thousands of miles away, might be feeling really bad that he had yelled at her.

The Land Rover suddenly slowed and we were again on the rutted dirt road that led to our home. We took a quick right, past little shacks with tin roofs, and then came to a stop in front of our house, guarded by the high stone wall and black iron gate with spikes on top. Captain Hills leaned on the horn and the gate was slowly opened by Assefa, who must have been working in the garden because his hands were covered in dirt.

We pulled into our driveway and Tim scrambled over me and ran into the house yelling:

"Mom, we have to get help, they have Dad!"

I got out of the Land Rover feeling small and unsteady and, as if I were drifting rather than walking, followed my brother into the house. Bewildered, my mother looked over at Captain Hills, and he motioned to her to go into Dad's study. He followed her in and closed the door. I sat down on the steps of the front porch. My little dog Poupee ran over to me and I tried to calm myself by holding her in my lap and stroking her ears. Mom and Captain Hills emerged from the study and I looked at my mother's face and could sense the terror and anguish that she was feeling even though she wore a mask of complete control. But I looked down at her hands and saw her rub her thumb back and forth over her index finger, a gesture I had come to associate with her feeling frightened.

"We have called the Minister of State," Captain Hills told us, "and he is sending some soldiers out to get your father back".

Suddenly I turned and ran down toward the stable looking for Mamo, thinking that he might be in one of the rooms behind the stables. When I got there the half-dozen horses were quietly munching on straw.

I sat down next to my favorite and nodded to Worku, who looked at me and without asking me why I was here said, "Mamo has gone to the market."

Everyone who worked for us had by now heard what had happened, but Worku was impassive.

I wanted to ask him, ""Are they very bad people?" but my fear of his answer kept me silent.

I heard the low rumble of a truck and quickly climbed to the top of the stable roof and looked out toward the army barracks that was about a quarter mile from our home. About two hundred yards away I saw a military truck moving quickly down the road. As it passed by me, squinting into the back of the truck I realized that it held about twenty soldiers armed with semi-automatic weapons heading now in the direction of the Soluta plains.

I must have hung around the stable for a couple for hours, hoping that Mamo would come back. I played hopscotch by myself. Something about my feet landing in a rhythmic pattern of one, one, one then two, seemed somewhat comforting because of its monotony. At six o'clock the back door opened and Beheilu rang the bell that meant dinner was on the table. We barely spoke through dinner as I pushed my food around my plate. A couple of times my mother tried to engage me in conversation and asked me about school. I answered my mother's questions about my homework but it felt as though someone else's voice was speaking.

Time seemed to drag, each minute ticking by as slowly as a snail moving towards its destination. I went to my room and turned the small alarm clock on my bedside table towards the wall so I would stop staring at it.

I was getting ready for bed, folding my clothes and putting them neatly on my dresser, when I suddenly heard the sound of a vehicle pulling into the yard and voices at the compound gate. I got to the front door just as the Jeep pulled up and my father and Colonel Nolan got out. I felt a sob begin deep inside me as I ran over to Dad, but before any sound could burst out of me, my throat tightened and I stopped in mid-tracks. My father's face wore an expression that I could not remember having seen before, but somehow recognized nonetheless. I stared at him and suddenly I knew, I just knew, that history was about to be rewritten. And then he laughed.

"Come on over here you kids," he said. "Give your old man a hug."

Tim raced into his embrace and I followed hesitantly.

"I never thought I was in any real danger," he told us. "I figured they would hold me for a few hours, ask me to pay a sum to the man I had struck and that would be it." I looked at him carefully hearing a hesitation in his voice even though it lasted just a fraction of a second.

We all moved into the dining room and sat down at the table. And I watched Dad because somehow his words didn't feel quite right. His eyes seemed a little out of focus. Then I thought that maybe he was just tired. Mom brought out the hastily heated leftovers and put them down on the table in front of Dad and Colonel Nolan.

"Anyway," he continued, "it was not a work day — Sunday. It was too early for plowing, and the few cattle could be left to their own devices, so lots of herdsmen joined the ring of spectators. I was put in a small room," he said, "but there was a small window and a short distance away I could see the elders, the *chika shums*, who administer village affairs grouped in solemn enclave. I knew it was going to be a long day because nothing brightens an Ethiopian's life like a good dispute. At least three sides can be found on any argument and each must be analyzed, dissected and presented. Books have been written about the intricate style and method of communication among the Amharas, the ruling tribe, in which few things are ever stated directly but only by allusion and suggestion. And even though these people were from another tribe, that culture had found its way into their method of settling disputes."

Dad reached for the pitcher of water and poured himself a glass. His hand shook slightly and he took a quick sip and put the glass down.

Colonel Nolan now joined in on the story. "It was clear to me that they were not going to let us leave. I asked if we might be permitted to send a message to Addis Ababa. 'Ah no,' they had responded, 'that is out of the question. This is a local affair.'"

Colonel Nolan caught Dad's eye and Dad nodded, and I suddenly wondered if they had already rehearsed this version of the story.

"Here is the funniest thing," Dad suddenly interrupted. "They decided to take me to a hilltop administration building so we all piled into the Jeep with some of the elders and they put this really

177

heavy woman in the back, I guess so we couldn't speed away. And the worst moment was when I was sitting in the building and I asked for something to drink and was brought this foul smelling goat's milk. But having asked for it, I felt I had to drink it."

He was now chuckling, but it somehow felt forced.

"Anyway," he said, suddenly intent on ending the story, "before we got to the administration building we saw an army truck up ahead and within minutes everyone fled."

He turned to my mother and asked if she had any dessert left. I had been silent the whole time Dad and Colonel Nolan were talking. A thousand questions churned in my mind.

"But Dad," I began, "why did they send soldiers?" and then I stopped in mid-sentence.

Dad held my gaze for a few seconds, his hazel eyes unblinking.

"Not another word," he said quietly but his eyes did not soften.

I wanted to yell at him, to demand that he tell me what had happened. For a few seconds, we stared at one another. A slight scowl creased his brow but then just as quickly disappeared.

"Not another word," he said again, his voice low.

Dad's discipline was never harsh or brutal but often came masked as gentleness. For many years I had been finely trained to obey him, and I felt my resolve fade away. Submission was my only option. I lowered my eyes, my face flushed as I swallowed hard sealing the pain and confusion for many years.

~ Chapter 10 ~

RUNNING

My father's way out of West Warwick had been as a football star and his scholarship to Wesleyan University in Connecticut had been as a scholar athlete. I had inherited some of his natural athletic ability and could sense how important it was to him that I always push myself to give it my best effort. He never said anything directly but I could tell that my successes meant something to him in much the same way that so much of what I experienced from my parents was not spoken directly but implied through physical expression and tone of voice.

All the running down to the river and around the compound had made me fast. Sometimes it worked against me though. On Christmas Eve when I was nine I wound up with six stitches above my right eye because I ran straight into Tim who was holding his pocketknife with the blade out. I must have hit him on an angle because the blade sliced into the skin right above my eye. I thought Tim had run into me but when I mentioned that to him later that week he said,

"Why would I be running with an open knife in my hand?"

I guess he had a good point.

I heard my mother gasp as I came into the living room holding my hand over my eye with the blood streaming down my face.

My father gently pulled my hand away and said, "Thank God it is her eyebrow not her eye, but she will need stitches."

So off we went to the Swedish clinic where a young doctor sewed up the gash. He didn't do a very good job though. A few months later I looked in the mirror and saw a crooked scar running through my eyebrow.

"It gives you character," my father said when I pointed it out to him. "Like a battle scar."

"Or in this case a brother's scar," I said to Tim later that day.

It was a tradition at our school that the athletic department held three days of track and field competitions. We were lectured on the importance of a strong body as well as a disciplined mind. As a small school this meant that everyone, including all the middle and high school classes, competed in a common series of athletic events. The days were grueling, but I did my best, jumping as far and as high as I could, running as fast as I could, and thrusting my chest out at the last moment as I crossed the finish line. But at the assembly after the final day of competitions, I was stunned when my name was announced as the overall winner of the girls' events, winning out over girls who were so much older than me. I stood there motionless for a moment until two of my friends pushed me forward to accept the medal. An older Ethiopian student named Kasai won for the boys. After we had gone forward to receive our awards from the headmaster, he took us aside and told us that we would be representing the German School on the days of competitions held at the big stadium where students from schools all over Ethiopia would be competing.

"There will be hundreds of students competing from every province in Ethiopia," he said. "Make us proud."

No one said much to me about the upcoming competition and I didn't know what to expect. Maybe they didn't either. The birds woke me the first morning of the competition. I went to the window and looked out and saw a flock of blackbirds sitting in the back yard. Suddenly they all started making a loud warbling noise and began rising into the air. For a moment total chaos filled the sky but then they organized themselves into a single file and I watched them fly off toward the river. I stood holding my breath and saw them become a single speck in the sky.

"Hmmm, blackbirds," Tim said when I told him about it at the breakfast table. "Maybe that is a bad omen."

"Don't say that," I barked, glaring at him.

Tim had a piece of waffle with a piece of bacon on top and he started to mash it all up.

"Why do you always mutilate your food before you eat it?" I asked.

"That way I don't have to waste time chewing," he answered grinning widely at me, bits of waffle and bacon in his teeth, "and anyhow it all gets mixed up in my stomach."

"Ugh gross," I said. "Don't let Mom and Dad see you eating like that," which prompted Tim to let bits of waffle and bacon drop out of his mouth.

Dad and I pulled out of the driveway at seven-thirty sharp. We drove by the big field at the top of the road. The cattle were all lying down and I watched a few of them begin to scramble up, their ribs sticking out. It had been a long while since the rainy season and the grass was yellow and dry, the few bushes in the field prickly and sparse. We drove past one of the *Tej Bets*, a few drunken men already with a bottle of *tej* in hand standing out front of a nondescript low-slung building. A beggar crossed the road, his left leg dragging behind him and his clothes reduced to grey rags. I wondered where he lived and if he had a family. Every so often we would have to stop and wait for a whole herd of cows or sheep to cross the road. Inevitably one of them would stop in the middle of the road and just stare at us. When that happened my brother and I liked to stare right back, and if the animal lowered its head and moved on Tim and I would whoop and holler that we had won the "stare down."

We pulled up to the big stadium where the soccer matches and track and field events were held. Dad had made small talk along the way but I wasn't really listening. When the car pulled up I saw Kasai waiting by the entrance. I got out and Dad motioned for Kasai to come over. He leaned in toward the window and I watched Dad's mouth move up and down, and Kasai nod his head over and over, and then Dad extended his hand out of the window, his gold wedding band glinting in the sun for a second, and Kasai shook it.

Dad pulled away and Kasai said, "Come on, let's go."

"What did my father say to you?" I asked as we waited in line.

"He said I should guard you with my life," he answered, but he wasn't looking at me and I couldn't tell if he was serious or joking.

I thought about a story that my father liked to tell about a trip we had taken to a part of Ethiopia where people had rarely seen a car much less someone who looked like me. We stopped by one of the villages and with our interpreter asked for directions to a monastery set in some mountain caves. My legs were cramped from the long car ride and I had gotten out to stretch them. I looked over to where Dad was speaking to an older man who kept pointing in my direction.

When Dad got back into the car, he was smiling.

"What's with the smile?" my mother asked.

"I was offered two camels for Martha," he said.

And that was it — from that day forward, anytime Dad was annoyed with me he'd say, "I should have taken the two camels."

Kasai went through a small entrance with turnstiles and then came to an area where long rows of benches had been set up. Kasai motioned for me to sit down while he went to see where we had to register. I looked around at the sea of kids in different colored t-shirts depending on the team they had been assigned to. The day was already hot and sticky, the air a little thick. Voices overlapped until it was one loud buzzing noise. My stomach felt a little queasy and I sucked in a breath and squinted against the bright sun. The stadium before me blurred and I blinked until it came into focus. A group of soldiers pushed their way through the crowd, their guns held high over their heads. I looked at a young guard who was stationed beside the windows where kids were lined up. His black hair was thinning a little at his temples and there was a sheen of oil to his skin.

I took in a long deep breath and thought about a game my brother and I played when we had time to kill. We'd pick someone we had seen that day and make up a story about who they were. The other night Tim had decided that a very tall, thin boy he had seen from the school bus on the ride home who didn't move a muscle in his face when Tim repeatedly waved at him and smiled, was the son of one of the leaders of one of the provinces in Ethiopia. I had told him that a beautiful young girl I had seen out on one

182

of my rides who seemed mysterious and elegant was actually a princess who was in hiding because she did not want to marry the much older man who had been chosen for her.

"She'd better stop acting so dignified," I said to Tim, "or she will give herself away."

I looked at the young guard again, thinking about how I would describe him to Tim — "He is around mid-twenties and is wearing a tan uniform with a gun strapped casually over his shoulder" — and I began to memorize his angular features.

The young guard caught my eye and winked. I quickly looked away. It was embarrassing to be caught watching someone. But when I glanced back a few seconds later, he was still staring at me. He winked again and smiled, but rather than feeling relaxed I felt unsettled. I put my head down, praying that Kasai would come back soon. When I looked back up the guard had moved closer to me and was leaning up against the metal gate.

I was just about to get up and go look for Kasai when I heard his voice behind me, "Over here, Martha. You have to sign in and get a pass that will give you entry to the stadium every day."

"You'll be coming with me?" I asked, looking up into eyes that were as dark as roast coffee, suddenly feeling panicked.

"Unless I get disqualified in the first heat," he said, and I watched his eyes soften in response to the slight quiver in my voice.

"That's not likely," I said feeling my shoulders relax. "You are way too fast."

Kasai took me over to the team I had been assigned to. There were so many kids there and he pressed my shoulders gently to the left, then right, as if guiding a boat through rapids. I suddenly felt an elbow in my ribs and looked to my side but could not pick out who had poked me.

The competition took place over the next three days. Uncharacteristic of Addis weather, the raging furnace of a sun overpowered the few clouds above, and heat boiled down baking my shoulders through the white t-shirt I wore with my number pinned on the back. The sweltering humidity made my hair stick to my forehead and my shorts bunched up on my legs. Even the earth seemed to perspire. The track looked like a blistering strip of heat. Surrounding the track were bleachers about thirty rungs high and I knew that the Emperor was seated somewhere in the middle with his entourage and many of the ministers Dad worked with. Mom was once again up visiting Nancy at boarding school, but I knew that Tim and Dad were sitting about twenty seats to the Emperor's right. Dad hated being in the midday sun and I knew he was wearing a suit and could well imagine how much he was perspiring. I also knew that Sileshi was seated with his high school on the side near the long-jump pit. There was something comforting to me knowing that the three of them were watching these events.

The next two days passed in something of a blur. I took first place in the long-jump event. Kasai and I had developed a ritual in which he stood on the grass on the side of the sandy pit and as soon as I hit the board and took off he lifted his leg and only returned it to the earth as I landed. At the fifty-meter line was the platform where the medals were awarded and I received a gold medal attached to a tricolor ribbon of green, yellow, and red along with an expensive looking watch presented to me by one of the Emperor's retainers. For a split second I wondered if the Emperor recognized my name when we were announced. He knew Dad of course, and how many people named Paradis could there be in Addis? I was also the only Caucasian on the field and even though Sileshi had told us that unlike other Africans, the Ethiopians consider themselves white, with my blond hair I knew I still stood out because of the way some of the kids would stare at me. I had trained myself to ignore it.

"What are we then?" Tim had asked Sileshi, laughing.

"We call you the pink people," Sileshi told us.

I was so tan these days that in fact my skin and Sileshi's were almost the same color.

The stadium was packed, and I had read that almost twenty-thousand spectators watched the events. In the same way that *berbere* is made up of dozens of spices, Ethiopia itself is a fine-grained mixture of tribes each with its own language, so while I could understand what many of the kids speaking Amharic were saying, there was something unsettling about not understanding what was being said as I walked past a group who pointed at me.

The announcements over the loudspeaker were first given in Amharic and then English which was the official second language in Ethiopia, the one that the kids learned in school after Amharic. Of all the competitive events, the one I was most excited about would be the final heats of the 100 meters, about twice the distance Tim and I could shoot our slingshots. The fastest runners would make up the relay team and I had been told that they would move on to compete in a bigger, more impressive competition. I won my first heats, but was up against the best runners in the final heat.

There were six of us, but only four of us would make the relay team. I paced around before the final heat waiting for the starter to order us to our marks. I was on the inside lane and the girl who had the fastest time was two runners away. I got to the start and taking in a deep breath I began to envision the Kebena River at the finish line.

"Just pretend you are running down to the river," Worku had said to me the evening before when I was feeding the horses with him. "And if you want to run even faster, imagine there is a fire behind you."

It was so quiet that I heard the wings of a dragonfly as it went by. The stands were silent as though all the spectators were holding their breath. I heard a loud shot from the starter's pistol. The track blurred as I pushed off and I surrendered all thoughts to the beat of my feet against the ground. I could feel a shadow at my shoulder. My blood felt like it was boiling along with the sweat that poured down my face, but I lifted my elbows a little to give my lungs more space and pumped with my arms, and for the last fifteen meters began to kick off the ground with all my strength with each step. I did not see myself cross the finish line and would have run on and on had I not felt Kasai's strong arms around me. I bent over, heaving, my breath coming in short little gasps. My shirt was soaking wet and my mouth parched. I had not remembered to drink enough water that morning. I stared up at Kasai and then slowly other faces came into view. I looked up toward the stands where I saw Dad and Tim both on their feet with their arms up in the air.

Suddenly blinded by a flashbulb as the photographer from the *Ethiopia Herald* took a picture, I managed to whisper to Kasai, "Do you know my time?"

"You made it," he said, smiling broadly.

Sweat stood in little beads on his brow and nose.

"Here," he handed me a slice of orange.

It tasted as tart as a lemon and I let the juice run down my throat and my stomach contracted. I heard the names being announced and realized I had come in second in the final heat with a time fast enough to qualify for the relay team.

"I can't believe it," I said to Kasai as we walked over to where the medals for the 100 meters would be awarded.

My breathing had returned to normal and I stood stiffly on the platform and sang along as the military band played the Ethiopian National Anthem. The entire crowd, bigger than anything I had ever seen, rose as one, a sea of vibrant colors blended together, and I felt emotions swelling up that I had competed on the same ground as people I did not know but felt a great love for.

A few minutes after the medal ceremony, two official looking men in dark business suits approached me. For an instant I thought I had done something wrong and my heart raced.

"You are Martha Paradis?" one of the men asked. Deep dark shadows had found a home beneath his eyes.

"Yes sir," I said stiffly.

"Congratulations on your time. Your school and parents will be very proud of you."

And then my mind went blank and while I have tried for the past forty-seven years to remember exactly what he said to me, all that my memory retains is something about being American and not Ethiopian.

"But I live here," I said stunned. "I have lived here my entire life." I bit my lip.

The second official began speaking but my hearing had shut down for a few seconds as I watched his lips move and then I heard the words, "We are sorry," and his tone told me the conversation was over.

I waited for my brother and Dad at the side of the arena. I had put on a light grey sweatshirt and pulled the hood up over my head hoping that no one would speak to me. When Dad pulled up I quickly climbed into the back seat. Tim was sitting in the front seat and I stared at the back of his neck, red with sunburn. We were all quiet for the first ten minutes or so of the drive home but something in Dad's demeanor told me he already knew what had transpired. Tim didn't turn around to talk to me either. We drove in an uncomfortable silence.

Finally Dad spoke.

"You know, Martha, Mexico City where the Olympics will be held in 1968 is at the same altitude as Addis. The track team from the United States will be coming here to train. I asked the Ambassador if you can come to the track and meet them."

"Okay," I answered, and I tried to squash the empty feeling that had settled in my stomach.

"You don't sound very excited," he said.

"They don't mean anything to me," I blurted out, shaking my head. "I don't know them the way I have heard of Abebe Bikila my whole life. He is the great Ethiopian runner I know. I don't even know who the American runners are."

Dad looked straight ahead out the window and then said almost to himself, "I think we may have outlived our time in Ethiopia."

That night when Tim and I were sitting in my room I told him that I couldn't remember exactly what the two officials had said to me. I was on the floor leaning up against the wooden slats of my bed.

"It was like I suddenly went deaf. All I know is I won't be going wherever the relay team next goes and that's going to be international," I said.

Tim slid off the foot of the bed, knelt down beside me and gently put his arm around me but didn't say anything, which was the first moment of comfort I had felt. And I shared something with Tim that I had realized.

"I have always known somewhere in the back of my mind that I am American and not Ethiopian," I said to him. "But today, Tim, was the first time that I really felt it."

If there are moments that transform us into a different person than we were a second ago, I will always believe that the moment the two men told me I could not compete because I was not Ethiopian was one of those times.

When I returned to school I was treated as something of a hero but I always had a bittersweet recollection of those days, even as I ran around the track with an American long distance runner named Jim Ryun who would go on to win a silver medal in the Mexico City Olympics.

And I stuck by my family's unspoken creed that painful emotions must be swallowed.

~ Chapter 11 ~

THEATER

I was in Athens with my family when I was about eleven years old. We had gone out to see *Doctor Zhivago*, an intense and disturbing film about true love and loss in the Russian Revolution. I can still remember Lara in a red dress dancing with the character Victor Komarovsky and the scene at the end where Yuri is on the tram and sees Lara through the window. I remember I cried as he bolts off the tram chasing her, and then suddenly clutches his chest, collapses and dies, as she continues walking away. At age eleven I loved the drama.

So I was filled with excitement a few months later when my father told my brother and me that since our mother was away from Addis — again visiting my sister in Rome where she was now in boarding school for the high school years — he would take us to the movies. The movie was *Zorba the Greek* with Anthony Quinn. I looked in my closet for something special to wear.

There were no department stores in Addis Ababa so my wardrobe consisted of hand-me-downs from my older sister and her friends, and once a year I was permitted to look through the Best catalogue and pick out three or four new items. I would pore over the choices and then carefully fill in the order sheet which would be sent off to the U.S. and about three months later a box from Best Catalogue Company would arrive. My usual outfit was jeans or jodhpurs and a t-shirt, because I spent most of my afternoons riding, but tonight I picked out a white skirt that had recently arrived and a turquoise top. Turquoise was always my favorite color.

About forty-five minutes before the movie was to begin, Tim and I climbed into the back seat of Dad's Jeep and we set off on the twenty-five minute drive to the theater. Whenever we drove in Addis I'd be reminded that the city was sharply divided by class and ethnicity, with informal settlements concentrated near the center and wealthier districts to the southwest and southeast. Most of the population lived in mud huts with no running water or electricity. Unlike many other African capitals, Addis Ababa's founding and growth were not rooted in colonization. For a brief period between 1936 and 1939, the city was occupied by the Italians under Mussolini, but because their rule was so short-lived the Italian influence on the city was minimal.

"Except," Dad would tell us as he talked about the history of the city, "Enrico's ice cream parlor," located near the movie theater we were now headed towards and serving the most delicious gelatos. "That was the Italians' greatest contribution," he'd chuckle.

"Maybe we'll stop by after the movie."

Located in the heart of Addis Ababa, the Empire Theater was one of the city's oldest. It was built in the 1930's as a huge warehouse, but shortly after World War II it was renovated. The seats were red velvet, there were two big chandeliers hanging down from the ceiling, and red drapes hung on either side of the screen.

When we got to the theater, I asked if we could sit upstairs, in the mezzanine.

"Sure," Dad said, "why not."

We sat down in the third row, and then a rather tall man sat down in the seat in front of me, blocking my view.

I looked over at my dad and mouthed, "I can't see."

Dad stood up and moved two seats to his left gesturing that Tim and I should do the same. The theater darkened and I settled back, a carton of popcorn nestled in my lap. A newsreel began and a clip of Emperor Haile Selassie on some state visit somewhere flickered onto the screen. For less than a second I saw a flash of light to my right followed by a deafening explosion. I flung my head forward towards my lap and put my arms over my head hearing screams all around me. The popcorn I had been eating spilled out of the carton.

Dad stood up and yelled, "Don't panic," and for a few seconds the entire room quieted down, like a wave receding in the ocean.

I was just beginning to lift my head up when there was a second blast and I screamed, although I don't know if a sound came out because the echo of the second explosion drowned out any noise for a few seconds. The serenity of silence surrendered to terrified cries and people began to push forward.

Maybe it was the sound, maybe it was the terror, maybe it was God, but I flung my body forward and began scrambling over the rows of seats in front of me, squeezing past people who were barely moving although some seemed frozen in place. My eyes were fixed on an "Exit" sign that was lit up and cast a pale glow around the theater. I reached behind me desperately trying to locate Tim.

My hand flailed back and forth in the air for what felt like forever although it was probably no more than thirty seconds, but I could not locate him. The crush from the crowd behind me was now so forceful that I was pressed up against the railing of the mezzanine. I scrunched my body down just as the person next to me was pushed over the railing into the orchestra below. I closed my eyes trying to block out the horror of the image of his body being catapulted over the railing. Now on my hands and knees and pressed up against the front of the mezzanine I inched my way forward unaware until much, much later that someone's shoes or boots must have stepped on my fingers for they were sore and swollen.

I finally managed to get to the exit and stood up although my legs felt weak and shaky, and for a few seconds I thought I was just going to sink back down. My stomach felt contorted but quickly changed to the sense that I was being smothered by a huge hand as I tried to get in a deep breath. The panicked crowd turned left into the corridor that led down the ramp to the outside, but I suddenly turned right. I stood very still pressed up against the wall and leaned around the corner, straining to look back into the theater. Every instinct in my body said to keep moving, to just get out of the theater, but the need to find Tim and Dad was stronger. A part of my mind kept repeating, "This can't be happening, this can't be happening." The people were still pushing toward the exit but it looked like they were all moving in slow motion even as my own body felt like it was in high gear. I knew people were screaming but I didn't seem able to hear the sounds, until a sudden crash and I watched helplessly as eight or ten rows of seats collapsed onto each other.

I could not see Tim or Dad anywhere in the dimly lit room and as the crowd thinned I began to push my way back in. I was still small and slender enough to squeeze my way between two people if I turned my body sideways. As I neared what I thought must be about the seventh row where we had been sitting I heard low moaning coming from somewhere on my right. Suddenly the emergency lights came on and I saw the outline of the man who had been sitting in my original seat. A wave of nausea rose up into my throat and I felt suddenly faint as I looked at him and realized that his leg was split open hanging by a piece of skin. His arm was badly mangled as if it had been stuck in a wood chipper.

I turned away and for the first time started screaming, "Dad, Dad! Tim, Tim!"

I tried to move to my left but a woman was lying in the row bleeding from her stomach and I was afraid to step over her. I knew that the explosions had been to my right and Tim and Dad had been sitting to my left so they had not taken a direct hit. I began to climb over the seats, many of which had collapsed.

"Martha, over here," I suddenly heard Dad's voice and I began to feel my way towards it, grabbing the back of a seat and hoisting my body over it.

The emergency lights kept flickering on and off. As I neared him I saw that he was kneeling down by one of the seats that had collapsed.

"Tim's leg is trapped under here," he said as I reached them. "Martha, see if there is anyone who can help me."

I looked around wildly and then saw a man walking down the aisle from the back of the theater. I was trembling as I pushed my way towards him, willing my legs to keep moving.

"Please help us," I whispered, and I reached out and tugged at his jacket. "My brother is trapped over there, my father needs help."

Dazed, as though he was a robot, the man turned into the row and went over to Dad and together they lifted the seats up and Dad pulled Tim forward. I felt something warm on the side of my face and reached up and realized that the whole right side of my face was wet, and pushing my tongue out toward the side of my cheek, in the corner of my mouth I tasted my own blood. I reached up and began to feel around my ear and side of my head trying to locate the place where the blood was coming from.

"Daddy, I am bleeding," I said to my father who was feeling Tim's right leg.

"I don't think anything is broken," he said.

He turned toward me and said, "Let me take a look."

I turned the right side of my face towards him and he said, "Shrapnel. Here, press this up against the side of your head."

He gave me a handkerchief with his monogrammed initials in the corner. I pressed it to a place that was beginning to throb.

"Press down hard," he said. "Come on, kids, let's get out of here."

He was holding my brother under his arm, supporting him as Tim began to limp toward the exit. The corridor that led to the outside was empty now except for a few people who seemed to be walking slowly as though they had forgotten their destination, and a woman who was sitting on the ground with her legs curled up under her. When we got outside there were people milling around. In the distance I heard a siren. We had parked about two blocks away and Dad now lifted Tim up from around his waist, and holding me with his other hand quickly got us to the Jeep.

Dad told us that he was going to go to the hospital.

"What was that?" Tim suddenly asked.

"I am pretty sure those were two grenades," Dad answered.

It always seemed to me that Addis had its own heartbeat. At night it was slow and steady with only a few people venturing out into the darkness as only limited places had electricity and there were no streetlights. But when dawn came the city would spring to life as the beggars began their rounds, the tradespeople scurried to sell their wares and schoolchildren hurried to their classes. At dusk the rhythm seemed dangerously erratic, with drivers navigating past the multitude of child beggars, disabled people, cattle, goats, donkeys and stray dogs. You had to weave your way through traffic, most of the time without traffic lights, crossing chaotic intersections with your hand on the horn. In the busy business district, homeless women and children sat in the gutters begging for food and money. In the more upscale parts of the city, beautifully dressed men and women socialized at cafes and nightclubs. It was common to see shacks next to big luxury hotels. Tonight the temperature was very mild — my parents always referred to the climate as "San Francisco weather" — and we were a couple of weeks away from the beginning of the rainy season.

It was still early evening but the traffic seemed much more jammed than usual. I looked out of the window. It felt to me like we were driving through gauze. The bleeding from my head seemed to have lessened but my head had begun to throb. We crawled along. I watched as a bus groaned to a halt. Fifty or so people tried to get off at the same time that fifty tried to get on — like two rivers flowing in different directions. Dad kept laying on the horn to try to maneuver his way along faster and I heard him cursing quietly under his breath.

I leaned back in the seat, glad of the comfort of my brother's body next to mine. We came to Arat Kilo and I stared at the monument at the center of the square commemorating the victory over the fascist Italian invaders. A policeman was trying to direct traffic. Dad pulled up to him and rolled down the window and asked the officer what seemed to be the problem.

"There has been an explosion," was the curt answer. "Keep moving." He waved us on.

It took us another thirty minutes to get to the Empress Zewdito Memorial Hospital. Dad got out and went up to the door and rang the bell. After a long while it was opened by a woman wearing a white dress. I saw Dad speak to her for a few minutes and gesture over towards the car. Dad came back to the car and helped Tim out of it and then took him under the arm again as Tim limped toward the front door. We went into the waiting room and Dad started filling out some paperwork. A doctor stuck his head out and motioned that we should follow him to an exam room. He had salt and pepper hair, and the white coat he was wearing was stained. He first looked at Tim's leg. I could see my brother wanted to cry out as he moved the leg this way and that but then gratefully Tim slid off the table when the doctor said, "Nothing broken; use ice and rest and I'm going to give you an ace bandage and you can have someone wrap it tightly."

"Climb up here," the doctor told me and I dutifully climbed up onto the exam table.

He looked at me quizzically and said, "You look familiar. I'm a colleague of Doctor Calmar Nielsen. Do you happen to know his boys, Kenn and Jarl?"

I felt the color rushing to my face, and mumbled, "Yes, I know Kenn. And Jarl."

The doctor's hair was unkempt as though he has been roused from sleep and had not taken the time to comb it. His eyes were a watery hazel behind thick glasses. I wanted to turn my head away but did not dare do so as he picked up a pair of tweezers and began methodically extracting small pieces of metal and wood from the side of my head. It was then that I looked down and saw that my white skirt was covered in dirt and congealed blood. The whole time the doctor worked on me I kept trying to distract myself by imagining how long it was going to take for me to scrub that skirt white again. In my mind I could see myself moving the skirt over the washboard in the laundry room in our home and watching the water run bright red but then gradually turn pink and finally run clear.

Dad in the meantime had asked to use a phone and I could hear his muffled voice on the other side of the door. He came back into the room just as the doctor was beginning to shave a small patch of my hair. He told me to lean to the side, and poured alcohol over the side of my head which stung so badly tears rushed into my eyes; then he placed a bandage over the wounds.

"We were lucky," Dad said as he came back into the room. "The grenades they used were training grenades so the force was substantially less than it might have been. I have spoken to the U.S. embassy and there have been threats called in to a number of restaurants tonight as well."

Dad picked up one of the tiny pieces of metal from a steel bowl and handed it to me.

"Here, a souvenir," he said.

I took it from him, wishing that I was wearing jeans so I could put it into a pocket. Instead I held it in my hand, and moved it around in my palm feeling the jagged edges and cold metal.

For the thirty minutes it took to drive back to our home we rode in almost complete silence. Dad seemed to have a lot on his mind and was preoccupied with his thoughts. I started thinking about how calm he had seemed throughout the whole evening and wondered if it was because he had been in World War II.

"Maybe he is used to explosions," I thought to myself.

I tried not to think about what had happened back in the theater, but the images kept intruding. For a few minutes my thoughts drifted to the little that Dad had told us about his time in the Navy. He had enlisted shortly after graduating from Wesleyan University at age nineteen, and was ordered to Chicago for officer training at Northwestern University. He thus became one of the so-called ninety-day wonders, Dad had said at dinner once, but added that wasn't completely accurate because for thirty days they were apprentices, followed by ninety days as midshipmen, a total of one hundred and twenty days.

Dad had been asked to stay on as an instructor, but turned it down. "If I'd known then what I know now, I might not have been so rash and patriotic," he said.

He said that all the trainees asked for assignment aboard destroyers, but only one of them got his wish. He was killed six weeks later in the Pacific. Most of them were sent to Little Creek, Virginia, for landing craft training, but Dad and about six others were ordered to minesweepers, where he stayed for the remainder of the war.

"What was it that you didn't know then that you know now?" Tim had asked.

Dad had suddenly gotten this faraway look in his eyes and after about thirty seconds had said, "That is something I am never going to talk about. Ever."

Tim and I had later pulled down the "M" of the *Encyclopedia Britannica* from the high bookcase in Dad's study and looked up "minesweepers." We read about how those vessels neutralize mines. It seemed pretty clear that terrible things happened during the process.

I leaned up against the back seat of the Jeep, and I tried to picture what it would look like if something exploded in water. "It probably catapulted a giant foamy wave straight up out of the ocean," I now imagined, shuddering to think what that wave might contain. I wondered if Dad was seeing terrible things that he had witnessed during the war when he had that faraway look in his eyes.

"I will talk to Tim about it later," was my last thought as I began to doze off, my head resting on Tim's shoulder, my feet feeling tingly at the same time that my legs felt like they had a hundred-pound weight on them. I woke up with a start and began reciting the Lord's Prayer to myself. Memorizing that prayer in Sunday School felt like the only preparation I'd had for the possibility of death.

I awoke just as we pulled into the driveway. Dad helped my brother out of the car and got him up the front steps and into the house. I hurried in behind them because suddenly the house looked dark and foreboding. Usually I liked to stay outside, especially on a night like this one when the sky was clear. I would lie down on the front porch and look up into the heavens. Tim would frequently join me and we could spend over an hour debating which star we thought was the brightest one.

But tonight I did not want to be outside alone. Once inside I thought I would calm down, but I felt on edge and every time I heard the slightest noise it felt like my body went on alert, like there was a low electrical current buzzing through me.

Dad had gone into his study and I heard him on the phone. I was hungry and thirsty but was afraid to go into the kitchen — which was in the back of the house — by myself.

Dad came out and told us that he had to go to the prime minister's office. "You two will be okay here and I will only be gone a couple of hours."

I looked at Dad, trying to take in what he was saying.

He must have seen the expression of panic on my face because suddenly he said, "You and Tim can sleep in Mom's and my big bed tonight or at least till I get back."

He grabbed his jacket and hurried out the front door. I heard it slam and then the roar of the Jeep starting up.

I looked at Tim, "Are you scared?" I asked him.

"Not really," he said, "but I am really hungry."

"If I help you can you make it to the kitchen?" I asked.

"I think so," he said. "Just let me put my arm on your shoulder and hop so I don't put all my weight on the leg."

It took us a long time to get to the kitchen that way. Tim had put his arm on my shoulder and leaned into me and then on the count of three I had slowly stepped forward and he had pushed off with his good leg and jerked his body forward, holding the leg that hurt in the air. When we got into the kitchen I helped him over to one of the chairs at the kitchen table and then opened the fridge and got out a glass bottle of milk. I poured us each a glass and then went into the pantry and came back with a box of crackers and peanut butter. For about half an hour we made peanut butter and cracker sandwiches, piling them as high as we could to see if we could still fit them into our mouths. My limit was eight, but Tim managed to cram in a sandwich of ten before they crumpled and his mouth was covered in peanut butter and cracker crumbs.

"Okay, you win," I said, and fetched him a wet paper towel.

He wiped his mouth and I then wiped off the table and threw the remains of our feast into the trash.

"Do you think Mom and Nancy know anything that has happened?" I asked my brother as we hobbled back to Mom and Dad's room.

"I don't think so, not yet. Dad would not want them to worry," he said.

I helped Tim to get off his shoes and then lie down fully clothed under the covers. I went around to the other side and got in.

I was just about to turn off the light when Tim said, "Can you leave it on? Maybe Dad will need to have a light on when he gets back."

I looked at my brother for a second. He had just gotten his hair cut, a crew cut, and it made him look younger and more vulnerable than his ten years. I wished he could just tell me that he was scared, but he was already learning never to admit fear.

I could hear my dad's voice, "Never give in to fear," as I settled back on the pillows. I wanted Tim to keep talking. His voice calmed me.

I must have dozed on and off for a couple of hours. I kept waking up and thinking, "How long have I slept?" I picked up the book that I had been reading. It was from a series of mystery books that had appeared one morning on the dining room table after one of Dad's trips to the States. At the end of the first chapter you could choose one of five possible options for the main character to take and then, depending on the option you chose, you had five possible endings. Sometimes I would skip to the end and choose the outcome that I liked best. I wished that was how life was. I wished I could pick the best possible ending.

I looked over at the bedside clock to see that only ten, or fifteen, or twenty minutes had gone by. I went to my room and found my diary and wrote quickly but then put it away. I got back into the bed next to Tim whose sleep seemed unsettled, his breathing rapid. Every little noise would startle me out of sleep, and I kept listening for the rumble of the Jeep coming down the road that led to our home. Three or four times I climbed out of the bed and went to the window and peered through the metal shutters hoping to see that the Jeep had somehow pulled into the driveway unnoticed. A couple of times I was awakened by the laughter of the hyenas that roamed around the homes in our neighborhood eating any trash that had been left out.

At 4 a.m. I was sitting in the big armchair by the closet and suddenly the whole day's events came flooding back to me — getting dressed to go to the theater, choosing my seat and then moving to another seat, the first explosion, the second, getting out of the theater and then forcing my way back in, the sight of the bleeding flesh of the man's leg. I felt sick to my stomach. I opened the shutter and looked up into the night sky as though searching for a sign that might help me make sense of it all. But at that moment, the night sky that I loved gazing up into with Tim revealed nothing.

I slowly crawled back into bed and fell asleep only to wake up again in a sweat. The sheets were twisted around my body and I was clutching my pillow up to my chin. My mouth was dry and I felt feverish although when I reached up and felt my forehead it was cool. I so wished that Nancy and Mom were not in a different country on a faraway continent. I longed for Mom to be sitting by my bed wiping my forehead the way that she would when I was sick. I guess it must have been about five in the morning when I finally fell asleep.

"Martha, time to get up," I felt Dad's hand on my shoulder and slowly opened my eyes.

"You have a horse show this morning."

I rubbed my eyes. Dad was still dressed in his clothes from the night before and for a moment the events of the previous night were forgotten, and then suddenly it all came rushing back and I felt weak. I couldn't imagine taking Ben Hur over a six-foot fence at the show at the Italian Embassy this afternoon.

For a split second I thought about just saying, "No," but instead asked, "But what about my helmet, maybe I can't wear it and they won't let me compete without one?"

Dad looked at the bandage and said, "I don't think it will touch where the bandage is. Come on, get up."

I didn't meet his gaze, but in a low voice said, "I don't think I can ride today, Dad, I don't feel so good."

Dad looked at me and I could see that he was debating something in his mind.

"Martha," he said, "do you remember I mentioned to you once about the feud I had with Jimmy Romero when I was in seventh grade?"

I nodded.

"Well, we finally decided to have it out. He was a lot bigger than I was and probably a lot stronger and it was a really long afternoon."

I waited for him to continue and then he said, "Now, let's get going and I will have Worku ride over with you and I will meet you there before the first event."

I slowly swung my legs over the side of the bed and began to get up. Dad turned and began to walk out of the room.

"Who won the fight between you and Jimmy Romero?" I suddenly asked.

He stopped with his hand on the doorknob, turned around to me slowly and said, "I did."

He took a step forward, smiled at me and added, "He quit."

Then he walked out of the room.

We found out a few days later that, while there had been plots all over the city that night, the Empire Theater was the only place where plans had been carried out. There were reports that four people had been killed and more injured. I didn't know if the deaths were from the force of the explosion, from falling over the balcony from the mezzanine into the orchestra seats, or from being trampled by the crowd, and I tried not to think about it.

About three months later I began experiencing symptoms of what many years later would become known as post-traumatic stress. I did not know what it was and I never said a word about it to anyone. I was beginning to keep more and more to myself. The flashbacks of being in the movie theater carried the most intense kind of fear and horror, containing all the helplessness, loss of control, and threat of death that the original grenade explosion had carried. I would be at home doing my homework in my bedroom and all of a sudden I would start to "hear" screams and "see" the mangled arm of the man who had been sitting in my original seat. I had difficulty with sudden movements and unexpected noises, and always felt on edge. I never knew when my mind and body would suddenly be pulled back in time with a terrible sense of panic accompanied by a massive charge of electricity running through my body. And I felt guilty that because I had moved my seat a man had probably lost his leg.

One time I talked to Worku about it although I did not tell him about what I would see or hear. We were coming home from a long ride.

"I keep thinking about the seat," I said to him. "About the man who took my seat. If I hadn't moved that would have been me with my leg and arm blown up. He just took a seat and look what happened to him. I moved and was spared that."

It felt like I was trying to find some kind of meaning to how random it all felt to me.

Worku had been quiet for a few moments and then said, "Every day when we go riding, when we reach the top of the hill we have to pull the horses to a complete stop so we are sure no cars are coming around the corner."

I nodded wondering why he was telling me this.

"So perhaps every time you are able to pull Martini to a full stop, without knowing it, you just missed a bad accident. Maybe this man has missed something bad happening to him every day. But this time for no real reason that we can understand, he was the one that something terrible happened to."

That afternoon I had ridden in the horse show and I had taken first place. I had seen my father in the front row of spectators smiling and applauding as I went forward to receive the first-place trophy. For years I couldn't understand why Dad had insisted I ride that day and it was not until many years later that I could see that he was telling me something important about myself — that I was tough and resilient and that it was important not to quit.

Today, years and years later, among all the complex feelings I have about my father, I feel grateful he instilled that lesson in me.

Worku leads me on my first horseback ride at age 2.

Feeding Taffy and Mac from baby bottles.

Me on Palomine in our front yard.

Franco, my trainer, and me.

Tim and me in the ceremonial parade before the show jumping finals.

Ben Hur and I clear a fence in the final jump off.

Nancy, Tim and me horsing around.

My parents' favorite picture of me at age 12.

Kenn, around the time I met him at summer Bible school.

My father out hunting with local villagers.

My father and his buddy Nick at the end of a hunting trip.

My father, Nancy, Tim and me with our dog Jambo (the Solulta plains in the background)..

My father on the piano with the jazz trio.

Our dining room decorated for the French bistro party.

The 100-meter finals at the National Stadium (me on far left).

Receiving my 2nd-place medal for the 100-meter race.

The medal winners of the 100-meter finals.

Our family leaving Ethiopia.

Sileshi with my children, Alex and Becca, soon after his arrival in the U.S.

Sileshi, Tim and me in 2016.

~ Chapter 12 ~

MARINES

I was beginning to feel a greater and greater sense of unease, as though the flowers and trees and dirt were hinting at something happening in Ethiopia that had not yet fully appeared, and whose ultimate form was as yet unknown. Unsettling spirits born of this land's history seemed constantly to drift in and hover like dark clouds, and I was too impossibly young to understand why I felt personally threatened by what was happening in Ethiopia. I knew from past experience that clouds gather until a storm breaks, but I never knew when it would come, or how deadly it would be. That night at the movie theater had seemed like just another evening — until suddenly it wasn't. And Dad's mundane hunting trip had instantly changed into a waking nightmare. And then there was that day when three American Marines showed up at our compound, bringing yet more ominous shadows.

The day before the Marines came, I was awakened by sunlight streaming in through the slats in the metal shutter that was pulled down over my window every night. Squinting as my eyes began to adjust to the bright light I quickly got out of bed, pulled on my socks and, still wearing the pair of sweats and a t-shirt that I liked to sleep in, crept down the hall carrying my rubber boots in my hand. Once outside, I pulled them on and then quickly ran down the side yard splashing through the puddles that had left the ground still wet and soggy after a torrential rainfall during the night. I arrived at the stables just as Worku was coming around from the back carrying a huge bale of hay over his head, his biceps visible through the thin shirt he wore.

"Start filling the buckets with clean water," he instructed, and I grabbed the hose and did as I was told.

I loved spending time with Worku. He was an Amhara, like Beheilu, Mamo, and Belaynesh. Dad told me that most of the men he worked with were Amharas and that they possessed great political skill and were the traditional ruling class. Worku seemed very proud of his Amhara heritage and he loved explaining Amharic phrases to me. He told me that personal names had meanings beyond the name.

I told him I had a friend at school named Asfa Wossen and he told me that Asfa Wossen meant "to expand the border," and that the popular name for a girl Asselefech meant "she made them line up."

Now I watched Worku divide up the hay and throw a section of it into each stall. Half an hour later, the six horses were fed and their stalls mucked out and, suddenly realizing that the rest of the household would be getting ready for breakfast, I tore back up to the house and into the kitchen.

"French toast if you get here in time and Nancy and Tim have not eaten it all," Beheilu called after me laughing, and snapped a dish towel in my direction as I ran through the room and back to my bedroom.

I dressed quickly and got to the dining room table where Tim and Nancy and my mother were already eating.

"How long is Dad going to be away?" Tim asked my mother.

"He is in New York now and will be stopping off in Athens on his way back a week from now," she answered.

I looked at Nancy out of the corner of my eye. After finishing junior high in Switzerland Nancy continued at Saint Stephen's Boarding School in Rome. But now she was back, having been expelled from Saint Stevens for sneaking out with three other girls. They were unlucky enough to get caught up in a police raid of the drug dealers and prostitutes on the Spanish Steps in Rome and had landed themselves in an Italian jail for a night. The morning after Dad received the phone call that she had been expelled and that he needed to fly up to Rome to get her, I had heard him playing a mournful song on the piano, and when I said goodbye to him as he left for the airport his eyes seemed red and puffy as though he had been crying. Or maybe it was just my imagination.

So now Nancy was home, fifteen going on sixteen and totally rebellious, using every occasion when Dad was away to sneak out at night. She'd put an extra blanket to look like a body under her covers and, leaving Tim and me with strict instructions and veiled threats to divert our mother from coming into her room, she would climb over the back wall and meet up with some of the other American and European teenagers, most of whom were a good three or four years older than she was. The one time Dad caught on that she was gone, he drove around Addis for two hours going into all of the local bars and joints where the U.S. Marines and older teens hung out until he had found her. He threatened the young Marine with his arm around Nancy that he would report him to the Marine colonel for luring in under-age girls if he ever saw him around his daughter again. Holding Nancy tightly by her shoulders Dad marched her out of the bar and drove her home. I'd heard the front door slam and an angry exchange between them.

"What did he say to you?" I asked my sister the next afternoon when we were alone in her room.

"He told me to wipe off the lipstick I was wearing and then he didn't say a word to me that made any sense," she told me dejectedly. "But I've been grounded for a month. What is this, a prison?"

Uh-oh, I thought to myself, now she'll figure out more creative ways to sneak out, and Tim and I will have to cover for her even more carefully.

"And now the young Marines will steer clear of me," she added in one of those rare moments when she almost treated me like a peer.

She was drinking a coke and pulled the bottle up close to her chest. I suddenly noticed that her face seemed to have become more angular than it was a year ago, her cheekbones more prominent, her eyes blue liquid under straight darker brows. And now her face was flushed with anger and frustration. She drew her lips together in a tight line and brushed her hair back with the sweep of a hand. I waited, hoping she would say more.

"But that won't ever stop me from having fun," she continued, fiercely throwing herself on her bed, the coke bottle held high above her head so its contents wouldn't spill out.

I looked at my older sister in awe. To me she seemed fearless and becoming more and more so. She was now attending the American Community School in Addis while Tim and I were still at the German School. I thought about the fact that we lived in a compound with a high stone wall around it to keep danger out. I wondered if Dad had hoped that the high stone wall would also keep Nancy in.

The bus ride to school one particular morning had been uneventful until about ten minutes before we got there. As the bus came around Sidist Kilo, we suddenly saw hundreds of police with bayonets heading in the direction of the university, which was a few blocks from our school. In the past month, the relentless drive of the university students, whose demands for change grew more and more intense, seemed to be spilling out beyond the university grounds. Sileshi told us that students were being rounded up suspected of painting anti-government slogans on walls and for distributing pamphlets.

Twice in the past month, while we had been out for recess, our eyes started stinging and watering as the tear gas being used to quell the rioting had drifted down to the grounds of our school. When we got back to our homeroom, our teacher asked if any of us wanted to see the nurse. He wanted to say more. I could sense it by the way his eyes focused on each of us, but then he turned to the board where the geography lesson was laid out. There had been a time when I felt as though I could tell what was going on outside our home by what went on inside, by the mood of those who worked for us, by how much they laughed and teased me and chatted with one another.

But now the riots and demonstrations seemed to make everything feel more unpredictable; and the prior week, when the bus had pulled out of the school driveway for the trip home, we were suddenly surrounded by students with banners, their surging bodies an invisible force moving the throng forward. They pounded their fists on our bus. Suddenly the soldiers were among them and the soldiers pushed and shoved anyone who was in their way. A few of the students fell to the ground. Right in front of me a student yelled something at one of the soldiers, who lifted his rifle and hit him in the head with the butt of his weapon. The student fell to the ground and a dark pool of blood oozed onto the pavement. I both wanted to look out of the window and was afraid to, and not until the bus made a right turn while the rioters and soldiers continued straight did I realize that my shoulders were hunched up and I was gripping the headrest of the seat in front of me.

I looked over at Tim.

"Are you okay?" he mouthed at me.

I nodded although I didn't feel okay and wished that I was sitting with Tim. I looked at the boy next to him. He was staring at his hands folded tightly in his lap. For the rest of the ride home, I pulled my legs up toward my chest and rested my head on them telling myself that my fear was nothing compared to the fear that the students must have been feeling. I tried to silence the noises in my head, and felt a wave of relief when Tim and I walked through the gate into the compound and I saw that my mother's little blue Volkswagen buggy was parked in the driveway, and, when I came into the kitchen, saw that Nancy's schoolbag had been thrown carelessly across the back of one of the wooden chairs.

"Good," I said to no one in particular, "that means we are all home."

A few nights earlier I had been eavesdropping outside Mom and Dad's bedroom door. At first their voices were too low for me to make out what they were saying but then I heard snippets of sentences about "political unrest," and "things in this country are not changing fast enough," and "our family's safety will always come first." I had snuck back into my room and when I couldn't fall asleep read my Nancy Drew books for what seemed like hours.

It was a Friday and because we had just finished our midterm exams that meant no school the next day. I had thought earlier about telling Mom what we had seen from the school bus, but decided I didn't want to worry her, especially because she always seemed a little more on edge when my father was out of the country. The rest of the afternoon passed uneventfully. We all ate an early dinner together. Beheilu had made meatloaf, and after a couple of rounds of hearts, which was a favorite family card game, we went to our own rooms for the rest of the night. I wanted to get a good night's sleep because Saturday night a costume dance was being held for the sixth, seventh, and eighth graders. I wished that Kenn was going to be there but no one who didn't go to the German School was permitted to come.

"Don't go falling in love with someone else," he said when I told him about the dance.

I shook my head, and said softly, "Of course not."

My best girlfriend at the German School, Makeda, who was a boarding student but would occasionally spend her weekends with us, told me that you always wanted to keep a boy guessing whether you really liked him or not. That didn't make any sense to me. If you liked someone why not just tell them? Since Makeda lived at the boarding school I wondered whether maybe you felt differently about things when you lived so far away from your parents. Somehow the boarding school students seemed a little older than the rest of us.

During the years that Nancy was away at boarding school I would often watch Makeda and the other boarding students and wonder what Nancy was doing. Did she miss me as much as I missed her? There were always so many questions that I wanted to ask her, especially once I started liking Kenn. Makeda and I had an easygoing friendship and we tried to sit next to each other in as many of our classes as we could. I loved having a best friend that I could talk to about the things girls like to talk about. There were just some things that you wanted to know another female's opinion of. And on the weekends that Makeda spent with us we would stay up late into the night talking and laughing.

My mother had taken me to a material store and I had picked out a velvety leopard print, and the dressmaker had skillfully transformed the cloth into a skirt and top and mask that covered the top half of my face. She had cut holes into the mask around the eyes so I could see out, and sewn short little feathers above the eyes to look like lashes. Nancy was going to lend me her brown knee-high suede boots, and while her feet were two sizes bigger than mine, with two pairs of socks they fit me.

When Nancy saw my costume she said, "That mask will get pretty warm. I will do your eye makeup like a cat and then even once you take the mask off you will be in character."

I fell asleep fairly easily that night. Saturday morning seemed like any other morning. I helped Worku feed and groom the horses. He left after his chores were done. Everyone who worked for us alternated having Saturdays and Sundays off unless my parents were hosting a big party, or there was a horse show and then Worku got the Monday off. I started a big history project that I had for school. My leopard outfit was hanging on my closet door and, as I carefully drew and colored in a map of Europe during the Middle Ages, I would glance over at it every now and again and let my mind wander to the upcoming dance.

It must have been close to twelve noon when I heard what sounded like a Jeep or a Land Rover come into the compound. I couldn't imagine who it was since Dad was out of town, but I heard the vehicle pull up to the front door and then the sound of men's voices. By the time I got to the front door my mother was standing there with three men in uniform.

"Martha, go get Nancy and Tim," she said quietly.

Nancy and Tim must have heard the vehicles as well because they were already coming down the hall when I went to get them.

Once back on the porch we all stood in a row looking at the men. One of them stepped forward. He was lean and his close-cropped hair was barely visible under his cap. He took off the cap and ran his hand through his silver hair, the color reminding me of the tea service that Mom was always asking Mamo to polish. He was wearing a green coat, green trousers, a khaki web belt, khaki tie and black shoes. He had a number of ribbons on the epaulette.

"I am Captain Philips, and this is Lance Corporal Johnson, and Private First Class Davis," he said formally. "And we are stationed at the American Embassy."

He paused for a few seconds but none of us said anything, and clearing his throat he continued, "And I have been asked to speak to you on behalf of the ambassador."

Again he stopped speaking, but it was as though the four of us had been struck mute.

Only Tim leaned over and whispered to me, "They are Marines."

Captain Philips started speaking again. "You most likely are not aware of this, but a coup against the Emperor has been uncovered, the two generals who were planning it arrested, but we do not know how many others were involved yet."

He shifted uncomfortably.

I suddenly wondered if any of these Marines had been in the bar the night Nancy had been hauled out by Dad.

"The city will have a curfew tonight and there has been a ban on all demonstrations."

He stopped speaking and my mother said, "Go on." But she leaned up against the back of one of the porch chairs as though to steady herself.

He stiffened his shoulders and continued, "We do not think you are in any danger, but when the list of families to be taken hostage was found, because of your husband's position in the prime minister's office, your name was on that list."

He bowed his head ever so slightly as he finished speaking.

None of us spoke. I watched my mother drift backwards and I thought she might fall over but then she regained her balance as she reached out and put her hand on Tim's shoulder and left it there.

Captain Philips spoke in a commanding tone and told us that one of them would check on us throughout the day.

"Why can't you stay here the whole time?" my mother asked quietly.

The Captain must have sensed the fear in my mother's voice because his tone became gentler as he explained that unfortunately most of their unit was up in Asmara at the U.S. base and that he was needed at the embassy. "We have no concrete reason to think you are in danger," he said, "but we are being very cautious."

"What should we do?" my mother asked.

"We understand that your husband has a lot of hunting shot-guns and ammunition in your house."

I watched my mother nod at the Captain.

"You don't want anyone to get access to firearms so we want you to empty the guns and hide all of the bullets."

"Hide everything?" Nancy spoke for the first time and stepped forward, and I watched her closely to see if there was a hint of rec-ognition on her or the Marines' faces.

I noticed how much taller than my mother she was now.

"Yes," Captain Philips said to Nancy, "hide everything or at least empty the guns and hide all the boxes of shells."

"Does your husband own a revolver?" he turned his attention back to my mother. "One of you needs to be prepared to use it."

"Yes," she said, and I sensed her anxiety.

"I'll get it," Tim turned and ran back into the house reappearing a few minutes later with Dad's gun.

"He keeps it in his bedside table," Tim said and handed it to the Marine.

My mother shrank slightly back away from the gun, her hands locked in a tight fist. The Marine started to say something.

"You can teach me," Nancy said and stepped in front of my mother. "I already know how to use a shotgun."

I was suddenly aware that I had been holding my breath and I tried to force air deep into my lungs, but my chest was tight. It felt as though the scene in front of me was suddenly enveloped in a thin wispy layer of haze. I squinted to try to bring everything into focus, but the mist I was trying to peer through was too thick. The Marine named Lance Corporal Johnson stepped forward. He seemed way too young to be a Marine; he looked like he couldn't be more than nineteen or twenty years old. The shirt that peeked out of the collar of his jacket was blended with his deeply tanned skin where his neck met the top of the shirt. His eyes were green with brown flecks in them.

He asked Tim and me to show him where the guns were and I noticed that his eyes didn't seem to blink. Nancy and my mother had moved over to the side of the porch with the other two men.

221

My brother and I turned and led the Marine silently in the semi-darkness down the hall towards Dad's office. The hallway was unadorned and felt barren and lonely to me. The only sound was the "clack-clack" of the Marine's boots on the hard wooden floor as he walked behind us. I was moving so slowly that Tim nudged me along, no doubt sensing the reluctance in my step. My legs felt clumsy and stiff, so unlike the legs under me when I ran.

We got to the office and Tim pointed to the far wall where the case that held Dad's six shotguns was. The Marine tried to turn the knob, but it was securely locked. I suddenly thought about the time Dad told me that power in Ethiopia was almost always gained militarily.

"The poorer people would often place themselves under the protection of a powerful landowner and using arms was unquestioned in a feudal society," he had said.I had asked him what a feudal society was and he said that the peasants didn't own the land but worked for the big landowners who kept most of the profits.

"That doesn't seem very fair," I'd said.

"No," Dad had answered, "it isn't."

I was jarred back to the present by the young Marine's voice. "Do you know how to open this?" He directed the question to Tim although his eyes watched me, and I lowered my gaze and crossed my arms across my chest. I felt uncomfortable with the way that older boys and men had begun to notice me. I tried to study the Marine without making any kind of eye contact peeking out through the lashes of my lowered eyes.

Tim went over to Dad's desk and found the drawer that held the key. He rummaged around for a few seconds and then pulled out the key and put it in the Marine's outstretched hand. Opening the case, the Marine lifted the guns one after another off their racks and then handed each gun to Tim who lined them up against Dad's desk.

The Marine found an empty box and instructed, "I am going to empty the guns; pick up the cartridges and put them in the box."

Each gun held about eight cartridges and as they fell one after another Tim and I scrambled to retrieve them from the hard wooden floor.

When the guns were emptied the Marine said to us that there were about fifty boxes of shells and he wanted us to hide them, five boxes at a time. He turned, stiffening his posture, and marched out of the room.

Tim looked over at me and he shifted from one foot to the other.

Then we heard three shots from the area near the porch and Tim said, "I guess Nancy knows how to shoot Dad's pistol."

I felt my stomach contract, and a lump in my throat made swallowing difficult.

"Where should we hide these?" Tim asked, gesturing toward the boxes.

I had been thinking about that from the moment we had first been told to hide Dad's ammunition. My mind roamed around the back yard thinking about various possibilities.

"Let's get these outside first," I said to Tim.

We could each carry five boxes at a time, so it was five trips back and forth to get the boxes out of Dad's study, down the hallway and through the main part of the house, through the kitchen and then down the back steps. Neither of us spoke until we had all the boxes piled up at the foot of the stairs. I surveyed the back yard, my eyes moving from the large lawn to the eucalyptus trees where the tree house was.

"What now?" Tim asked.

"I'm thinking, I'm thinking, give me a minute," I said sharply, and immediately regretted my tone when I saw a hurt look sweep across my brother's face for a second.

"Sorry," I mumbled quickly.

Dad always told me to think about books when I wanted to find a solution to a problem and suddenly I thought about Nancy Drew, a series I was currently reading about a young girl who always had to find her way out of some kind of difficult predicament. I wondered what she might do in this situation. I closed my eyes and waited for an image to appear.

"Go get the bread knife," I said to Tim. "I have an idea."

Tim ran back up the stairs and, collecting five of the boxes of shells in my arms, I walked out onto the yard toward the eucalyptus grove. The ground was covered with grass, but as you got closer to the trees the grass was not as thick and the ground became much softer. I stumbled over some roots hidden by leaves, and my legs felt unsteady.

Tim was back with the serrated bread knife and I said, "Okay, let's get some shovels and a wheelbarrow from the shed."

"Are you scared? "Tim asked me.

"Yes," I answered. "You?"

I looked at him.

"Not really," he answered, but I knew he was lying by the way he avoided eye contact.

And in any case, Tim was not only my younger brother but my best friend, and I could sense things about him that betrayed what he said. Under his thin white t-shirt I could I see his chest fluttering.

We got the supplies from the shed and then I took the knife and carefully cut a square about one foot deep into the earth. I gently pushed the knife back and forth trying to keep the patch of grass and dirt intact. I glanced around a couple of times feeling as though there were eyes watching my every movement.

"Okay," I said to Tim, "try to lift this grass patch up and after we have buried the boxes we'll put it back and hope it will camouflage that anything is buried here."

"Which one is your favorite of the two Hardy Boys, Frank or Joe?" I asked Tim, referring to the series he was currently reading. Tim and I both loved to read. Sometimes if Mom and Dad were out late at night we'd read aloud to each other. We would slip into character as we read and I'd throw my arms in the air, stomp my feet or pretend to cry or rage as it seemed to me the character in the book might have.

Tim thought for a minute and replied, "Joe. He'll jump right into a situation whereas Frank tends to stand back and think about things."

"Good," I said. "So pretend you are Joe and I will be Nancy Drew and we are going to hide all these bullets."

I wished I was Nancy Drew; I wished I was anyone but Martha Paradis right then. Over the next three hours I operated like a person with only one goal, a goal that was driving me above all else. I worked like a madwoman, bathed in sweat, fighting hunger and thirst. But a question kept coming into my mind unbidden: If we were taken hostage, would we all be kept together, or would we be separated? Would they put us in different rooms and slam the door shut like a giant mouth enveloping each of us? I just kept telling myself that back on the Solulta plains they had let Dad go, so maybe we'd all be okay.

Tim worked beside me as we moved from one patch of ground to another covering about a twenty-five foot area under the eucalyptus trees. Looking over at Tim from time to time I realized how much he was beginning to look like Mom. He had her same soft clear blue eyes, and her chin, and the slant of his head was hers. A few birds flew over us, coming so close that we almost could feel the breeze of their wings in the arid, stagnant air. I thought about the fact that Sileshi had not shown up as he usually did on Saturday afternoons. I wondered if he knew what was happening. I lay down on the grass for a few minutes, hoping that the earth would somehow calm me. I must have dozed off, because I awoke with a start. I had dreamed about Astatke, our former cook. Although I could barely remember him and could no longer summon up even the palest image of him, he sometimes appeared in my dreams as though I was trying to call him up from the emptiness. I had been trying to touch him, to find his face in the darkness.

"Are you okay?" I heard Tim's voice above me. I wanted him to keep talking so I just nodded wearily." His voice calmed me.

Tim and I were about to head up to the house when Nancy appeared, carrying a pitcher of lemonade for us.

"Where is Mom?" I asked her.

"She called Dad, but it took her about an hour to reach him," she said. "And now she has gone up to Colonel Nolan's."

The U.S. air attaché was our closest American neighbor and lived about fifteen minutes away. Nancy squatted down on a nearby tree stump and surveyed the area where we had dug the holes and hidden the ammunition.

"Try to pack the dirt down more," she said. "That way it won't look like the earth has been disturbed."

I heard the rumble of two cars coming down the road and looked up toward the iron gate at the front of our compound. Followed by Mom's little buggy was a military Jeep and seated in it was Colonel Nolan with Sandy, his daughter, in the seat next to him. Sandy was Nancy's friend and a partner in many of her crimes.

Nancy, Tim and I walked up to the vehicles and Colonel Nolan asked Tim and me, "Everything buried?" as he stepped out of the Jeep.

We both nodded.

"What do we do now?" Tim asked, looking back and forth between Mom and the Colonel.

"I got off the phone with your dad a few minutes ago," Colonel Nolan said, "and he wants you all to proceed as though everything is normal."

My mother turned to me, saying, "I have asked Frau Dietrich to give you a ride to the school for the dance."

Frau Dietrich was a German neighbor whose son, Thomas, was in my class.

"She will be here in an hour. Nancy can help you get ready."

My mother looked visibly shaken. I did not want to make it worse for her so I didn't say a word but just turned and began to walk back up to the house.

As children what do we really know about our parents, the father and mother who brought us into this world and have known us since our birth? If we are lucky, many, many years later we may be blessed with a deepening clarity of who our parents were, of where they came from and the events that shaped and molded them, of the demons and wounds that were part of their history.

And how well when we are children do our parents know us? Did mine know that sometimes my mind would be pulled back to the day of the coup, or the night of the grenades, or the terror of watching Dad being led away during the hunting expedition? Those memories were like ghosts that had settled in my mind uninvited, or perhaps I just kept summoning up demons because I was trying to overcome them. In those next moments, though,

226

as I trudged back to the house, I could not comprehend how they could not know that, for me, the most terrifying thought was to be separated from my family in the midst of possible danger.

I thought back to the time that Mom and Dad had been in Israel and something called the Six Day War had broken out. I heard something about it at school but when I asked Captain Hills, who I was staying with, what was happening, he had basically ignored my question. That night after everyone else had gone to bed, I had gotten my small transistor radio and tried to tune in to Radio America to find out what was going on and whether my parents were safe.

And now Colonel Nolan had told us that Dad wanted us to proceed with our lives as though everything was normal. But it didn't feel normal. I sensed that Dad did not like to see fear in us and wondered if perhaps there was a message in his insistence that I go to the costume party even though it was the last place in the world I wanted to be. I wanted to be home with Mom, Nancy and Tim. But maybe he was telling me that even though I was afraid I needed to not give in to the fear but overcome it.

I glanced at my watch as I entered my room, and saw that I had about half an hour before Nancy would start doing my makeup for the dance. I climbed into my bed, hoping I could fall asleep, but instead a recent conversation with Dad came back to me. I had heard snippets of conversation over the years about the coup of 1960. These conversations between my parents always came to an abrupt halt if Tim or I came into the room. From the little I had managed to overhear, though, I knew that my father had been directly involved in some kind of hostage negotiation. I wasn't even sure what that meant. I kept hoping that I would find an opportunity to ask Dad about it more directly, and a few weeks earlier that moment had presented itself.

In the neighborhood one day, an Ethiopian friend of mine whose father had not survived the coup had told me a story about Dad. He said that Dad had brought his mother her husband's gold wedding band and a note hastily written on the back of an envelope one night after the attempted coup.

I then asked Dad about it and he had reminded me that this was the time when we had gone to stay at the American Embassy for a few days during the coup of 1960, when I was about six.

"A message had been sent to the embassy," Dad said, "from the rebels who were holed up at the Guenette Leul Palace, asking the American Ambassador to try and stop the fighting. Bill McGhee, the number two man at the embassy, and I agreed to go with him. I was told that many of my friends from the Prime Minister's office and other ministries were being held as hostages."

Dad had paused and taken in a deep breath before going on with the story.

"When we arrived at the palace the military officers who had staged the coup asked us to take a message to the loyal army headquartered out on the Bishoftu Road. We went in the official embassy car with flags flying."

His voice sounded deeper, almost unfamiliar. I didn't want Dad to stop talking and I held my breath as if any movement might spoil this moment of candor with Dad when he seemed really to be answering one of my questions.

I probed hesitantly. "What did you see along the way? Was there fighting?"

"There were tanks at the square guarding the Ministry of Defense and foot soldiers marching up the hill alongside armored vehicles. Tragically, the leaders of the army said no to a cease fire. I told them that I thought a blunt 'No' would leave the rebels no choice and that their first act would be to kill the hostages they had at the palace. I refused to go back to the palace with the Ambassador because I felt so strongly that the message they were delivering would seal the fate of the hostages, my close friends, men I worked with every day and who have been in our home for cocktail parties and dinners."

"What happened?" I asked Dad quietly.

"Well, when the army tanks broke into the compound of the palace, fourteen of the sixteen hostages were killed by the two rebel generals."

Dad was staring out of the window and I wasn't even sure that he knew he was talking to me.

I waited and then asked as softly as I could, "Why did you have their wedding rings?"

Dad looked up, cleared his throat and shook his head as though wiping away a memory. He paused, as though he needed to overcome some obstacle within himself. He picked up the glass of water on his desk and drained it quickly.

"I think they suspected they might not get out of the palace alive and they wanted something to be given to their wives and families."

He stopped speaking and I waited, not daring to breathe lest I stop him. He was silent and it was clear he was not going to say any more. In the hush that followed. Dad seemed to pull all of his external self into his core and then it was almost as though he managed to absent himself from himself and his eyes seemed vacant, devoid of all emotion as he looked at me. I wanted to wrap my arms around him, but instead I got up and quietly left the room leaving Dad with his thoughts. I knew better than to press for places where Dad's feelings had taken refuge.

As I lay in bed I felt my legs ache from the hours of kneeling on the hard ground as we hid the bullets. But Mom had told me that I would be going to the dance.I got out of bed and slowly put on my leopard costume.

Nancy had all her makeup spread out in front of her. As frequently happened in Addis, there was a power outage and our faces glowed in the candlelight. Nancy had positioned Dad's gun right next to the compact of powder. I reached forward for a second wanting to touch the cold metal but she shook her head.

"Don't," she said quietly, "it is loaded."

She put dark black eyeliner on my eyes and then took an eyebrow pencil and drew cat's whiskers above and below them. We didn't say much to each other as she worked on my face.

"Close your eyes, stop squirming, try to keep still," she instructed me.

"Did you learn how to shoot the gun?" I asked her.

She nodded.

"Would you shoot someone if it meant protecting us?" I continued.

She looked at me for a few seconds, her mouth a tight line and then she nodded again.

When we heard Frau Dietrich's car pull up to the gate, I twisted away from her.

Nancy stood up, reached out and put her hand on my shoulder and, as I turned in response to her touch, she looked straight at me and said in a voice much gentler than her usual tone, "Martha, you look nice. Try to have fun."

I stared out the window. The moon illuminated the front yard, making the eucalyptus trees appear to extend into the heavens, and casting a silvery glow over the gravel driveway.

I still didn't move and Nancy reached out and took my hand and squeezed it gently, a secret gesture that let me know that she loved me and would do all she could to protect me even as she and her school friends would tease and torment me. I didn't answer her but went to the front of the house and out onto the porch and then down the four steps. I could see my own pale reflection in the living room window as I turned towards the car. I heard the phone ring in some distant part of the house. And then, as the car pulled out of the driveway and I looked back at my home, it felt as though time had just stopped.

There are flickering moments of my childhood that I cannot capture entirely unless I open my diaries. Without the words that I had put to paper I can recall them only as fragments of memory. Or sometimes I feel a sudden flood of emotion when something happens today that feels unrelated to the present event and I find my thoughts pulled back to Ethiopia, and the past and present become somehow confused. And I pull out my diaries to try to make sense of what I am feeling.

What I do know for sure though is that the terror that I held in my body seeped into my cells that night as I refused invitation after invitation from the eighth-grade boys to dance. I couldn't eat or drink or keep my mind focused on the music. Makeda sensed that something wasn't right with me and asked me about it, but I just shook my head. And she didn't ask me again but stayed close by me the rest of the night as though her presence might provide some comfort. No one broke into our home that night but my prayers for my family's safety became more pleading and the fear of ever being held hostage became a theme of my nightmares.

Dad returned a week later and that Sunday told my brother and me to go and dig up all the ammunition we had hidden. While it had taken us hours to bury the boxes of shells, it took us days to find them all. The earth had settled, a rainstorm had soaked the ground and because we had not marked the bullets' graves, Tim and I dug hole after hole trying to find them.

~ Chapter 13 ~

LEAVING

In everyone's childhood there are certain events that leave an indelible impression and have a lifelong impact. I remember the day we left Ethiopia a lot better than I remember what happened a few days or a month ago. It is still crystal clear, the way children etch moments as if in a block of granite — the temperature that day, the sound of people's voices and the encompassing emotion. If I close my eyes, almost half a century later, it all comes back.

At the end of my seventh-grade year Dad and Mom told us that we would be leaving Ethiopia, and moving to England. The political situation in the country was far too unstable for us to remain, and I also think our parents had wanted us to experience another culture before we went back to the States for our college years. Dad told us London would be a fun city, but I was unmoved. Nancy seemed a little more excited about it.

"The Beatles live there, and Eric Clapton," she told me. "And there will be so many more things for us to do, and Dad says he will have to travel so he won't be able to keep me on such a short leash."

Whenever I saw Belaynesh, Mamo or Beheilu I would fling my arms around them, sobbing. They tried to comfort me but it was of no use as their eyes would well up and I would cry harder. I think we all knew that we might never see one another again.

I was sitting on the steps of the front porch one late afternoon and Beheilu came and sat down next to me. We sat in silence for a few minutes and then I turned to him. The wind picked up, causing the branches of the eucalyptus trees to sway back and forth, the sound like a hoarse whisper.

"I don't want to leave," I said. "Ethiopia is my home."

He put his arm around me and said, his voice husky, "Go into your life, Martha, with an open heart. Life will break your heart, but if you let it, it will also open it."

I didn't answer him and we just continued to look out towards the mountains and listen to the sound of the swaying branches.

Tim did not cry once — at least I didn't see him cry — but seemed to turn all of his feelings inward. He had gotten quieter and quieter and rarely laughed or joked with me.

"Tim, tell me what you are thinking," I said to him one evening as we rode home from Jan Hoy Meda.

"Look there, Martha, the moon is about to come over the hill," he said softly, ignoring my question.

"Don't change the subject," I persisted. "What are you feeling?"

Tim was quiet for a minute, a puzzled expression creasing his forehead.

"That's the problem," he said. "At moments I start to feel and then I don't feel anything."

We rode along in silence. It felt like my brother was withdrawing into a world where I could not reach him and it frightened me. Was it possible that a family could suffer a collective nervous breakdown and was that what might happen to us?

Together Tim and I had been told to take on the responsibility of giving away all of our pets — the three bigger dogs, six horses, the ostrich and chicken and three sheep. Each separation was agony for me. I was so afraid that the animals' new owners would not treat them well, except for the little bit of comfort I felt that Martini would be going to a girl named Ellen, who was roughly my age and rode at Jan Hoy Meda. I knew she would be good to him. Every time we had found a new family for one of the horses I went to the stable for a final goodbye. Leaving Taffy was especially hard for me because she had been a baby when we got her. The night before she would be picked up I slowly walked down to the stable after dinner. I sat down on a bale of hay next to her. She took a step toward me and gently nuzzled my head, and I reached up and began to stroke the silky-smooth hair behind her ear.

Jambo, our golden Lab, came into the stall with a ball in his mouth and looked up at me tilting his head.

"I'm sorry," I said, "I just can't play right now."

Dropping the ball, Jambo flopped down on the floor, his ears drooped and he looked up at me again, then put his head down on his paws and let out a whimper. The three of us just stayed like that for about half an hour. Before I walked out of the stall I clipped off bits of the horses' manes and put them into baggies so that I would be sure to remember exactly what the soft hair felt like. Only little Poupee, my scruffy little dog, would be shipped to England where she would have to spend six months in quarantine.

I couldn't imagine ever sleeping in a different bed from the one that I'd slept in the past nine years. I found it hard to sleep at night. I started getting up an hour earlier than I needed to and I ran back and forth to the Kebena River. I ran until my legs hurt and my feet had blisters on them. It was almost as if I hoped that by punishing my body I could keep my heart from breaking.

Two weeks before our departure I asked my brother to go down to the river with me, but this time instead of running we walked slowly through the fields and down the hill that led to the river. On the horizon I could barely see where the path we were on disappeared into the mountains. It was midday and hotter than usual. When we got to the river we waded out to the middle. I swam out into the deeper waters and dove down, and opening my eyes I could see the bottom clearly. My body felt like I was swimming into a veil of pure silk and when I surfaced I floated on my back for a few minutes.

Often after swimming on a day like this one when it was hot, we'd climb up on a large rock that rose out of the water with a platform on top large enough for Tim and me to lie on. We'd let the breeze and the sun dry us. Sometimes we'd talk and sometimes we'd just sit there listening to the water rush by below us. Today it was hot and sticky. Even the few flies seemed to be suffering from the heat, their buzzing listless and sluggish. I thought about how many hours we had spent skipping stones at the river, how we could spend a half hour first finding the right stone, not too light with the proper edge so you could spin it off your finger, how you'd have to twist and bend to throw it at just the right angle.

I looked over at my brother.

"I read that it rains all the time in London," I said, startling Tim.

He turned and looked at me, droplets of water glistening in his hair.

"Not like the rains here," I continued, "where the water pours out of the sky for weeks and weeks. Not the way you and I watch the clouds grow thicker and darker, more and more bloated until they burst and the water that comes pouring down is so fresh and clear. No, it sounds like a nonstop drizzle. And it is grey a lot of the time."

"Ugh," Tim said, "I hate playing soccer in the mud. I hope our new school will at least have a decent soccer team."

"Who knows," I shrugged my shoulders. "It will be weird though to have all of our subjects taught in English."

"Do you think we will forget how to speak Amharic?"

"I don't know," I said, a wave of sadness washing over me.

At night for the past couple of weeks I had started writing down all the Amharic words and phrases I knew, slowly filling up one of my school notebooks that had a portrait of the Emperor on the front.

"Sometimes I feel really mad at Mom and Dad for making us move," I said. "I don't think they get it that we're not like the other American families who just come here for a couple of years and leave."

"I think Nancy will like London though," he answered turning his face away. And for a second I thought I heard his voice crack but when he looked back at me his face was blank.

"Do you think you'll like London?" I asked Tim. He made an attempt to speak but no words came out and he just slowly shook his head.

I then told Tim about a conversation I had had with Dad a few weeks earlier when he had been in a talkative mood and I decided to take a chance and ask him something that I'd been wondering about for years. I wanted to know what had happened to Astatke, about how he had just disappeared when he'd been arrested. In my mind, it was almost as if he had ceased to exist, or had never existed. I was sitting in the armchair and suddenly the words had rushed out of me.

"Why was Astatke arrested during that coup?"

Dad looked startled but quickly regained his composure.

"For no good reason," he said. "Maybe he looked like a Body Guard officer, or maybe he was out after curfew, or maybe whoever was making the arrests had to fill a quota."

"What would have happened if we hadn't gone to get him?" I asked in a hushed voice but pressing on even though I was afraid of the answer.

"Who knows, he might still be sitting there." Dad had paused for a minute his voice faltering, and then asked me if I remembered that time that we were out hunting on the Solulta plains.

I nodded. "Yes, I saw an army truck going out to get you back."

And then Dad told me that about two months after that day he and his friend Kirk decided to go back to the Solulta plains to see if they could find the police officer who had arrested those men. They had a bottle of alcohol as a thank you.

The police officer was thrilled with the gift but as they were leaving asked, "So what do you want me to do with the men I am holding?"

And Dad said he was shocked and blurted out, "What? Are you telling me you have had those men in jail this whole time? For God's sake, let them go."

Dad had paused and I waited for him to speak.

"We're dealing with a traditional society that doesn't have all the laws and legal protections that I was taught at law school. Whoever has the power makes the rules as they go. And if you are an average person you just hope that you don't get caught up in the net," he'd said.

I looked over at Tim who was stretched out on the rock letting the sun warm him.

"I feel really worried about everyone we are leaving here. I know Dad has gotten Mamo a job at the Italian Embassy and Beheilu will be working for Ethiopian Airlines. What will happen though if someone gets arrested for something they have nothing to do with when they are walking home and we're not here to get them out?" I asked.

Tim got up, reached out and touched my shoulder. "Come on, let's swim a little while longer."

We dove into the water and for a few seconds I couldn't tell where my tears ended and the waters of the river began.

The week before our departure I went for a long ride with Kenn. I rode a horse borrowed from Franco De Santis for the day because all of our horses had already gone to their new owners. We were out for about three hours galloping along our favorite trails. We stopped for a while and sat under one of the trees and let the horses take a rest. Suddenly I turned and kissed him. His lips were soft and moist.

"Do you promise to write to me?" I asked quietly.

"I promise," he said, "but I am not much of a writer, unlike you who have so many notebooks and diaries filled with words."

"How much longer do you think you will stay in Ethiopia?" I asked him.

"I overheard my parents say we'll probably stay here another year."

"You are so lucky," I said leaning my head up against his chest, listening to his heartbeat.

"Do you know what I'm going to miss the most, besides you?" I asked Kenn. He shook his head.

"The eucalyptus trees," I said. "I am going to miss them so much."

When we got back to the hospital compound where Kenn lived and it came time to say goodbye, I walked over to Jarl who was outside standing by their front door. I gave him a long hug and then quickly walked away from both of them refusing to look back. Neither Mom nor I spoke during the whole ride back to our house and I was grateful she seemed to sense there were no words of comfort.

It felt like some kind of awful countdown had begun in earnest. At school I tried to pretend like nothing was happening and I would join in the chatter about next year as though I was going to be there. I wanted to totally avoid saying goodbye to Makeda It just felt too hard.

Mom and I drove out to the Cheshire Home one last time. When I said goodbye to Sofiya she wrapped her little stumps around my waist and held tight. She also gave me a picture she had drawn. It was of a *tukul* under a yellow sun and then two figures standing together, a smaller girl wearing a blue dress and an older girl with yellow hair.

A few days before we left I dug a big hole in the soft earth under the tree house. I took one of Dad's empty cigar boxes and put my best marbles, my slingshot, and a picture of myself with Tim into it.

I also included an index card and on it in Amharic I wrote, "My name is Martha Paradis." And then in English, "This is the home where I grew up."

I buried the box in the hole, digging my hands deeply into the soil as I covered it up. I let the dirt run through my fingers slowly and then watched it pour over the box.

Two nights before our departure date my parents were at a farewell party thrown by some close friends of theirs and Nancy was out with her friends. "Let's go look at the stars," I said to Tim, and I got our ponchos from the front hall closet.

The early evening rain still lingered in the grass and the ground was wet as we spread our ponchos out and lay down on the ground. The heavy rains were still a few months away. I felt the curve of the earth under my back and pressed my spine into it. Darkness fell around us except for the small light from the flashlight we had with us. Sometimes in the dead of night I felt as though there were spirits around me, and for a long time now I had wondered if they might be the ghosts of the soldiers I had seen hanging from the trees or the people who had been pushed over the balcony in the movie theater. Perhaps ghosts and demons dwell around all of us and we never know what might awaken them.

For a long while we lay silent, letting the cool night air fill our nostrils and lungs. We watched our breath move in and out. I felt the light of the moon move across my face, my heartbeat barely a murmur in my chest. A low-lying fog crept in and lingered.

"Doesn't that look like a horse?" my brother whispered, pointing towards a hazy shape. My body felt almost weightless, and gazing out toward the sky it was as though I was looking through a glass that was not transparent.

"It is so peaceful," Tim mumbled, mostly to himself. I turned my head toward my brother, suddenly aware that my heart was beating much faster.

"What do you think is going to happen in Ethiopia after we leave?" I asked quietly.

He didn't answer for a minute and I wondered if he had heard me. But then he said almost in a whisper, his voice husky, "I don't know, Martha, but I don't think it is going to be good."

I reached out and took my brother's hand the way I used to when we were much younger, and returned my gaze to the sky. I felt Tim's hand but wasn't really sure that I was touching him. Neither of us spoke for a few minutes.

"I love so many things about life here," I whispered. "Running down to the river, taking one of the horses on a wild gallop, the scent of the flowers from Mom's flower beds in the morning. What will you miss the most?"

"Eating injera and wot every day," he answered, "and the taste of berbere." He stopped speaking for a minute and then said, "It is so beautiful tonight."

I was quiet for a few minutes alone with my thoughts. And then I murmured, "Maybe this is a glimpse of heaven, maybe so death doesn't feel so scary."

Tim was still but I could hear him breathing in and out. His breath sounded almost like a soft whistle.

I turned towards him. "I hope it will be like this. I hope and pray that heaven looks and feels and smells like Ethiopia," I said, my voice barely a whisper.

We both continued looking up into the sky. I couldn't really believe that we were leaving. I felt the slow dampening of my mind, the fading of my body. Over the past months I had found myself thinking about death more and more often. I didn't speak out loud, but in my mind quietly said a prayer, that in the same way that I used to imagine Tim and I were really twins and had floated together in our mother's womb, one day far off in the future we would float up to Heaven together.

I didn't sleep much the night before our departure, but spent hours tossing and turning in my bed. I got out of bed and for one last time slowly pulled the heavy metal shutters up from my window and opened it. The sun cast a pinkish glow over the yard as it made its slow ascent. The surrounding silence was broken by odd rustlings and what sounded like the crackling of twigs.

With dawn came the sounds of waking. Far off in the direction of Belaynesh's village I heard a rooster crow and from somewhere else another answered. From right under the window there was a rustling and scratching as some animal rose from its bed. I took in a deep long breath, filling my lungs with the eucalyptus scented cool air. I held it in for as long as I could and then let it out in short little puffs.

I dressed slowly and joined the rest of my family for breakfast although I barely ate anything. The dining room looked like it had been stripped naked. All the paintings were off the walls and just the bare wooden table and chairs stood in the center of the room. Boxes filled with plates and silverware that would be shipped to London lined one wall. I felt strange wearing the green corduroy suit that Mom had the dressmaker make for me. I knew she was trying to give me something to focus on other than the pain of leaving and I loved her for it. But I much would have preferred to be in my jeans and t-shirt. Mom and Dad always insisted we dress up when we traveled though.

When the time came, I walked out of my room refusing to turn and look back. I just wanted to slip quietly out the front door, without anyone really noticing, and then wake up when it was all over. I couldn't even begin to imagine saying goodbye. I stumbled as I stepped down from the front porch to the gravel driveway, and walked over to Assefa and Worku who would not be coming to the airport with us. I moved toward Assefa. At the corners of his mouth flickered an expression of sorrow and pain that I recognized from the time we had surveyed the locust-ravaged circular garden bed. I hugged Assefa first. He stepped back and reached into his tunic and pulled something out, and holding my hand gently pressed something into it. I looked down and saw a flower that had been pressed flat and was dried out. I immediately recognized it as one of the pink roses from the garden.

Assefa looked at me and said softly, "Martha, when ugliness and pain come in your life, always remember that in all of us there is beauty. Just like this flower."

His voice wavered, choked with the same sadness that had seeped into my body during these weeks leading up to our departure. Tears rimmed his eyes and he fought them back. My own tears spilled out of my eyes and ran down my face. I closed my hand around his, and for one last time I felt the rough callouses on his palm that had brought so much color into Mom's gardens.

I slowly pulled my hand away and took a step toward Worku, my head down. Through wet lashes and a furrowed brow, I looked up at him. His mouth moved trying to say something, but no words came out.

Behind me I heard Dad's voice. "It's time to go."

Worku held onto me, his shoulders quivering, and I finally whispered, "I have to go, I promise I will never, ever forget you. I will always pray that you are well."

I took in a deep breath, and turned around slowly, holding Assefa's flower softly in my hand. I got into the car and sat sandwiched between Tim and Nancy, but felt none of the comfort their bodies pressed up on either side of me usually provided. It felt like a weight had settled in my stomach. I reached into my bag, pulled out my book, and placed the flower between the pages in the middle. And then suddenly as the Jeep's motor went from a low purr to a roar and the car began to move toward the gate, I saw the moment. I saw the moment that we would be gone. We were barely out of the compound but I could already envision what it would be like without us and I felt like a stranger in my own life.

The car moved slowly along the dirt road and then up the hill, and I turned my body around and looked out the back window and I watched our home begin to recede. I could see the grove of eucalyptus trees and the tree house where Tim, Sileshi and I had spent so many hours. I saw the flower beds where I had watched Assefa weed every afternoon. They were now a sea of color after everything had been replanted since the locusts. I could see the top of the roof at the back of the stables where I went every day for my second lunch with Worku and Assefa, where they laughed and gossiped and took a break from their chores. I caught a glimpse of the patio and the grey metal shutters over the window of my room.

I closed my eyes for a few seconds and imagined the shelf Dad had put up for all my trophies that were now packed in one of the suitcases in the trunk of the car. I sat up as straight as I could and caught a glimpse of the stables but with the stall doors open since the horses were no longer in them. And then at last, the roof of the guardhouse that I used to sit upon watching the cars go by, waiting for someone in my family to come home. I could see the small figure of Kadir standing by the gate where he always stood. He seemed to be watching us and then slowly he turned and closed the gate.

The road was fairly deserted because it was early morning. We were on the first flight out. I had asked Nancy if I could borrow her sunglasses because my eyes were so red and swollen from the constant tears. She seemed to understand because she gave them to me without threatening me with what she would do to me if I broke or lost them.

Sileshi had come to the airport with us. He was wearing his one suit and stood with the others who had come to see us off. Mamo, Belaynesh and Beheilu were there and they hugged me, and Belaynesh wailed and repeatedly beat her chest the way the Ethiopians do at funerals. About forty of Mom and Dad's closest friends had come to the airport to see us off, including many of the ministers Dad worked with and whom I knew from cocktail and dinner parties in our home.

Mom and Dad were both saying goodbye to them, and then Dad came over to where Tim and I were and gently put his hand on my shoulder, nudging me in the direction of the plane.

"Come on, Martha, it is time to go," he said.

I looked at him and for a second I thought about bolting and just running as far away as I could down to the Kebena River. In my mind, I could feel the ground under my feet as I moved further and further away from the plane and back towards the sights and sounds and events of my childhood. It felt like a hand had a tight grip on my throat and it was hard to swallow.

"Come on, Martha," Dad's tone was sterner.

I forced myself to walk up the stairs following Tim and Nancy with my parents behind me. My body and mind felt strangely disconnected, my legs moving without conscious intention. When we reached the top, Dad instructed us to turn around, smile and wave. A friend of his who worked for the airlines took a photograph. I felt sure that it would probably be on our next Christmas card. I took a few steps forward and stumbled into the plane; but then, regaining my balance, I reached out and grabbed Tim's hand pushing my way past Mom and Dad who were behind us. I didn't care if Dad was mad at me.

I stepped back out onto the platform at the entrance and tore off the sunglasses, my eyes searching for Sileshi, Beheilu, Belaynesh, and Mamo. I found them still standing as though rooted like statues. Beheilu and Mamo had turned their faces away and Belaynesh was swaying back and forth. I stared at Sileshi and held his gaze as I tried to memorize his face. He slowly raised his arm and waved to Tim and me and shouted something but we were too far away and I couldn't understand what he was saying. I waved back and, holding onto my brother, turned away and stepped back into the plane.

AFTERWORD

I don't think I realized it then, but now I see that it was the deep bonds forged during our early life among the proud and gentle Ethiopians who took care of us, along with our parents' love and guidance, that shaped the people Nancy, Tim and I would become. Our shared belief in the essential worth of all human beings, no matter what their circumstance, didn't emerge with any single event, any one moment, or exceptional words in all those years that we lived in Ethiopia. It was just a long unfolding of experience — of both the loveliness and tragedy of life — that began and stretched on for almost twelve years and then ended.

We left Ethiopia in the late 1960s. The forces of revolution that had been gathering pace — and that we had witnessed as children in the demonstrations by young students in the streets around Addis Ababa — would sweep away the Imperial government. The reforms that Emperor Haile Selassie had introduced, in education, the military, and a strengthened parliamentary system, had been too little and too late. And the famine which we had heard about in fragmentary conversations when we lived in Ethiopia had badly tarnished the image of the Emperor's government.

Tragically, the bright idealism that motivated young Ethiopians to demand change was extinguished by the dictatorship that replaced the ancient aristocratic order. The history of Ethiopia in the decades after we left was one of hope betrayed and terrible suffering.

In the mid-1970's, Colonel Mengistu Haile Mariam came to lead the military regime that overthrew the government of Emperor Haile Selassie. The military dictatorship — or *Dergue* as it was known in Ethiopia — inaugurated its rule by sending

245

sixty senior officers, one the father of my friend Asfa, and many of the men my father had worked with every day, to the firing squad. Shortly thereafter, Emperor Haile Selassie and the head of the Ethiopian Orthodox Church were secretly murdered. In 1976, Mengistu unleashed what was known as the Red Terror. If you had even a modest education and were young, that alone was enough to send you to your death.

In the words of the Human Rights Commission that investigated the abuses of this era:

"Many of these young prisoners were detained in unspeakable conditions, packed by the hundreds in airless, lightless cellars where they could hear the screams of those being tortured as they themselves awaited torture. During one week of the Red Terror, Mengistu's secret police and security squads murdered 5,000 high school and university students and imprisoned 30,000 others."

Amnesty International reported that during Colonel Mengistu's reign over half a million people were brutally murdered or mutilated, including thousands of children. These executions frequently took place in front of the victims' families, who were then required to pay for the bullets that had killed their child, or brother, or sister, before the bodies were returned for burial.

Mengistu was found guilty of genocide in 2007 by the International Criminal Court in the Hague, and sentenced to life in prison. He remains in wealthy exile in Zimbabwe.

The move to London was extremely difficult for our whole family, and it felt to me at times as if we had had a collective nervous breakdown. My father was devastated by the personal losses of so many friends he had worked with, and for the rest of his life was tormented by the knowledge that everything he had tried to do to have a positive impact in Ethiopia was simply wiped away. My mother coped as best she could by being supportive of him and by throwing herself into managing the household in London. Nancy continued her rebellious ways and my admiration for her continued to grow. Tim decided at age sixteen to return to the United States for the remainder of his high school years. His departure was a huge loss for me. I missed everything about Ethiopia and for years would take out my scrapbook and

246

try to relive my happiest memories. But I was also haunted by the knowledge that people I knew — the parents of classmates, children I had seen playing stickball in a field across from our home, women in their shamas and men simply on their way to work — had been tortured and murdered. Their faces came to me in nightmares. Unable to really talk to anyone about what I was feeling, I continued to write in my journal every night.

My brother and Sileshi had corresponded while we were living in London. Dad had started giving us an allowance and every month Tim sent half of his to Sileshi. Sileshi had been forced to join the air force, had his name changed, and was sent to India for training. In June 1991, I received a heart-wrenching letter from him. He described the horrendous atrocities that had taken place in our neighborhood, and said that our home had been taken over by Mengistu's henchmen. He begged us to help him. Most of his friends had been killed and if he returned to Addis and refused to join the ruling Communist Party, that would seal his fate. He said he simply could not return and count the bodies of dead children, that he would go out of his mind.

I had thought that the moment at the airport was going to be the last time I would ever see Sileshi. But life had something else in store for us. All credit goes to my brother Tim who began the arduous process of bringing Sileshi to the United States where he received political refugee status. I remember the first reunion when I saw Sileshi and the rush of memories that came back to me as he smiled. I asked Sileshi what he had shouted to Tim and me from the tarmac at the airport the morning we had left Ethiopia.

"I shouted that I would pray for the rest of my life that one day we would see one another again," he said simply.

He also told us he knew that Beheilu, Belaynesh and Mamo had survived the terrible years of the military dictatorship, but no one knew the fate of Assefa, Worku or Kadir.

A few years later he was able to bring his wife and two sons to the U.S. We now see Sileshi often and he recently came to New York for the interment of my father's ashes. As I stood in the church with my brother and Sileshi, and looked at the names of my parents and sister inscribed on the steel plate behind which their ashes rest, I thought about how life is a mysterious circle and we never know where our stories will end.

But we always know who the most important and beloved people in our lives are, and we know that they remain a part of us forever.

ACKNOWLEDGMENTS

Every book has its own inspiration and presents its own challenges. I had never thought about writing a memoir. My sister Nancy, a journalist, always planned to, believing we had a unique story to tell. She never got the chance, but before she died she asked me to promise that I would attempt it. I have felt her with me every step of the way. But there have been so many others whose help and support have been invaluable, and to whom I will always be grateful.

To my husband Bob, and children Alex and Rebecca, who were a constant source of encouragement, who made me tea as I worked, and never complained about the scraps of paper littering the dining room table, goes my lifelong love. You are my deepest source of joy and inspiration.

I was blessed to have two of my sister's closest friends as a constant source of guidance. I am deeply appreciative to Margo Hammond and Carl McClendon for all the time they took at critical points to offer feedback and support. And to Carl goes lifelong gratitude for lending his expert skills to the final editing of the book.

Heartfelt thanks go to Sileshi Tefera and Makeda Diggs Nichols, friends for over fifty years, who experienced many of the events recounted in this book alongside my family. And love and affection to Kenn, Jarl and Roy Nielsen, who lived many of the adventures and misadventures with us.

I am beholden to Prince Asfa-Wossen Asserate, Vincent DeFilippi, Jessica Heffernan Ziegler, Melissa Mertz, Chris Wriggins, Andie Evans, Henry Matthews, and David Karraker, for providing generous reviews of the book from their unique perspectives.

When the manuscript was barely in rough draft form, Lisa Beth Vanesky Meisel and Iris Segall Wormser encouraged me to keep writing. Thanks go to Roz Ginsberg, Deborah Aronson, Kathy Leventhal and Linda Benezra Wachtel for convincing me that this was a memoir worth the effort of seeing into print.

My gratitude goes out to dearest friends Felice Toonkel, Nancy Napier, Dorothy Pietracatella, Kathleen Turley, David Johns and Michel Kassett, who have been with me on this journey from the first sentence. Thanks also to Judy Kurzer for her encouragement and Bob Willis who has been a sustaining support for many years.

At a time of sorrow after Nancy's passing, treasured friends Beth Lazarus and her daughter Rebecca, Robin Rever DeFilippi, Deborah Scher, Michelle Riesner Osian, Caroline Norden, Shelby Nelson, and Sally Orme, flew to Florida for her memorial service, and compassionately understood why fulfilling my promise to Nancy was so deeply important to me. Much gratitude goes to Lodovico Balducci for being such a cherished friend and spiritual guide to Nancy, and to members of her parish who walked together with her on her journey of faith.

I am indebted to Pamela Powell, Rosemary James, Steve McLaughlin, Nick Ciminello, David James, James Madsen, Elizabeth Evans-Olivier, Charles Dodgen, Zeb Schachtel, Bernadette Janovic, Hope Shaw, and Teddy Flamingo – all of whom took the time and effort to read the manuscript at different stages, and each of whom offered invaluable feedback.

Warm thanks to Trevor James who did an initial edit, Jessica Moore who set up my first website, and to Sonny Kui and Coy Pittman who helped with technical issues and never lost patience with my technophobic questions. I also want to commend Katie Tota and Taylor McCown of Salem Publishing who went above and beyond in tending to the details of bringing this book to print.

My appreciation of enduring friendship also goes to the Dodgen, Childers, Lazarus, Peters, DeFilippi, Aronson, Maxfield, Scher, Osian, Sparkman, Demar, and Roth families, and to David Johns and Kathleen Turley, Terhi Edwards, Victoria Royal Boyt, Darleen Thomas, Susan Henderson, Robin Bado, Alison Upright, and the women of the mother/daughter book group – Sarah

Lafferty, Judi Herrmann, Tonja Blankenship Feingold, Nancy Landau Gillon, Iris Wormser, Angela Bianco Smilen, Shelly Volerich Gershon, and Pam Caine.

This book was written not only in my home state of New Jersey, but also in Maine and Florida, where dear family friends Mary Corbett, Marian Baker, Shelly Elmer, and Curtis Bohlen were a supportive presence. And it's always been a delightful diversion on my New England trips to spend time with my god daughter Katrina and her sister Sarah.

To my colleagues in my psychotherapy supervision groups – Jennifer McDermut, Elizabeth Buonomo, Felice Toonkel, Steve Darwin, Ruchi Nadella, Nancy Napier, Camilla Brooks, Susan Lemak, Stephen McFadden, and Melissa Mertz – I extend thanks for your backing. I also have been enriched in my understanding of spiritual healing and the resolution of trauma by the members of Devedana Sanctuary and the Somatic Experiencing community.

I am blessed to have Tita DeGavre and her family, Heidi Plante Blank, our cousins the Derochers and Holts, John Quinlan and Janet Crawford, as well as the Ciminellos, the Domenechs, the Jameses, and the Saracinos as part of my extended family..

The deep friendship of family friends the McGhees, Wilson, Nelson, and Miler families, and Adey Imru Makonnen, Bella Endeshaw, Franco DeSantis, Imru Zelleke, and Isaac Kifle, has resonated since our time in Ethiopia. And, the Powell, Loughran, and Jepsen families shared deeply meaningful years with my parents in Paris, and have remained a part of our lives. In more recent times, we have developed a special bond with Abebe Mamo and Azeb Setegne, and the Davids and Matthews families from South Africa, who intuitively understand our bond with Ethiopia and the African continent.

And finally, to my brother Tim, who corroborated memories because he also lived them. But he also conducted research, organized my folders, helped me on the darn computer, was a source of editorial feedback and literary insight, and in much the same way that he was my companion during childhood, was a steady and humorous presence throughout. This book would not have come to fruition without him, and I cannot thank him enough.

251